Indigenous Responses to Western Christianity

ALSO BY THE SAME AUTHOR AND PUBLISHED
BY NEW YORK UNIVERSITY PRESS

THE BETA ISRAEL (FALASHA) IN ETHIOPIA
FROM EARLIEST TIMES TO THE TWENTIETH CENTURY
Steven Kaplan (1992)

SURVIVING SALVATION
THE ETHIOPIAN JEWISH FAMILY IN TRANSITION
Steven Kaplan and Ruth Westheimer (1992)

INDIGENOUS RESPONSES TO WESTERN CHRISTIANITY

Edited by Steven Kaplan

NEW YORK UNIVERSITY PRESS
New York and London

NEW YORK UNIVERSITY PRESS
New York and London

Library of Congress Cataloging-in-Publication Data

Indigenous responses to western Christianity /
edited by Steven Kaplan.
p. cm.
Includes index.
ISBN 0-8147-4649-7 (hard : alk. paper)
1. Missions—History. 2. Christianity and Culture. 3. Asia—Church history.
I. Kaplan, Steven.
BV2100.I53 1994
270.8—dc20 94-11718
CIP

New York University Press books are printed on acid-free paper,
and their binding materials are chosen for strength and durability.

Manufactured in the United States of America

10 9 8 7 6 5 4 3 2 1

The editor and publisher gratefully acknowledge permission to reprint "The Africanization of Missionary Christianity: History and Typology," which appeared in the *Journal of Religion in Africa*, vol. XVI, no. 3 (1986).

Dedicated to R.J. Zwi Werblowsky

Contents

ACKNOWLEDGMENTS

Most of the papers published in this volume were first presented in a workshop on "Indigenous Responses to Western Christianity" held from June 29–July 3, 1987 at the Harry S Truman Research Institute for the Advancement of Peace of the Hebrew University of Jerusalem. Inevitably in the case of a project that has taken so long to come to fruition, the list of those to be acknowledged and thanked is long.

The idea for this workshop grew out of discussions held over brown bag lunches at the Truman Institute. Professor Harold (Zvi) Schiffrin, Chairman of the Institute's Academic Committee encouraged the participants to develop these informal exchanges of information into a proposal for a formal meeting. He was also instrumental in securing the Institute's approval and support for the workshop. Professors Irene Eber, Avraham Altman, and Fred Bronner joined me in taking up this challenge and shouldered the burden of much of the correspondence and initial organizational work. Professor John B. Carman, Director of the Center for the Study of World Religions, responded to our initiative with enthusiasm and secured funding for three scholars affiliated with the Center to attend the workshop.

In addition to the contributors, others who presented papers at the workshop included: Michael Ashkenazi, Richard Gray, Alfredo Tiamson, G.P.V. Somaratne, Daphne Tsimhoni, Matthew Elbow, Tu Wei-Ming, John B. Carman. Avraham Altman, Irene Eber, Fred Bronner, Miriam Hoexter, Benjamin

Z. Kedar, Hava Lazarus-Yafeh, Nehemia Levtzion, Harold Z. Schiffrin and Gedaliahu Stroumsa were also among the participants and contributed to our discussions and attempts to formulate the issues at hand. The administration of the Truman Institute, led by Dr. Edy Kaufman, Executive Director, and Ms. Dalia Shemer, Administrative Director, handled all the technical arrangements for the workshop and made it possible for both local scholars and guests to devote their attention to scholarly matters, rather than luggage, planes, hotels, etc.

Norma Schneider was the Director of Publications at the Truman Institute at the time of the workshop and continued to show interest in the papers even after her formal responsibilities were over. In particular, she was instrumental (yet again) in establishing the connection with New York University Press. Chaia Beckerman inherited these papers when she became Director of Publications and has carefully and conscientiously seen them through the lengthy process of publication. Leah Bowman worked with her to prepare camera-ready copy. The staff at New York University Press, particularly Niko Pfund and Despina Gimbel, have handled all matters concerned with this book (my third published with them in recent years) with characteristic efficiency and enthusiasm.

Finally, I would like to thank the authors whose papers are published herein. Throughout a lengthy process of submission, editing and manuscript preparation they have demonstrated unstinting patience and understanding. The quality of this volume is a testimony to both their scholarly achievments and their generous forbearance.

Steven Kaplan
Jerusalem, February 1994

INTRODUCTION

For over five hundred years, since the great "age of exploration," Western Christians have visited, traded with, conquered, and colonized large parts of the non-Western world. In virtually every case this movement of Christians has been accompanied at some point by an attempt to spread Christianity. The precise composition of the European community varied from region to region and from period to period. But whatever the mixture of traders, explorers, soldiers, politicians, and settlers, there was rarely, if ever, a European presence without a missionary component. The encounter with Western Christianity therefore represents one of the major themes in the history of contact between Western and non-Western civilizations.

Despite intensive Christian efforts all around the globe, the extent of positive response has varied tremendously. While in some areas—including Latin America, Korea, the Philippines, and parts of sub-Saharan Africa—large numbers have converted to Christianity, India, China, Japan, Southeast Asia, and the Muslim Middle East have produced only a limited number of converts. While in some cases, such as Latin America and the Philippines, conquest appears to have been a major contributory factor to Christianity's success, the British occupation of India produced no torrent of converts in its wake. Nor can conquest be used to explain the extreme variability in local responses to Christianity in colonial Africa.

In general, Christianity appears to have enjoyed much greater success when confronting small-scale tribal societies than in the encounter with great civilizations. To date, however, the mechanisms whereby these and other societies resisted Christianity remain obscure.

The impact of Christianity has varied not only because of differing rates of conversion, but also because of the extreme selectivity which has frequently characterized local responses. It seems crucial to distinguish, for example, between the spread of Christianity as a system of religious belief, behavior, and patterns of worship on the one hand, and its role as a transformer of the basic premises of the civilizations and societies on the other. Catholicism, as introduced into much of Latin America and the Philippines, largely succeeded (often with the help of massive displacement of the local population) in irrevocably altering the cultural dynamics of the regions effected. In contrast, in sub-Saharan Africa the acceptance of Christianity by a significant proportion of the population has usually not been followed by a radical restructuring of local society and culture.

Of special interest in this context are the wide-ranging responses to Christianity, lying somewhere between the extremes of complete transformation and total rejection. Confronted with a Christian "package deal," local populations have demonstrated a remarkable ability to select certain elements while rejecting others. A variety of changes frequently took place on both the individual and societal level without formal conversion. Millenarian movements, which have been so prominent a feature of local religious activity during the period of European influence, frequently reveal the acceptance of Christian concepts of time, history, and salvation, without significant movement in the direction of Christian doctrine, ritual, or myth. In other cases, elements of Old Testament and New Testament narrative have been incorporated into the local mythology not as precursors to the acceptance of Christianity, but as new adhesions to traditional belief systems. Selectivity has appeared not only in the incorporation of elements from Western Christianity by traditional believers, but also in the retention of aspects of local culture by local converts to Christianity. At times it has been traditional beliefs (in demons, witches, spirits, for example) which have proven most resistant to Christian influences. In other cases, traditional rituals, such as funerals, initiation rites, exorcism and healing, have proven especially durable. In general, it would appear that although Western Christianity frequently arrived with a clearly articulated civilizing mission, in many cases it also displayed a remarkable openness toward "indigenization." Lacking either a stated code of laws such as Jewish Halachah or Islamic Sharia, or a single holy language such as Hebrew or Arabic,

Christianity repeatedly absorbed elements from the cultures it entered, and thus numerous local or national Christianities emerged.

The seven essays contained in this volume explore the manner in which Western missionary Christianity has been shaped and transformed through contact with the peoples of Peru, Mexico, Africa, India, Sri Lanka, Thailand, China, and Japan. They demonstrate how local populations, who initially encountered Christianity as a mixture of religion, culture, politics, ethics, and technology selected those elements which they felt suited their needs. Moreover, since even those aspects of the missionary program which were accepted were rarely incorporated totally unchanged, the essays demonstrate how the conversion of the local population was usually accompanied by a no less significant indigenization of Christianity.

Although this book is not the first to view the missionary enterprise in a broader comparative perspective, it nevertheless represents an important departure from general trends of scholarship in this field. On the whole, the historical study of Western Christian missions and their impact has tended to be treated as a subtopic in the history of a particular region or country. Patterns of scholarship have accordingly followed general trends in the study of the relevant areas. Thus in the period of Europocentric studies, much attention was lavished upon the activities of the missionary "heroes." In the 1960s and 1970s, as scholars became more sensitive to the destructiveness of foreign intervention in many parts of the world, nationalist critiques emerged emphasizing the collusion of missionaries in the spread of racism, imperialism, capitalism, colonialism, and so forth. Perhaps more significantly, such studies began, for the first time, to describe how the introduction of Christianity transformed local cultures and societies. Attention was also given to the importance of local responses and initiatives, as well as to the role of local Christians and native agents. While the numerous local studies undertaken uncovered several important areas of inquiry, with few exceptions they made little attempt to examine indigenous responses to Christianity beyond the confines of a single region or period. This book seeks to depart from this format by examining indigenous transformations of Christianity in several lands within a single volume.

As the essays in this volume indicate, the transformation of Christianity has not been uniform in all periods and regions. Rather, it has taken many forms and used various of methods. Yet underlying this apparent diversity have been several common themes and processes which span both time and space. Through the detailed examination and comparison of a series of case studies, this book seeks to provide some materials for comparative study and in this fashion point the direction toward a deeper understanding of mission history and the dynamics of Christianity's expansion.

Forms

The transformation of Christianity as a result of local initiatives has assumed diverse forms and has been guided by a variety of principles and motives. While blanket terms such as inculturation, adaptation, indigenization, and contextualization may be of some use in characterizing the general processes which occurred, when applied to specific cases they tend to obscure rather than clarify important distinctions. Under different conditions, Christianity was transformed in different ways. In the first essay in this volume Steven Kaplan proposes a six-fold typology for the modes of mutual adaptation of Christianity and African culture. Loosely moving from the more limited forms of adaptation to the more extensive, he begins with the mere *toleration* of African practices, continues with the *translation* of Christian ideas and concepts into African terminology, considers *assimilation*, *Christianization*, and *acculturation*, and concludes with the *incorporation* of African models into the main body of Christian thought and practice.

Many of the analytical possibilities only hinted at in this essay are elaborated upon in Erik Cohen's examination of Christianization and indigenization in Thailand. Cohen sets out to explore the parallel processes whereby Christian churches absorb indigenous elements (*Christianization*) and indigenous religions absorb Christian elements (*indigenization*). Through a detailed examination of the Christian-Buddhist encounter in Thailand, he demonstrates how different types of adaptation are the product of different sets of circumstances. Thus, for example, "in those relatively few instances in which elements of doctrinal Buddhism have been adapted to Christianity, the more central types of Kaplan's typology, particularly 'incorporation' were involved; whereas in the process of adaptation on the level of popular religion the more peripheral types, ranging between 'Christianization' and 'translation,' predominated." From the Buddhist side, attempts to indigenize elements of Christianity were totally lacking at the level of doctrinal philosophical Buddhism. Moreover, even at the popular level Thai Buddhists showed less interest in Christianity than their Christian counterparts showed in Buddhism.

Although Cohen's and Kaplan's chapters, which lead off this volume, limit themselves to the discussion of Thailand and Africa, the processes they analyze are of obvious relevance to other periods and regions. Indeed, while none of the other authors make explicit use of the categories suggested in the first two chapters virtually all of them offer additional examples of the various forms of adaptation they describe.

Points of Contact

Cohen suggests that the lack of adaptation he describes in Thailand can at least in part be ascribed to "the fundamental and pervasive contrast between the presuppositions" of Christianity and (doctrinal) Buddhism. Certainly it must be acknowledged that where major differences exist between the religions in contact with regard to central core concepts or beliefs, the possibilities for extensive adaptation are greatly decreased. Indeed, in such circumstances it may well be that the intellectual and philosophical abyss created by such fundamental differences can only be overcome by a "leap of faith," for example, conversion in the classic Nockian sense.

Most of the chapters in this book however, indicate that almost everywhere Christianity has arrived it has found shared or similar concepts which have served as useful bridges to the local religious systems. Dennis Hudson, writing about Sri Lanka, notes that "Śrī Vaiṣṇavas stress the predominant role of divine grace...[a position which] closely approximates that of the nineteenth-century evangelical Protestants." Eric Van Young and Daniel Bays, writing about nineteenth-century Mexico and twentieth-century China, respectively, both describe the confluence of indigenous and Western Christian traditions of millenarianism in local religious movements. Shared concerns with healing and other practical techniques have also tended to transcend the normal boundaries of faith communities and open the possibility for reciprocal influences.

In some cases, particular figures or symbols have served as crucial links between indigenous and Western Christian traditions. Thus in Mexico and Peru the cult of the Virgin, with its echoes of ancient mother goddesses, functioned as a link between initially separate belief systems. In early nineteenth-century colonial Mexico the figure of King Ferdinand VII of Spain served as the unlikely focus for popular Indian messianic expectations. As Eric Van Young vividly illustrates, the symbol of the king was able (as symbols so frequently are) to unite seemingly disparate concepts and dissolve logical contradictions. Nowhere is this ability more clearly captured than in the memorable call, "Long live King Ferdinand VII and death to all Spaniards."

Alongside their recognition of these and other points of contact, however, most authors also note that the ease and extent of mutual understanding should not be exaggerated. Attempts to translate fundamental theological doctrines have often foundered, producing only inadequate and neutered approximations. As Jacques Gernet has remarked in his recent book which examines Chinese responses to Jesuit missionaries, "The missionaries had tried to adapt, but by using a particular method of conversion and unconsciously borrowing from deeply rooted Chinese traditions, the meaning of which they failed to understand...The doctrine of the Master of Heaven [i.e., Christianity] appeared [to the Chinese literati], essentially, to be a mixture of misunderstood Buddhist and Confucian ideas."[1]

The Word

Of all the techniques used by indigenous Christians to transform missionary Christianity, none would appear to be more important than independent interpretation of the Bible. When Western missionaries arrived in foreign lands, they brought with them not only the biblical text, but also an accumulated tradition of commentaries and "orthodox" interpretation. Translation of the Scriptures into local languages both created new questions of interpretation and placed the texts firmly in the hands of the local population. Some authorities have suggested, for example, that the existence of vernacular Scriptures has been virtually a *sine qua non* for the emergence of independent (separatist) churches. Others have noted the manner in which direct interpretation of Scripture has enabled local Christians to identify links between their own traditions and those of the ancient Israelites or early Church.

Several contributors to this volume explore the process and consequences of direct interpretation of Scripture for the transformation of Christianity. In the chapter concerned with sixteenth-century Peru, Jan Szemiński analyses the manner in which two Andean Catholic noblemen reinterpreted the "salvation history" of the Bible through traditional Incan concepts of history and cosmology. In some of their writings the main figures and themes remain Christian (Jesus, Mary, the Holy Spirit, Jerusalem), but the basic structures and relationships are Andean. In others, traditional Andean deities (Thunder, Tunapa, Mother Earth) were assimilated to Christian concepts (St. James, St. Thomas, the Virgin Mary). John Howes describes how Uchimura Kanzo, twentieth-century Japan's foremost student of biblical literature, sought to purify Christianity and return it to its biblical and apostolic roots through direct and original interpretation of Scripture. In this fashion he sought to remove "the accretions which had taken place in the name of 'Christianity' after the events in the Bible" and had distorted the true faith.

The conviction that their understanding of Christianity was even more authentic than that of their Western counterparts led Uchimura Kanzo and his Incan predecessors to appeal directly to the authority of the Bible. The original interpretations they produced enabled them to reject jarring elements in Western

Christianity and create a more appropriate local form which could still claim a biblical mandate. Their methods were similar, but not identical. While the Andean nobles sought to indigenize Catholicism by assimilating distinctively Incan ideas, Uchimura sought to de-Westernize Christianity and produce a more pristine and universal (although not necessarily Japanese) faith.

An even more remarkable response to original interpretation of Scripture is chronicled in Dennis Hudson's discussion of the Sinhalese Tamil intellectual Āṟumuga Nāvalar. Although initially attracted to the Wesleyan mission, Nāvalar's reading of the Bible, and in particular his work as a translator, convinced him that the Bible was not an authority that the Protestants could reasonably appeal to in support of their faith. Indeed, he concluded that the temple-centered cult of the Old Testament was far closer to the religious culture of Śaivism than that of Evangelical Protestantism. Eventually he left the mission and applied the lessons he had learned from it concerning educational methods, printing, and preaching to the revitalization of Śaiva culture.

The Spirit

At first glance the claim to a direct revelation would appear to have little in common with the direct interpretation of Scripture discussed above. While the latter is a drawn-out, highly intellectual process, largely confined to educated elites, the former is usually characterized by dramatic eruptions and emotional outpourings with a broad popular appeal. Yet despite their apparent differences, both processes can be shown to have functioned similarly with regard to the transformation of Christianity. Direct revelation has, like direct interpretation, served as a method of "cleansing" Christianity of its post-Apostolic accretions. Both processes have, moreover, formed the basis for a claim to possess a pristine, more authentic form of Christianity.

In his analysis of Pentecostalism in early twentieth-century China, Daniel Bays devotes considerable attention to the manner in which both American and Chinese Pentecostalists transformed Western Christianity. Of particular interest is his discussion of (Paul) Wei Enbo, a founder of the True Jesus Church, who received "direct revelations, along with direct visual sightings of Moses, Elijah, and others, calling him to be a warrior for the True God, to defeat Satan and his forces, and to 'correct' (*geng-zheng*) the mistaken path of all the world's churches." Together with his fellow Chinese Pentecostalist, Zhang Lingsheng (Peter), Paul Wei succeeded in creating an indigenous Christian religious movement with a clearly defined and highly original creed, and a large membership spread over several provinces.

Bays's discussion of the True Jesus Church also raises a number of points touched upon by other essays in this volume. Firstly, his consideration of the manner in which popular Christianity found points of contact with popular, even heretical, aspects of indigenous religion is strikingly similar to phenomena discussed by both Erik Cohen and Eric Van Young. While clearly the transformation of Christianity was not confined to the popular level alone, all three essays seem to indicate that, around the periphery of the starkly defined "truths" of the different religions, existed a relatively hazy popular faith which could provide a fertile matrix for contact and mutual adaptation.

Secondly, by analyzing in some detail the relationship between Chinese Pentecostalism and similar twentieth-century American movements, Bays reminds us that the transformation of Christianity has not been limited to areas outside of Europe or the United States. Western Christians, particularly those critical of the values prescribed by Western "civilization," have also sought to liberate Christianity from its culturally imposed limitations.

Although the essays presented in this volume are concerned with local responses to Christianity during the past five hundred years, the themes and processes they describe have a significance which extends far beyond the historical and geographical contexts with which they are directly concerned. Many of the questions they raise and forms of analysis they suggest would appear of relevance to other periods in Christian history and perhaps to other religions as well. The typology which I suggest, and which Erik Cohen has expanded upon, may well be of use in understanding the early Christian encounter with classical culture and civilization. The theme of direct interpretation of Scripture figures prominently in the teachings of the Protestant Reformation (*sola scriptura*), and throughout history may well have been the most important means of transforming Christianity. The worldwide success of Pentecostalist churches during the twentieth century offers ample testimony to the continued importance of direct revelation in the ongoing renewal of Christianity. Christianity, like every living religion, has throughout its history been in a constant state of transformation. The chapters in this book attempt to point the direction to a deeper understanding of this process by exploring some of the forms, methods, times, and locales in which this transformation has taken place.

Note

1. Jacques Gernet, *China and the Christian Impact* (Cambridge, 1985), 50.

CHAPTER 1

The Africanization of Missionary Christianity: History and Typology

STEVEN KAPLAN

Of the many issues confronting African Christians today, none would appear to have received more attention than the problem of defining the precise relationship between Christianity and African culture. The lively, sometimes heated, debate that has developed over this issue has produced in its wake a substantial body of literature on diverse aspects of a process variously labeled as "Africanization," "incarnation," "contextualization," and "adaptation."[1] As with almost any large corpus of literature, the writings on this topic vary significantly in scope, intention, and quality. Yet, almost without exception, these works are consistent in their avoidance of any discussion of two topics: historical precedents and typological distinctions.[2] Whatever the differences in the authors' stands in present-day debates, they are generally united in the limited attention they give to early attempts at Africanization and their lack of interest in defining different forms of adaption. It is with these two issues that this chapter is primarily concerned.

Western missionaries have frequently been condemned as cultural imperialists incapable of or unwilling to fairly evaluate and respect the cultures of the peoples with whom they came in contact. A. J. Temu's claim that "almost all the Protestant missionaries to Kenya viewed all native customs and traditions with abhorrence" has been voiced by students of missionary studies with regard to Christian activity in almost every area of the continent.[3] Missionaries, it is charged, were unable to separate the Christian religion from such European trappings as monogamy, Western dress, and etiquette and accordingly sought to impose an all-inclusive package upon the African population, rather than confining themselves to religious change *per se*. In the main this picture is an accurate one. The extreme ethnocentricity and cultural arrogance of many Western missionaries cannot be denied. However, in conceding this point we should not be led (as many have been) to ignore the evidence for sincere attempts by numerous foreign evangelists to come to terms with the African setting in which they worked. The contributions of Western missionaries to the "Africanization" of Christianity were far more numerous than is generally acknowledged. Indeed, as we shall demonstrate below, the more famous attempts at indigenization, such as that of Bishop Lucas of Masasi, are often dramatic pointers to many lesser-known and less-publicized episodes.[4]

The process of relating Christianity to an African setting has assumed diverse forms and has been guided by a variety of principles and motives. While blanket terms such as "Africanization," "adaptation," and "incarnation" may be of some use in characterizing the general processes, when applied to specific cases they may obscure important divergences.[5] Different aspects of African culture were "adapted" in different ways. In this chapter six terms have been chosen to describe what appear to be six different modes of adaptation: toleration, translation, assimilation, Christianization, acculturation, and incorporation. Each term is discussed and illustrated with historical examples in the appropriate section below.

The typology presented in this essay is, of course, tentative and intended to provoke discussion. Some readers may challenge the categories I have suggested; others may attempt to characterize the various historical episodes. Such debate is welcome. As the study of African independent churches has demonstrated, efforts to create an analytical framework, while no substitute for case studies, are a valuable supplement. The phenomena discussed in this chapter are of obvious relevance to the history of Christianity in other periods and regions and, while no attempt has been made to apply the typology outside Africa, this should be understood as a product of my own limited knowledge, rather than a function of inherent limitations of this framework.

Toleration

"Toleration" is the term I have chosen to characterize those cases in which missionaries agreed to accept the continued existence of certain African social customs, while at the same time maintaining that they were essentially incompatible with a true Christian life. Such acceptance, usually defended on grounds of expediency or functional necessity, differed in one crucial aspect from the other forms of adaptation we shall examine below. No attempt was made to argue for the positive value or Christian potential of the customs involved. Rather, it was claimed that although such customs were non-Christian in character, abolition was at present impossible or impractical. The best that could be hoped was that they would eventually wither away.

Several good examples of toleration are revealed through an examination of the missionary encounter with polygamy. In theory, virtually all missionaries were opposed to polygamy and most were opposed to the baptism of polygamists.[6] Indeed, numerous mission conferences and mission board decisions reaffirmed this stand. However, we should not be misled into reading decisions passed by a majority as if they had unanimous support. Acrimonious debate and bitter controversy often lay behind the passage of antipolygamy resolutions. Twenty-one of 104 voters at the Lambeth Conference of 1888 favored the baptism of polygamists in at least some circumstances.[7] The minutes of the Centenary Conference of Protestant Missions, also held in 1888, reveals a similar range of opinions on the topic.[8] The very frequency with which the issue of polygamy was debated is another indication of how troublesome the issue was felt to be.[9]

Moreover, whatever the official policy over polygamy, missionaries in the field were frequently forced to make *ad hoc* decisions based upon the realities which they faced on a daily basis.[10] Thus, for example, Church Missionary Society (CMS) missionaries in Kenya in 1907 "expressed the view that baptism should not be denied to a man having more than one wife though any church member subsequently taking a second or additional wife would be subject to church discipline."[11] In 1909 the same missionaries were party to a joint Protestant resolution to "in no case urge heathen men to put away [abandon] their wives with a view to baptism."[12]

The German missionary, Johannes Bachmann, began his career as a rigid advocate of the imposition of European standards of morality and discipline.[13] In time, his attitude softened and he eventually proposed the toleration of polygamy during the transitional stage in Christianization.[14] A similar practice of tolerating polygamy on a temporary basis during the first stage of mission work also existed among missionaries in the Portuguese Congo whose custom it was "in opening up work in a heathen district to receive into Church membership a man with more than one wife, but prohibit him from taking any further wives and holding before him the ideal of monogamy."[15]

Perhaps the most famous advocate of the toleration of polygamy and the baptism of polygamists was Bishop Colenso of Natal. In his Journal *Ten Weeks in Natal*, Colenso criticized the usual practice of enforcing the separation of wives from their husbands and advocated the admission of polygamists to Communion, although not to Church offices.[16] In 1855 he published his

Remarks on the Proper Treatment of Polygamy, one of the most cogent arguments for the toleration of polygamy.[17]

Colenso and those who shared his views were often the victims of vituperative attacks and condemnation.[18] Indeed, were one to read only the attacks of their opponents, one could hardly escape the conclusion that such lenient missionaries favored polygamy and looked favorably upon the baptism of polygamists. In fact, almost without exception, they viewed polygamy as evil and such baptism as a temporary expedient. As Colenso himself wrote:

> I believe, of course, that the practice of polygamy is at variance with the whole spirit of Christianity, and must eventually be rooted out by it, wherever it comes, as speedily as possible.... But I certainly expressed a doubt in my published Journal, whether requiring a man, who had more than one wife to put away all but one, before he could be received to Christian Baptism, was the right way of accomplishing this end.[19]

In the main, such advocates of toleration put forward three arguments with regard to polygamy: practical, humanitarian, and moral. The practical argument, which was only infrequently voiced but must have figured significantly in missionary thinking, was that the refusal to baptize polygamists presented an insuperable barrier to successful evangelization.[20] Colenso even argued that if all converts were required to divorce all wives but one, the consequence of large-scale conversion would be the breakdown of the social order.[21]

Far more frequently voiced was the missionaries' humanitarian concern for divorced wives and abandoned children. "Whatever he, a convert, may be willing to do to secure his soul's salvation, he has no rights to sacrifice his wives, their feelings, their marriage bonds, their rights, and the rights of their children."[22]

Rev. D. D. Young of the Free Church of Scotland Mission in Kaffirland reported, "I have in my Mission district a very worthy elder. In his heathen days he had three wives, and when he became converted he put away two of the wives and remained with the first. But he had children by the other wives...they are without the fatherly care and fatherly attention."[23]

Mabel Shaw of Mbereshi wrote, "We do not look upon polygamy as wrong; the wrong would lie with her who left the husband of marriage and spent the rest of her life going from man to man."[24]

Thirdly, missionaries who advocated the toleration of polygamy argued that whatever the status of polygamy in Church canons, divorce was clearly forbidden. Accordingly, the African convert could not be required to discard any of his wives:

> Our American friend told us that he was willing that a polygamist who had discarded all his wives should marry any other woman. I must say it appears to me, with all deference and humility[,] that that would be directly violating the

> command of our Lord that 'He that puttest away his wife save for fornication and marrieth another, committeth adultery.' They are his wives.[25]

"What scripture do you refer to when you say a man can put away a wife?"[26]

> We must look to whether it is right or wrong and consider what our Head and Master, the Lord Jesus Christ thinks of the matter—and I will take up this verse, "Whosoever, putteth away his wife and marrieth another committeth adultery." But I think, when we bring forward that text, we must not forget that our Lord Jesus Christ was speaking to a nation where polygamy was allowed; and if that is so then the verse cuts another away; [*sic*] because if those women are the wives of that man, *we are forcing him and them to commit sin in putting them away*.[27]

Whatever the arguments put forward by such missionaries, it must be stressed again that they strongly differed from those (usually African) clergy who favored polygamy and viewed it as fully in keeping with a truly African form of Christianity.[28]

Translation

The second mode of adaptation to be considered in this chapter is "translation." In referring to "translation" I am not exclusively concerned with the process of rendering Christian literature in African languages, but rather with the more general attempt to express Christian ideas and concepts in an African idiom. Although rarely attempted in as consistent and systematic a manner as today's African Christian theologies, such restatements of Christian doctrine and terminology were a necessity from the beginning of the missionary enterprise in Africa.

As many authors have noted, the discovery of the right terms for basic biblical concepts was one of the most serious difficulties facing evangelists in the field.[29] Misunderstanding or improper attention to nuance could frequently result in the total misrepresentation of the message they attempted to convey.[30] The cautious missionary thus required a firm grounding in both the language and the culture of the people he worked with in order to accurately express Christian ideas. The translator of the Bible into Luba-Katanga (Southeast Congo) spent years looking for the right translation for "Holy Spirit." Although the local language contained many words for "spirits," none satisfied him because each appeared to have either wrong connotations or wrong associations. Finally, he learned that there was an official at the local court known as "Nsenka" whose function it was to meet those who had business with the chief, find out what they wanted, conduct them into the ruler's presence, and act as their advocate and intercessor. It occurred to him that the mediatory role which the Nsenka fulfilled on both a human and tribal plane corresponded to that which Christian theology assigned to the Holy Spirit. He therefore adopted the term and turned it to Christian usage in his translation.[31]

Locating the proper indigenous terms to be used in producing a vernacular Bible was only a small part of the translation work undertaken by the missionaries. Equally important, and certainly at least as difficult, was the identification of useful comparisons and analogies for explaining the essential elements of Christian belief. CMS missionaries in Tanzania compared God's word to a lamp or the medicine of diviners. God himself was described as a "chief," "diviner," or "shepherd."[32] Mabel Shaw, who ran the London Mission Society's famous school at Mbereshi, made extensive use of the image of God/Jesus as "Chief" and the Christian community as a "tribe" in her teachings among the Bemba.

> I told the children of the knights of old who pledged themselves to their chief *Bakalume ba mfumu* of their own land who lived near the chief to do his bidding. That to which our girls were giving themselves that day was the final act of initiation. They gave themselves to the Chief in the great congregation, and He, with all His people, the quick and dead, received them. It was for them to guard the Tribe's law and tradition, to obey their Chief's behests, to eat of the Chief's food, and be His good tribesmen forever.[33]

The God/Chief, community/tribe analogies are so predictable that it would be a mistake to view their usage as prima facie evidence of a missionary's earnest commitment to adaptation. Some translation of this sort was certainly inevitable and probably only a small percentage of missionaries viewed such analogies as anything more than an expedient way of communicating. Nevertheless, a few missionaries did exhibit tremendous thoughtfulness and originality in their translations.

In Tanzania some CMS missionaries compared God's sacrifice of His son to the local custom of giving cattle to redeem kinsmen who had been pawned for debts. "We know the Wamegi give cows for the redemption of men, but God gave His Son."[34] The remarkable creativity of Vincent Lucas, the UMCA (Universities Mission to Central Africa) bishop of Masasi, is clearly demonstrated in his discussion of the symbolism of Ash Wednesday in terms of the symbolic associations of ashes in local practice.

> I explained the meaning of ashes which seemed most likely to be understood in the country following the four uses of ashes here:
>
> (1) On the path to avert witchcraft from the home. We are to contend with the Devil in Lent.
>
> (2) Smearing a child's arm when a dream has been dreamed that evil has befallen the child and we wake to find it still safe. We only believe the judgements of God as a dream. Let us wake and while our soul is still safe use the ashes and guard it more diligently in the future.

(3) Ashes are used as a sign of joy when a traveller returns from a distant land on safety. Let us return like the Prodigal from the land of destruction.
(4) Ashes are used in the "Unyago" (initiation ceremony) rejoicing over the passage of children from childishness to manhood. Our ashes should mean the abandonment of the unworthy things of nature and the beginning once again of a new life of Grace, of the burial service where the use of ashes is closely linked to the hope of resurrection.[35]

Assimilation

I have used the term "assimilation" to characterize those cases in which elements from a non-Christian setting have been introduced into essentially Christian rituals. Through the assimilation of familiar African features the missionary sought to make the message of the Christian ritual more comprehensible and acceptable to his congregants. Although assimilation could be far-reaching and could involve numerous changes, it frequently represented a minimal attempt at accommodation. J. M. Welch, for example, while generally expressing little hope for the deeper adaptation of Christian marriage in Africa, did note the possibility of assimilating some customs "such as the leading of the bride by her father to the bridegroom with the Christians dancing and singing."[36]

The Dutch Reformed Church in Shonaland was generally negative in its attitude toward indigenous forms of religious expression. Nevertheless, one custom "that has been incorporated into the Church service is the sitting or kneeling with hands together, as a signal of respect during prayer. This practice corresponds to the way in which a Shona commoner expresses respect in the presence of a dignitary."[37]

Bishop Lucas of Masasi was far more ambitious in his introduction of traditional customs to Christian funerals. The digging of the grave was done with close attention to traditional practice. Customs related to ceremonial pollution, and petitions and offerings to the dead, were, however, not allowed.[38]

> Following the custom of the country, the friends and relations of the deceased dig the grave, and in the bottom of the grave they make a further excavation somewhat in the shape of a coffin. The body is laid out and wrapped in cloth: and when the service in church is over the graveside is reached, a near relation or, in the case of an adult, two go down into the grave and receive the body into their arms and lay it to rest in the hollowed-out earth coffin, placing rough hewn small logs of wood to form, as it were, the lid, and then covering all with a mat. The pagan custom is to lay the body on its side, and sometimes the cavity is hollowed out in the wall of the grave instead of in the floor, and before leaving

> the body a hole in the cloth is cut close to the ear, presumably in order that the deceased may hear petitions addressed to him: this custom is not allowed. In the pagan practice, when the grave has been filled in, a thatched roof on poles, sheltering the whole grave, is built over it, at any rate in the case of the most important people of the clan. There seems no reason to object to this, though the offering of tobacco and cloth are not allowed.[39]

What is important to stress here is that in the case of funeral rites Lucas was not engaged in the Christianization of a traditional ritual (see his treatment of rites of passage below) but rather in an attempt to incorporate African elements into the Christian rule. Although the end product might look the same in both cases, the two processes should be distinguished from each other for their starting points are diametrically opposed. In Christianization, missionaries began with an African ritual and sought to make it Christian; in assimilation, they began with a Christian ritual and incorporated African elements. Christianization was most likely to take place when no Christian ceremony existed which corresponded to the African ritual, assimilation could only take place when a Christian model existed.

Christianization

I have used the term "Christianization" to characterize those cases in which missionaries sought to create Christian versions of traditional African rites and practices. In such instances we are no longer concerned with the passive toleration or grudging acceptance of a non-Christian custom as was the case with polygamy. Nor are we dealing with a temporary expedient to be abandoned at some later date. The process of Christianization involved the adaptation of a traditional African ritual so that it became of value to the development of a Christian life in a Christian community. In the most successful cases such rites were not merely permitted to the believing African Christian, but almost required, and they achieved something resembling a sacramental status.

By far the finest examples of the process of Christianization involved the adaptation of traditional rites of initiation. Since no precise Christian parallel existed for such rituals, assimilation was not a viable means of adapting such rites. It was impossible for the missionary to incorporate African elements into an existing Christian ritual, for none existed. Accordingly, in each case the missionaries' starting point was the traditional African ritual, which they sought to cleanse of its inherently non-Christian character and mold to the purposes of the Church.

The most famous attempt to Christianize a traditional rite of passage took place under the leadership of Bishop Vincent Lucas of Masasi. Richly documented in Lucas's own writings and T. O. Ranger's well-known article, the Masasi experiment clearly illustrates the complexity involved in, and the successes possible from, such ventures.[40] Perhaps the crucial point to emerge from Ranger's article is that such endeavors to Christianize traditional institutions should not be viewed as the product of a single missionary's ideas or policies. Various groups, including foreign missionaries, African Christians, and practitioners of traditional religions, all influenced the fate of most such ventures.[41]

In fact, the Masasi experiment was so well known that it tended to overshadow numerous other similar ventures. Moreover, this tendency has been perpetuated in our own time, with Ranger's study being so extensively cited that one could scarcely escape the conclusion that it described a unique endeavor. In fact, this was far from the case, and several other examples of such Christianized initiations deserve attention.

The CMS attempt to create a "Christian and clean" *Jando* (initiation camp) among the Wagogo of Tanzania was typical of attempts at Christianization in several respects.[42] In particular, it clearly illustrates the ambivalence which characterized the adaptation of such rites. Advocates of the Christianization of such rites were not wholehearted supporters of traditional practices. While acknowledging the valuable social and educational functions of such rites, they also admitted that in their original form the initiation ceremonies contained much which was incompatible with Christianity. What distinguished the advocates of Christianization from the majority of missionaries was not only their sympathy for some elements in the traditional rites, but also their certainty that outright prohibition of such practices was ineffective. "Purely legislative measures or laying down of injunctions by people outside the tribe is of little or no value."[43] By Christianizing such rites they sought to cleanse them and purify them, eliminating the bad, substituting the good. The form generally remained African, the content became Christian. Although European intervention was prominent in the introduction of rules of hygiene and modern surgical instruments "stress was laid on the fact that it was to be a native (Wagogo) *Jando* run by natives throughout."[44] A model camp was made in the style of the Wagogo, male (non-Christian) relatives were allowed to attend, women were banned, circumcision performed. However, the entire ritual was given a decidedly Christian character. Ribald pagan songs were replaced by "healthy songs and hymns." During the period of the *Jando* definite teaching was given in religion and such subjects as "obedience, purity, honour, health, loyalty and temperance."[45]

A similar attempt to create Christian circumcision camps was also made by the CMS missionaries among the Kaguru of Tanzania. Although apparently less successful than the Masasi experiment, the intention was much the same: to replace pagan rites initiating youths as men of the tribe with Christian rites celebrating the entrance into the Church community. The Church even collected money in payment for the ceremony.[46]

In his discussion of the Masasi experiment, Ranger notes that similar attempts to create a Christianized *malanga* for females were far less successful.[47] It is interesting to note that this is not the impression one gains from reading the published and unpublished reports from Masasi. Speaking to a meeting on initiation camps attended by no fewer than thirteen missionaries and the distinguished anthropologist Audrey Richards, Miss A. M. Roe of the UMCA Masasi reported that parents were so pleased with the Christianized *malanga* that they tended to rush the girls into it. Accordingly, the missionaries had decided to limit the rite to those girls prepared to be baptized and become full Christians.[48]

Whatever the verdict concerning the success of the Christianization of female initiation in Masasi, there can be little dispute about the results achieved in other areas. Students of African religion are generally wellacquainted with Audrey Richards's classic study of initiation among the Bemba of Zambia.[49] It is therefore especially interesting to read Mabel Shaw's account of her creation of a Christian *Chisungu* and her own acceptance as a *Ba na Chimbusa* (initiation instructor). Although Shaw became aware of the Chisungu ceremony quite quickly after her arrival at Mbereshi for the London Missionary Society or LMS (girls absented themselves from school in order to participate), she initially took no action. "I did not question it, I was a newcomer and strange to them. I waited some years, then with Mwenya I was allowed into the house of Chisungu and heard some of the teaching."[50] Only gradually did a Christian ceremony evolve. At first the traditional ceremony was conducted with traditional teachings at the school. Next, Shaw herself gave the teachings but in a context which included medicines and food taboos. Eventually a Christian ceremony evolved in which the girl was initiated into the "tribe of Christ."[51]

Among the richest areas for the study of the Christianization of initiation rites are the missions to the Chewa of Nyasaland (Malawi). The UMCA, Dutch Reformed Church (DRC), and Roman Catholics all attempted to develop Christianized versions of the *Cinamwali* (initiation).[52] In fact, the existence of such parallel experiments raises serious questions as to the role competition between missions may have played in encouraging such flexibility. Although we possess only very limited information regarding the Roman Catholic venture, it appears clear that both the UMCA and DRC were extremely successful in their attempts to create Christian initiation rites. The DRC even reports that non-Christian parents frequently invited the Christian *Alangizi* (instructor) to instruct girls who refused to undergo pagan initiation.[53]

The Berlin Lutheran Mission in Uzaramo, Tanzania, made a carefully planned effort to develop a Christianized version of the traditional girls' initiation. As one missionary reported, "as much of the old ceremonial as was permissible in the opinion of the mission has been incorporated in the new system, so that the new shall be as far as possible an evolution from the old and not a complete break with the past."[54] Christian initiates found the traditional year of seclusion living with a *Kungwi* (female guardian) replaced by a two-month confinement, followed by transfer to a boarding school. Her "coming out," however, included many of the traditional elements, including dress, gifts, songs, manner of being brought out, and beer. Begun with three girls in 1932, by 1938 the experiment had grown to encompass 117 girls.[55] Once again, non-Christians were among the participants.

Even as controversial a ceremony as female circumcision was open to the possibility of limited attempts at Christianization. As recent studies of the Kikuyu Circumcision controversy in Kenya have shown, the CMS parted company with other missionary groups by refusing to adopt a uniform policy on female circumcision.[56] While some missionaries took an uncompromising position against the practice, others were far less dogmatic. In particular, W. J. Ramply of Kabarae station sought to retain the custom and conduct the ceremony under the auspices of the Church. While Ramply stopped far short of a fully Christianized ceremony and the creation of initiation camps, this seems to be as much a product of the Kikuyu understanding of the rite as a result of any hesitation on his part. Although less than 100 percent successful, Ramply's experiment, "was widely accepted in the mission community there and was continued for about twenty years."[57]

Acculturation

The fifth mode of adaptation to be examined in this chapter is that which I have designated as "acculturation." This term is meant to describe attempts by Western missionaries to preserve features of traditional culture which they felt to be valuable and compatible with the development of Christian spirituality. This type of adaptation can be distinguished from the forms previously discussed in a number of ways. First, acculturation is a much more positive attitude to African social institutions than tolerance. Advocates of toleration frequently accepted the assumptions of Western cultural superiority which motivated their less flexible brethren. The point on which they disagreed was not that of goals but of method. In contrast, advocates of acculturation openly challenged accepted ideas of the missions' civilizing role:

> There are times when one almost resents the coming of motor cars and steamers and aeroplanes.... The old days, the old ways, the old tribal life seem so very much more attractive; one deplores the rapid breaking-up and shattering of all that was.[58]
>
> Christianity is not the founder and chief carrier of civilization but its direct opponent.[59]

The process of acculturation also differed in at least one respect from the attempts at Christianization described in the previous section of this chapter. In the attempts to Christianize traditional rites of passage, the social context of the rites was the Christian community. The traditional social structure was generally circumvented and frequently undermined. Proponents of acculturation sought to work within the traditional institutional framework, seeking to preserve and even restore "traditional" tribal life.[60] For example, the American mission board responsible for work among the Ovimbundu of Angola sought to carry on much of its work through village kinship patterns. "In 1905 Elende Station was opened with the idea that the only natives to reside there would be a small number of teachers and other leaders and boarding-school pupils who would afterwards return to their own families to form new centres of work."[61] Indeed, throughout this area the dominant pattern has been for Christian elders to work within the kinship pattern of the village.[62]

This stress upon the inherent value of the traditional social system and the desire to work within its framework also distinguish acculturation from assimilation. However much the latter process may involve the incorporation of traditional *elements* into Christian ritual, it differs in essence from acculturation, which advocates the general preservation of the traditional society. Moreover, in assimilation African features were frequently integrated into a Christian setting situation. For the acculturationist, the preservation of the traditional social structure was an ideal, not an unavoidable compromise.

One of the most articulate advocates of this method of adaptation was the German missionary and anthropologist Bruno Gutmann. Unlike many missionaries, who viewed the acceptance of Christianity as an individual decision which necessitated the abandonment of past beliefs and social ties, Gutmann believed that whenever possible such ties should be maintained.[63] For Gutmann, the growth of personality and of morality were intimately connected to the primordial (*urtümlich*) forms of community life: clan, neighborhood, and age-grade. The creation of a successful Christian community in tune with the national spirit of the tribe could only be attained by working through, not against, the traditional native institutions and leadership.[64]

This "indirect rule" approach to missionizing among the Chagga of Tanzania held many of the risks involved in its more famous political counterpart. First, in those cases in which "desirable" social institutions had broken down (or had never existed) missionaries were forced to invent or revive them. "It would accord both with the dignity of the woman and the mission's task of protecting that dignity and maintaining the distinctive moral values of the primitive peoples if the mission were to attempt to *revive* and purify the old custom of the bride gift, maintaining the old fundamental idea."[65]

Secondly, many such missionaries combined their aforementioned skepticism regarding the values of Western civilization with a romantic idealism concerning traditional societies. "In the right context" or "properly reconstructed," the tribal society appeared Edenic in character.[66] Thus, for example, Gutmann argued that polygamy was a late degenerate institution among the Chagga and that in advocating monogamy the missionaries were reviving old customs.[67] Connected with this romanticism was a tendency among some missionaries to impose or reimpose African cultural features even in the face of native opposition. While Bemba women delighted in giving their babies Western names such as "Comin" and "Bunkum," missionaries insisted that a second Chibemba name also be given.[68] Some CMS missionaries were so eager to maintain traditional tribal cultures that they retribalized freed slaves, forbade Western dress, and encouraged traditional dances.[69]

Admittedly, few missionaries were as philosophically committed to the systematic preservation of African culture as Gutmann. Yet, such cases warn us against too simplistic a view of missionary cultural attitudes. Indeed, if many missionaries have been taken to task for their cultural imperialism, some may be criticized for their conservatism.

Incorporation

The sixth and final form of "adaptation" to be examined in this chapter is incorporation. Strictly speaking, incorporation carries the Africanization of Christianity beyond mere adaptation, for it entails the introduction of African concepts into the body of "normative" Christianity. Here we are no longer concerned with the attempt to contextualize Christianity on the African continent, but rather with the incorporation of African elements into the Church as a whole. The distinction is a crucial one. However much Shaw, Lucas, Gutmann, and other missionaries mentioned above may have demonstrated their flexibility and sensitivity, at no point did they consciously seek to introduce African elements into the wider Church.[70] The policies they pursued were designed to ease the way for the Africans' conversion, not to influence the development of Christianity in the West. However much African Christians might have to contribute to the development of an indigenous Church, they apparently, according to this view, had little of value to offer the Church universal. Supporters of incorporation, on the other hand, felt the African contribution to be of significance beyond the borders of the continent.

The outstanding example of incorporation in pre-independence Africa is the Jamaa movement, which was founded by the Flemish priest Placide Tempels in the Belgium Congo.[71] As several useful studies and Tempels's own writings reveal, the Jamaa was not the product of his first encounter with African culture. Rather, it developed over a lengthy period during which Tempels's ideas concerning African traditions and Africans underwent a gradual transformation.

During Tempels's first ten years as a missionary he enthusiastically accepted the dominant definitions of his role as white man and priest. Separated from the local Africans by race and robe, he sought to bestow upon them the twin gifts of civilization and Christianity.[72] Only after a decade of limited success did he begin to question the assumptions which lay behind his behavior. Under the influence of progressive colonial thinkers, especially a number of Belgian lawyers, Tempels abandoned what he characterizes as his "priest phase" and commenced his "adaptation phase." He turned his attention to the task of achieving an understanding of "native mentality."[73] These efforts culminated in 1945 with the publication of the now famous work *Bantu Philosophy*.[74] Focusing on the key concept of "vital force," Tempels attempted to explain Bantu ontology to a Western reader. In particular, he hoped to guide pro-adaptation officials and missionaries to a better understanding of Bantu thought.

> It has repeatedly been said that evangelization work should be adapted.... Adapted to what? We can build churches in native architecture, introduce African melodies into the liturgy, use styles of vestments borrowed from Mandarins or Bedouins, but real adaptation consists in the adaptation of our spirit to the spirit of these people. Christianity—especially Christianity in its highest and most spiritual form—is the only possible consummation of the Bantu ideal....[75]
>
> ...But it is essential to set out this perennial doctrine in terms of Bantu thought and to present the Christian life that we offer them as a vital strengthening and a vital uplifting.[76]

Unfortunately, relatively little is known about Tempels's missionary activities during his adaptation period.[77] The *Catéchèse bantoue*, which he promised to write in *Bantu Philosophy*, in fact only appeared in 1948, after Tempels's thought had undergone further development and he had entered a new phase in his missionary career, that of "encounter."[78]

The chief product of this encounter phase was the Jamaa movement. Although a detailed analysis of the Jamaa is, of course, beyond the confines of this chapter, several points should be emphasized. First, it should be noted that the Jamaa represents a reinterpretation rather than a mere restatement of the

Christian message. In his encounter phase Tempels experienced "a new vision on the *whole* of Christianity, a new discovery of Christ, or perhaps, a first discovery of Christianity, of God's good tidings to mankind."[79] This "new vision" finds expression in various aspects of the teachings of the Jamaa. According to Tempels, for example, the first and ideal Jamaa (Swahili term for family) was the encounter between Christ and Mary. "They were 'more than' mother and son; in a mystical sense, they were also linked as father and daughter, and husband and wife."[80] Such teachings should not be confused with the "translations" considered in the second section of this essay. While the latter represent an attempt to express existing Christian ideas and concepts in an African idiom, the Jamaa seeks to express new truths. In the example cited above, the application of the term "Jamaa" to the Christ-Mary relationship serves not to translate Catholic theology, but rather to elucidate the beliefs of a new movement of Christian thought and practice.

A second feature which distinguishes the Jamaa from the cases of adaptation we have considered previously is that its applicability is in no way limited to African Christians. The numerous African concepts and teachings incorporated into the Jamaa belief system and ritual do not represent an attempt to create a form of Christianity particularly suited to Africans. On the contrary, many of these elements are held to be of universal value and to be worthy of incorporation into the wider Church. The participation and place of European priests in the movement is one clear indication of this universalism. "The priest needs the *baba* (father) and *mama* (mother) to grow in priestliness just as the *baba* and *mama* need the priest to offer on the altar their love.... They are also spiritually equal."[81] Thus in the Jamaa movement unlike any of the other cases considered in this chapter, the European clergy stand not to the side, but in the heart of the movement, participating as members sharing in the encounter. The African elements of the Jamaa are held to be of relevance not only to the movement's African members, but to its European clergy as well.

As African Christianity moves toward the end of the twentieth century, the debate over the relationship between African culture and the churches shows no signs of abating. In this short essay an attempt has been made to highlight two aspects of that relationship. First, we have attempted to show that contrary to the rather one-sided picture which dominates much of the literature, early Western missionaries played a significant role in the "Africanization" process. Secondly, we have argued that attempts at Africanization/adaptation have varied in form and motivation. A six-fold typology has been suggested. It is hoped that both contributions, historical and typological, may be of value to the study of an issue whose significance extends far beyond the borders of a single continent.

Acknowledgments

I would like to thank the Harry S Truman Institute, the Lady Davis Fellowship Trust, the Humanitarian Trust, and the Baron de Menasce Trust for supporting the research which produced this essay. An earlier version of it was read at a seminar on African Religions at the School of Oriental and African Studies and published in the *Journal of Religion in Africa* 16, 3 (1986). I would like to thank Professors Richard Gray and Humphrey Fisher, for their comments. Ms. Esther Jacobovitz assisted in the gathering of sources on this topic.

Notes

1. K. Appiah-Kubi and S. Torres, eds., *African Theology en Route* (Maryknoll, N.Y., 1979); (Cf. the title of the French version *Libération ou adaptation? La Théologie africaine s'interroge* (Paris, 1980); E. Fashole-Luke et al., eds., *Christianity in Independent Africa* (London, 1978), esp. Part 2, "Traditional Religion and Christianity: Continuities and Conflicts."
2. Cf., for example, A. Shorter, *African Culture and the Christian Church* (London, 1973) or M. C. Kirwen, *African Widows* (Maryknoll, N.Y., 1979).
3. A. J. Temu, *British Protestant Missions* (London, 1972), 155; Cf. E. A. Ayandele, *The Missionary Impact on Modern Nigeria* (London, 1966), 242-43; W. L. Williams, *Black Americans and the Evangelization of Africa* (Madison, Wisc., 1982), 104-24; T. O. Beidelman, *Colonial Evangelism* (Bloomington, 1982), 133, and many others.
4. On Lucas, see T. O. Ranger, "Missionary Adaptation of African Religious Institutions: The Masasi Case," in *The Historical Study of African Religion*, eds. T. O. Ranger and I. Kimambo (Berkeley, 1982), 221-47, and see below.
5. Beidelman, 19, compares Tempels and Gutmann without considering the essential differences between them. E. Dammann in an important article which considers the foundations of today's African theologies makes no attempt to distinguish between the approaches of Gutmann and Lucas. "Vorläufer einer Afrikanischer Theologie," *Zeitschrift für Missionswissenschaft* 60 (1976): 138-48. Cf., however, S. Knak, "The Characteristics of German Evangelical Missions in Theory and Practice" in Tambaram Reports III (Oxford, 1939), 344, for such an attempt.
6. Two recent surveys on the subject are A. Hastings, *Christian Marriage in Africa* (London, 1972), 5-26; E. Hillman, *Polygamy Reconsidered* (Maryknoll, N.Y., 1975).
7. Ibid., p. 32.
8. Rev. J. Johnson, *Report of the Centenary Conferencer on the Protestant Missions of the World, London 1888* (London, 1889), 48-81.

9. A study of the archives of the Seventh-Day Adventists (Washington, D.C.) which I undertook in August 1982 illustrates this clearly. See also C. R. Maberly, "The Polygamous Marriage Variant: The Policy and Practice of a Church," M.A. Thesis, Andrews University.
10. "The lesson that we have been taught today is that we Christians at home must remember that our missionaries, who in our stead are preaching Christ to the heathens, have difficulties to contend with, practical difficulties, in this matter that we at home cannot estimate..." Johnson, 68.
11. R. Strayer, *The Making of Mission Communities in East Africa* (London, 1978), 79.
12. Ibid.
13. M. Wright, *German Missions in Tanganyika 1891-1914* (Oxford, 1971), 90.
14. Ibid., 105.
15. ICBM/CBMS (International Conference of British Missions/Conference of British Missionary Societies) (School of Oriental and African Studies, London) Box 21, File E.
16. J. W. Colenso, *Ten Weeks in Natal* (Cambridge, 1855), 140-1.
17. J. W. Colenso, *Remarks on the Proper Treatment of Polygamy* (Pietermaritzburg, 1855). For a similarly favorable report by the Catholic Bishop Jolivet in 1888 see W. E. Brown, *The Catholic Church in South Africa* (London, 1960), 248-50.
18. See, for example, *Reply by an American Missionary to Bishop Colenso's "Remarks on the Proper Treatment of Cases of Polygamy"* (Pietermaritzburg, 1855).
19. Colenso, *Remarks*, 3.
20. For the rejection of this argument see W. Holm in Johnson, 57.
21. Colenso, *Remarks*, 19.
22. Ibid., 17. Note that Colenso and the missionaries cited below recognized the validity of traditional marriage.
23. In Johnson, 72. Cf. Maberly, 11.
24. Mabel Shaw, *God's Candlelights* (London, 1936), 61.
25. Johnson, 63.
26. Maberly, 30.
27. Johnson, 71 (emphasis added). Cf. S. Axelson, *Cultural Confrontation in the Lower Congo* (Falkoping, 1970), 287.
28. For the tensions between toleration and outright approval in one area, see J. B. Webster, "Attitudes and Policies of the Yoruba African Churches towards Polygamy," in *Christianity in Tropical Africa*, ed. C. G. Baeta (Oxford, 1968), 224-48.
29. Dammann, 146-47; E. Fenn, "The Bible and the Missionary," in *The Cambridge History of the Bible*, ed. S. L. Greenslade (Cambridge, 1963), 3: 383-407.
30. M. Wright, "Nyakyusa Cults and Politics in the later nineteenth century," in Ranger and Kimambo, 158, 160.
31. Fenn, pp. 395-96.
32. Beidelman, 103, 146. On the work among the Ibo of Bishop Shanahan of the Society of Holy Ghost Fathers, see Ayandele, 265.
33. Shaw, 90, cf. also 78-84; Wright, 90.

34. Beidelman, 103.
35. Lucas, Masasi log-book, March 1, 1922 Ash Wednesday, quoted by Ranger, 229.
36. J. M. Welch, "Can Christian Marriage in Africa Be African?" *IRM* 22 (1933): 17-32, esp. 28.
37. M. L. Daneel, *Old and New in Southern Shona Independent Churches* (The Hague, 1971), 1: 262.
38. Lucas, "The Christian Approach to Non-Christian Customs," in *Christianity and Native Rites* (London, 1950), 19-21.
39. Ibid., 20-21.
40. In addition to the article cited in note 4 above, see Lucas's "The Christian Approach to Non-Christian Customs" and "The Educational Value of Initiatory Rites," *International Review of Missions (IRM)* 6 (1927): 192-98. Cf. the reply by J. Raum, "Christianity and African Puberty Rites," *ibid.*, 581-91, and the critical evaluation by Shorter, 73.
41. Ranger, 247.
42. W. Wynn Jones, "An Experimental Initiation Camp Held at Ugogo, 1930" (October 1932), 2. IMC (International Missionary Council)/CBMS (Conference of British Missionary Societies) (SGAS) Box 201, File F.
43. Ibid.
44. Ibid. For another example of the introduction of modern surgical techniques in traditional initiation, see R. Rotberg, *Christian Missionaries and the Creation of Northern Rhodesia 1880-1924* (Princeton, 1965), 94-95; K. N. Mufuka, *Missions and Politics in Malawi* (Kingston, 1977), 24.
45. Jones, 4. On the traditional Wagogo ceremony, see P. Rigby, *Cattle and Kinship among the Gogo* (London, 1968) 205-11.
46. Beidelman, 136.
47. Ranger, 247.
48. IMC/CBMS Box 201, File F (January 1931). Cf. *Central Africa* 45 (1927): 193; and 47 (1929): 24-26.
49. Audrey Richards, *Chisungu* (London, 1956).
50. Shaw, 57.
51. Ibid., 57-58. See also S. Morrau, "'No Girls Leave the School Unmarried': Mabel Shaw and the Education of Girls at Mbereshi, 1915-1940," History Seminar, Chancellor College University of Malawi 1982-83, No. 3.
52. G. Verstraelen-Gilhaus, *From Dutch Mission Church to Reformed Church in Zambia* (Franeker, 1982), 181-86; P. Pretorius, "An Attempt at Christian Initiation in Nyasaland," *IRM* 39 (1950): 284-91; A. M. Gathercole, "The M.U. in the Diocese of Nyasaland," in *The Mother's Union with U.M.C.A. in Africa* (London, 1956), 12-15, R. G. Stuart, "Christianity and the Chewa: The Anglican Case 1885-1950," Ph.D. dissertation, University of London, 1974, 210-18; M. Schoffeleers and I. Linden, "The Resistance of the Nyau Societies to Roman Catholic Missions in Colonial Malawi," in Ranger and Kimambo, 260, 272. Cf. also I. Linden and J. Linden, *Catholics, Peasants and Chewa Resistance in Nyasaland 1899-1939* (London, 1974), 169, 185.

53. Pretorius, 287.
54. C. M. Culwick, "New Ways for Old in the Treatment of Adolescent African Girls," *Africa* 12 (1939): 428.
55. A similar school existed prior to World War I at Kisserawe station, but was not restarted after the war.
56. R. Strayer (with J. Murray), *The Making of Mission Communities in East Africa* (London, 1978), 136-55. J. Murray, "The Church Missionary Society and the Female Circumcision Issue in Kenya 1929-1932," *Journal of Religion in Africa* (*JRA*) 8 (1976): 92-104.
57. Strayer, 145. Cf. Also Beidelman, 193, on Christian initiation in Ukaguru on the 1950s.
58. Shaw, 176.
59. Gutmann, quoted by M. Schlunk, "The Relations of Missions to Native Society," *IRM* 16 (1927): 354.
60. Cf. Knak, 343.
61. G. M. Childs, *Umbundu Kinship and Character* (London, 1949), 67.
62. Ibid.
63. J. C. Winter, *Bruno Gutmann 1876-1966* (Oxford, 1979), 39-41.
64. G. Wagner, "Dr. Gutmann's Work on Kilimanjaro: II. An Anthropologist's Criticism," *IRM* 26 (1937): 513. See also P. Hassing, "Bruno Gutmann of Kilimanjaro 'Setting the Record Straight,'" *Missology* 7 (1979): 423-33. For similar sentiments in the Swedish Missions's *Mission for Bundet*, see Axelson, p. 283.
65. Gutmann, quoted by Schlunk, 356-57 (my emphasis).
66. For the problems inherent in such contextual judgments, see E. Gellner, "Concepts and Society," in *Rationality*, ed. B. R. Wilson (Oxford, 1970), 18-49.
67. Quoted by Schlunk, 357.
68. Shaw, 41.
69. Strayer, 49.
70. All three appear to have valued the preservation of traditional customs insofar as these were compatible with and prepared the community for Christianity.
71. Two useful studies of the Jamaa are W. De Craemer, *The Jamaa and the Church* (Oxford, 1977), and J. Fabian, *Jamaa* (Evanston, 1971). A good example of incorporation in a non-African setting is the Jesuit reaction to Chinese religion and the introduction of insights gained in China to the religious debates of Western Europe and especially the development of Deism.
72. De Craemer, 14ff.
73. Ibid., pp. 18-31; Cf. Fabian, 23-32.
74. I have made use of the English translation of Placide Tempels's work: *Bantu Philosophy* (Paris, 1969).
75. Ibid., 25; cf. 36.
76. Ibid., 186.
77. It is perhaps significant that during this period Tempels argued for the recognition of traditional marriage by the colonial authorities; see "Le Mariage indigène et la loi," *Kongo-Overzee* 29 (1944-45): 245-82.

78. Tempels, *Bantu Philosophy*, 25; De Craemer, 33-35.
79. Father Frans (a Jamaa priest) quoted by De Craemer, 34 (emphasis added).
80. Tempels, "Le Renouveau communautaire," quoted in ibid., 59.
81. Ibid., 63.

CHAPTER 2

Christianization and Indigenization: Contrasting Processes of Religious Adaptation in Thailand

ERIK COHEN

The Issues

This chapter explores the processes of mutual adaptation of Christianity and indigenous religions in Thailand. It seeks to illuminate thereby some theoretical issues in the sociology of contact between religions which have heretofore remained unexplored.[1]

The voluminous literature on Christian missionary and evangelizing activities (e.g., Boutilier et al. 1978, Hvalkof and Aaby 1981, Whiteman 1983, Schneider and Lindenbaum 1987) is one-sided in one crucial respect: it is primarily concerned with the adaptation of Christian beliefs and practices to the local setting, and particularly the adoption of indigenous customs by the Christian churches. Christianization and indigenization are therefore used as interchangeable synonyms. The same is true for Christian theologians. Thus, J. E. Thabping, a Catholic bishop in Thailand, wrote that "Indigenization is only one among many aspects of Christianization" (Thapbing 1974, 80). I suggest that these processes are not only different, but proceed in opposite directions.

True enough, sociologists of religion were well aware of the fact that indigenous religions did adopt various aspects of Christian (and other) religions which have penetrated into their environment, but such processes were generally dealt with in the literature under the general rubric of "religious syncretism." The parallelism between processes of Christianization, as absorption of indigenous elements by Christian churches, and its reverse, indigenization, as absorption of Christian elements by indigenous religions has not been systematically observed and analyzed.

This problem was not resolved by Kaplan's otherwise excellent attempt to introduce some specificity and order into the study of adaptation of Christianity to indigenous religions. In his programmatic essay on the "Africanization of Missionary Christianity" (see chapter 1 of this volume), Kaplan proposed a sixfold typology of the modes of mutual adaptation of Christianity and native African religions. This typology is intended to overcome the application of "blanket terms such as 'Africanization,' 'adaptation,' and 'incarnation'..." (p. 10) to the processes by which Christianity related to African settings. It consists of six roughly ordered empirical types, ranging from mere "toleration" of African beliefs and practices, through their "translation" into Christian ideas and concepts, and their "assimilation," "Christianization," and "acculturation," all the way to their "incorporation" into the body of African Christianity.[2] The author does not propose an explicit rationale underlying his types and their order, but it appears that he seeks to order them by the extent to which the adaptations and adoptions become central to the theology and institutional structure of African Christianity: in this respect, "toleration" is the most peripheral, and "incorporation" the most central type. The typology does not, however, resolve the problem of the conceptual distinction between Christianization and indigenization (Africanization in Kaplan's case); in fact, from the viewpoint of this distinction, the title of his essay is a misnomer; he deals with the Christianization of African beliefs and practices, rather than with the Africanization of the Christian religion. The use the Africans made of Christian beliefs and practices in traditional African religious settings remained unexplored. No typology of indigenization, complementing that of Christianization, has been proposed by Kaplan.

A number of related issues remain similarly unexplored, whether in Kaplan's own work or in the work of other researchers. "Indigenous" religion and culture is in most of these studies conceived as a global, undifferentiated category. Relatively little attention is paid to the distinguishing characteristics of different indigenous religions and their impact on the extent and the specific types of Christianization. A distinction of crucial significance in this respect is that between "axial" and "pre-axial" indigenous religions (Eisenstadt 1982, 1986). In brief, "pre-axial" religions, a category which embraces most "primitive" or "pagan" religions, whatever their complexity, do not construe the world in terms of a fundamental chasm between an incomplete mundane sphere and an absolute and ideal transcendent sphere; nor do they possess a detailed soteriology, a systematic teaching regarding the route by which salvation from the mundane world could be achieved. "Axial" religions, a category including most world-religions, such as Judaism, Christianity, Islam, Hinduism, and Buddhism, do posit such a chasm between the two spheres, and propose a soteriological teaching by which it could be overcome.

Most detailed anthropological studies of Christian missionary activities dealt with "pre-axial" indigenous contexts, such as those of African (e.g., Beidelman 1982), Oceanian (e.g., Boutilier et al. 1978) or South American (Hvalkof and Aaby 1981; Shapiro 1987) tribal religions. Students of missionary activity have hence remained largely unconcerned with the difference between the encounter of Christianity with such "pre-axial" religions and its encounter with the great "axial" religions, such as Buddhism. Two basic questions can be asked with respect to that difference: (1) Are the processes of Christianization and indigenization more prominent when Christianity encounters an "axial" religion or when it encounters a "pre-axial" one; and (2) Which specific types of adaptation (of the kind discussed by Kaplan) will be most prominent in each of these situations?

Finally, studies of processes of Christianization and indigenization have not distinguished clearly between processes in which the *beliefs* of one religion are adopted by another, and the parallel processes of adoption of its *practices*. I argue that Christianity, being primarily concerned with correct beliefs (e.g., in "dogmas"), will find it easier to adopt some of the practices rather than the beliefs of other religions; a more practice-oriented religion, such as Judaism or Islam, in contrast, will find it easier to accept beliefs, rather than practices.

Christianity and the Thai Context

There are some important differences between the context of Christianity in Thailand and in most other countries in which intensive Christian missionary activities have been conducted.

Thailand is, first and foremost, a Buddhist country, which was never conquered or colonized by a foreign, Christian power, and in which Christianity played a minor role throughout modern history; the Christian churches in Thailand and their missionaries enjoyed the status of tolerated, but not particularly welcome, guests.

The religious and cultural situation which Christianity faced in Thailand is more complex and heterogeneous than that which it faced in simpler societies. Buddhism is an "axial" religion *par excellence*, with a complex theology, and soteriological teachings offering a way toward complete release from mundane existence. In its concrete popular manifestations in Thailand, however, Buddhism does not appear in its pure, doctrinal form, but in syncretistic admixtures with magic and "animistic" beliefs and practices (e.g., Terwiel

1975). Such popular Buddhism involves both "axial" and "pre-axial" elements. The latter are particularly prominent among the peasantry in northern and northeastern Thailand. Finally, the so-called hill tribes of northern Thailand (McKinnon and Bhruksasri 1983; Lewis and Lewis 1984), among whom Christian missionaries were particularly active, practice "pre-axial," "animistic" religions.

Christianity in Thailand thus faces a broad spectrum of religious beliefs and practices which form several completely divergent contexts for the promulgation and understanding of its message, and for the mutual adaptation between it and local religions. For present purposes, however, it is enough to distinguish only two contrasting types of contexts:

1. *Doctrinal Buddhism.* This is practiced by a small minority of sophisticated, intellectually minded individuals; it is "axial," philosophical, and oriented toward the higher goals of the Buddhist teachings—though only few of its adherents aspire to the highest goal of complete release (Sanskrit *nirvana*, Pali *nibbana*, Thai *niban*). This type of Buddhism is hence sometimes called "nibbanic" (Spiro 1970, 31–65).
2. *Popular Religion.* This, as practiced by the great majority of Thai people, constitutes an admixture at different proportions of "axial" and "pre-axial" elements. Popular Buddhism, among laity and monks alike, although grounded in an "axial" Buddhist worldview, is in many respects "pre-axial," practical, and oriented primarily toward the achievement of religious merit (Pali *punna*, Thai *bun*), which will benefit the individual in this or his future lives, according to the universal law of karma (Pali *kamma*, Thai *kam*). This kind of Buddhism is hence sometimes called "kammatic" (Spiro 1970, 66–139). Many Buddhists also practice straightforward magic, for the achievement of immediate, direct benefits (such as good luck), in a manner which lies, as it were, outside the framework of the world order regulated by *karma* (e.g., Terwiel 1975). Popular Buddhism represents a spectrum of admixtures of Buddhism and non-Buddhist, Brahmanistic, animistic, and magic beliefs and practices. "Animism," finally, is dominant in the religions of the non-Buddhist, tribal people (e.g., Chindarsi 1983; Walker 1976). No crisp dividing line, however, exists between the lower end of the spectrum of popular Buddhist beliefs and practices, and those of tribal "animists," and hence I do not, for present purposes, separate popular Buddhism and tribal religions.

Returning now to our pair of basic processes, Christianization and indigenization, and taking account of the diversity of local religious contexts, four specific subprocesses of adaptation between Christianity and local religions can be conceptualized. For reasons related to presentation of the empirical material in the main body of this essay, the pairs of subprocesses, listed under each of the basic processes, are not wholly symmetrical.

1. Christianization

(a) Christianization of Buddhism. Conducted primarily on an abstract theological level, this type will consist of attempts to integrate basic "axial" Buddhist concepts, beliefs, and practices with Christianity, often on the initiative of the Christian churches. However, it will be of little practical significance as a means of proselytization, or of improvement of the understanding of the Christian message, among the broader strata of the Thai people. Owing to the fundamental and pervasive contrast between the presuppositions of the two religions (Cohen 1991), such an attempt will necessitate considerable efforts and ingenuity, and will generally bear only modest fruit. In terms of Kaplan's typology, this process of Christianization, insofar as it takes place at all, will involve primarily the more central of his types, particularly "incorporation."

(b) Christianization of popular religion. Conducted on a concrete mundane level, this type will typically emerge as a response of the Christian churches to felt practical needs, and to an initially unauthorized penetration of non-Christian popular beliefs and practices into Christian worship. It will consist of the adaptation of these beliefs and practices as a means of enhancing the chances of proselytization, of bringing the Christian message closer to the local people, or of enabling converts to preserve their culture even after they have changed their religion. Owing to the less determinate and less "axial" nature of popular religion, both Buddhist and animist, this type of adaptation will be easier to achieve than the preceding one; it will also be more significant as a means of proselytization and hence more frequently encountered in practice.

In terms of Kaplan's typology, this process will involve primarily the more peripheral types, such as those he calls "Christianization," "assimilation," and "translation." An extreme border case would be "toleration," a situation in which non-Christian customs are not really Christianized in any positive sense, but merely tacitly tolerated by the Christian churches.

2. Indigenization

(a) Buddhification of Christianity. This process will consist of an attempt to reinterpret basic Christian concepts, beliefs, and practices in Buddhist terms, whether on an abstract "axial" philosophical, or "nibbanic," level, or on a less

"axial," more practical, or "kammatic" level. In the former case it will be initiated by Buddhist intellectuals and theologians, but will be of little direct relevance to the religious life of the ordinary people. It will involve the more central types of Kaplan's typology. In the latter case, this process of indigenization will be conducted spontaneously by rank-and-file Christians or Buddhists, who often unconsciously perceive Christianity in terms of the Buddhist worldview; this version will be more widespread than the theological one and involve the more peripheral types in Kaplan's typology.

(b) Animization of Christianity. This process will be conducted on a concrete, mundane, "non-axial" level. It will consist of a reinterpretation of Christian beliefs and practices within a popular religious, animistic, or magical framework, usually with the intent to reap a concrete practical benefit. The carriers of this process will be local people, Christians or even non-Christians. It will involve the more peripheral types of Kaplan's typology.

We shall examine these four processes of adaptation with the help of empirical materials collected in the course of a study of Christianity in Thailand conducted by the author in 1986 and 1987 (Cohen 1990 and 1991). The study comprised a survey of the extant written sources on Thai Christianity, including some unpublished material, in-depth interviews with missionaries and representatives of several Christian churches in Thailand, and some observations of religious events. Before presenting the findings on the processes of adaptation, however, some basic information on Christianity in Thailand is necessary.

Christianity in Thailand

The history of Christianity in Thailand has been told in several detailed publications (McFarland 1928; Thompson 1967, 646–72; Swanson 1984) and needs to be only briefly summarized here. On the whole, Christianity was spectacularly unsuccessful in penetrating Thailand (e.g., Lantern 1986), despite prolonged and intensive missionary efforts by both Catholics and Protestants. The Catholics were the first to arrive in Thailand, in the seventeenth century. French Jesuits attained considerable influence at the court of Ayutthya, and even attempted to convert the illustrious King Narai, but failed. They lost their position and influence in the xenophobic revolution of 1688 which followed Narai's death (Thompson 1967, 646ff.; Wyatt 1984, 113–17). This early failure to convert the Thais led to a stagnation of Christianity in Thailand for a century and a half. The Protestants arrived in the nineteenth century—first the American Presbyterians (1828) and then a host of other denominations (McFarland 1928).

They found a tolerant atmosphere and, at a certain stage, had even hoped to convert King Mongkut (Rama IV, reigned 1851-68) to Christianity (Thompson 1967, 660). Their efforts, however, bore no fruit: while the Thais eagerly accepted the missionaries' contributions to the "modernization" of Thailand, such as the introduction of the press (Winship 1986), and of modern medicine (Thompson 1967, 658-59), neither the king nor other members of the Thai elite adopted Christianity (ibid., 661). Enthusiastic Presbyterian missionaries then established themselves in the northern principality of Chiang Mai (McFarland 1928; Swanson 1984). After an incident with the ruling prince, in which two converted local Christians were martyred, and the subsequent proclamation under King Chulalongkorn (Rama V, reigned 1868-1910) of the "Edict of Toleration" (Swanson 1984, 28-29), Protestant missionaries enjoyed in the north greater success than they did in Bangkok. Even there, however, the number of converts remained limited (Swanson 1984, passim.). On the whole, relatively more converts were made among the Chinese in Thailand (Blanford [1976], 39) and later, among the hill tribes, than among the ethnic Thais.

Though limited in scope, Thai Protestantism became independently institutionalized. An autonomous Thai Protestant church, the Church of Christ in Thailand (CCT), incorporating the Presbyterians, the Disciples of Christ, the Baptists, and some smaller denominations, was formed in 1934. After the communist takeover in China, the Overseas Missionary Fellowship (OMF) became highly active in the central and northern regions of the country, while the Christian and Missionary Alliance (CMA) developed considerable activity in the northeastern region (Isan). An Evangelical Fellowship was established in 1970, affiliating some of the more fundamentalist Protestant sects. In recent years several pentecostal churches were founded by local preachers, mainly in Bangkok. Altogether there are presently more than fifty Protestant denominations and missions active in Thailand. But despite its manifoldness and activity, Protestantism remains a marginal phenomenon in Thai society—with less than one hundred thousand adherents in a population of over fifty-seven million people.

The Catholics are a bigger community than the Protestants, numbering about two hundred thousand members. Many of these, however, are of Vietnamese or Chinese origin; they or their ancestors were often already Catholics upon arrival in Thailand (cf., e.g., Ansuchote 1960, 6). The Catholic church does not at present engage actively in proselytization. Its missionaries restrict themselves primarily to humanitarian and educational activities. Recently, however, following the decisions of the Second Vatican Council, the Catholics attempted to open a "dialogue" with the Buddhists, an enterprise which provoked an unexpected controversy and attack upon the Catholic church in Thailand (Cohen 1991).

The failure of Christianity to make a significant number of converts among the Thais could be partly explained by the fundamental differences in the basic worldviews of Christianity and Therevada Buddhism (ibid.), partly by the salience of Buddhism in the Thai identity and way of life, and partly also by the often uncompromising attitudes of both Catholic and Protestant missionaries toward the "heathen" beliefs and customs of the natives whom they have sought to convert (cf. Hughes 1984). In the last two decades, however, these attitudes have begun to change, under the impact of a more open, "liberal" theological outlook of many churches, and the exigencies of the local situation. The processes of adaptation of Christianity to the local settings have thereby been accelerated.

Christianization of Doctrinal Buddhism

While most major Christian churches, Protestant as well as Catholic, at present manifest at least some degree of openness to the local situation, most, and especially the evangelical Protestant denominations, profess a strong abhorrence of religious "syncretism." This fear constitutes a major obstacle to any attempt at a Christianization of orthodox Buddhist conceptions and beliefs; any such attempt would be further hindered by the deep gulf separating the fundamental presuppositions of the two religions.

While no direct synthesis of Christianity and Buddhism was attempted on the Christian side, efforts at what may be called "partial synchronization" have been made. Several Christian theologians sought to show that Christianity and Buddhism are not in fact as radically different as they appear to be. Some even claimed to have discovered doctrinal resemblances between the two religions. Thus, in a book on the Christian approach to Buddhism in Thailand, Eakin, a Protestant missionary, listed a series of such resemblances, for example, "(a) Both Gautama and Jesus affirmed the inward, spiritual nature of religion as against mere formalism; (b) Both proclaimed a way of deliverance from the evil and burden of this life..." and so forth (Eakin 1960, 30). However, he simultaneously also listed a series of doctrinal contrasts (ibid., 31-38). Others stressed that, despite doctrinal differences, "Buddhism and Christianity have in common a number of moral precepts such as: 'Do not steal: do not speak falsehood" (Thirty-three Points 1962, 1); but the same source also points out that "because the doctrines of the two religions differ, the moral precepts differ also, either in emphasis or in interpretation" (ibid., 1). Christian missionaries in my interviews also pointed out the similarities in the moral precepts of the two religions, and saw in these—perhaps more than their theologically minded colleagues—a possible bridge by which the gulf between them could be spanned to some extent. Even so, such synchronization stops short of what Kaplan called "translation," since it is not accompanied by an attempt to express "Christian ideas and concepts in a [Buddhist] idiom" (p. 13), but only points out the parallels between the two religions. Such comparisons are sometimes intended by both Protestants and Catholics to serve as a basis for a dialogue with Buddhism (e.g., Nontawasee 1985, 14; Ulliana 1969, 14).

In the Catholic church the desire for dialogue has been given official approval and encouragement by the Second Vatican Council, which inaugurated a new era of openness of the church toward other religions (Déclaration 1966, III–160–1). The new doctrinal position, namely, that other religions contain elements of the truth, which was, however, completely revealed only in Christianity (ibid., III–161), engendered among some members of the clergy in Thailand the idea that Buddhism and other local religions could be considered as "stepping stones" to Christianity. A similar idea had been broached even earlier by some Protestant missionaries; thus Eakin (1960, 61), in a discussion of the missionary approach to Buddhists, says that: "Many have felt that the true and most effective approach is through the use of Buddhism as a stepping-stone to Christianity." Among the Catholics in Thailand, however, there were some who took this conception even further, and sought to employ it as a means to incorporate Buddhism into the religious history of Christianity: Buddhism was presented by them as a forerunner of Christianity in the East, just as Judaism has allegedly been its forerunner in the West. Buddha came thus to be seen as a prophet of Jesus. This most far-reaching, though perhaps not fully consciously intended, attempt at "incorporation" in Kaplan's sense, however, provoked a strong reaction from a group of militant Buddhist monks (Sobhon-Ganabhorn 1984; Catholic Plot 1986), who have been insulted by the implication that Buddha did not attain to the ultimate truth through full self-enlightenment. Following this anti-Catholic outburst, any further attempts at such theological integration have been given up by the Catholics, and even the dialogue between the two religions was considerably attenuated (see Cohen 1991).

The growing interest of Christian, mostly foreign, theologians in Buddhism generated some other attempts at a mutual adaptation of Christianity and Buddhism which, in Kaplan's typology, lie somewhere in-between "acculturation" and "incorporation." Especially worthwhile mentioning are the efforts on the part of some theologians to reconcile the alleged historicity of Christianity with the cyclical conception of time on which Buddhism is based (e.g., Koyama 1974, 30–31, 1976; Seely 1969, 139). However, whatever the theological import of such efforts, they seem to have had no significant impact on Thai Christianity, particularly since they were mostly published outside Thailand.

The general scarcity of attempts at an adaptation of Christianity to Buddhism on a doctrinal level stands in sharp contrast with the many, though diffuse and uncoordinated, attempts at the Christianization of selected aspects of Thai popular religion.

Christianization of Popular Religion

In the early stages of Christian missionary activity in Siam, Catholic as well as Protestant missionaries strictly prohibited their new converts from keeping any element of Thai culture, whether or not it had an express religious significance. They sought to prevent thereby a contamination of Christianity by "paganism" (cf. Hughes 1984, 325). Thus, even the use of Thai musical instruments and tunes in Christian churches was strictly forbidden, for fear that they might unwittingly produce among Thai converts some associations with their previous religion. The architecture of the churches and their internal physical arrangements were exact copies of those customary in Europe or the United States. Foreign missionaries, and later also the indigenous clergy, strenuously emphasized the difference between Christianity and Buddhism in every realm of life, in an effort to strengthen the distinct Christian identity of their new converts.

The meager results of prolonged and intensive missionary efforts to convert the Thai people, and particularly the Thai Buddhists, however, have in recent decades engendered much thought and soul-searching among Christian missionaries, and particularly Protestant evangelists on the causes and reasons for their relative failure (e.g., Gustafson 1970, 157–59; Chaiwan 1975, 33–37; Cooke 1978). Their deliberations frequently touched upon two major themes: on the one hand, the close association between Buddhism and Thai cultural and national identity was pointed out as a reason for the reluctance of the Thais to give up Buddhism; on the other hand, the identification in Thai eyes of Christianity with the West, and Christianization with Westernization was seen as a major reason why Christianity has been considered by the Thais as a foreign religion (e.g., Hughes 1984, 324–25). These deliberations pointed to a crucial dilemma facing Christian missionaries in Thailand: how to adapt Christianity to the Thai context, so as to divest it of its foreign character and enable Thai converts to preserve their national identity, while at the same time safeguarding the purity of the Christian message.

Ideas regarding such an adaptation ranged from a profound theological consideration of the need to take account of the living context of the Asian environment and culture (e.g., Koyama 1974, 30ff.), to prosaic criticisms of the inability of Christianity to "market" its message successfully in Thailand (e.g.,

Lantern 1986). The response of individual missionaries and of most denominations was an enhanced openness toward what they considered to be Thai "culture," even though they continued to reject those local beliefs and practices which they considered to be of a "religious" nature. Even so, the Christian churches differed considerably in their readiness to Christianize Thai customs and adapt them to Christian worship, and in the extent to which they actively initiated such innovations, instead of merely accepting and legitimizing those which had been spontaneously introduced into worship by the rank-and-file members of their congregations. I am presently not in a position to give a systematic account of those differences. But I would venture the hypothesis, based on the sect-church typology as originally conceptualized by Troeltsch (1961), that, in general, the more a denomination resembles the sect-type, the more closed it will be to the local Thai environment; and the more it resembles the church-type, the greater will be its readiness to adapt itself to the Thai environment. This hypothesis, if borne out by the data, would help integrate the cross-cultural study of Christianity with the mainstream sociology of religion. My data provide some support for this hypothesis. Thus, the oldest established denominations in Thailand, the CCT and the Catholic church, presently appear most open to innovation; while most evangelizing sectarian movements are much less responsive to local conditions. However, in reaction to this inflexibility, some of the most recently established sects evince a marked readiness and even eagerness to absorb local custom, though continuing to reject popular non-Christian religious beliefs and practices.

The strategy of adapting "cultural" customs, but rejecting "religious" beliefs and practices, however, poses an interesting problem of "negotiation of meaning." In Thai culture, no crisp line exists between popular religious and "merely" cultural practices: most such practices have, at least implicitly, some popular religious significance, although this may not be anchored in the tenets of doctrinal Buddhism. In an effort to open the churches to Thai custom, the Christian missionaries and clergymen—foreign, and later on local—set out to redefine the meaning of Thai customs and practices and to demarcate a line between what they considered to be the "cultural" as against the "religious" domain. In the words of one of the leading functionaries of the CCT in an interview: "We have to consider what is [religiously neutral] culture and tradition which belongs to all Thais and what are religious customs." Following this reconsideration, the church should, in this cleric's view, decided "which Thai cultural customs should be adopted or adapted into the church."

A Protestant missionary expressly recognized the negotiability of the boundaries between "religion" and "culture." In his opinion, "boundaries can be shifted around. When under Grace we have freedom to define boundaries"; the boundaries, however, could even in his opinion not be arbitrarily reset: they can be shifted only within the constraints of the historical experience of the Church.

The demarcation lines set by clerics of varying denominations and at different times, were not identical: In general, as the pressure upon the churches increased, they tended to interpret more and more local customs as "merely" cultural, arguing that they lacked any scriptural basis in Buddhism. Such customs were thereby made available for Christianization. Some of the newly established sects mentioned above went furthest in this respect, accepting as "cultural" custom even local practices such as *tham khwam*, the "binding of the soul" (Heinze 1982), which other denominations considered as unequivocally religious—and thereby provoked widespread consternation and criticism in more conservative Christian circles.

Efforts at the adaptation of local customs ranged from active attempts to endow them with an explicit Christian meaning, all the way to passive toleration; they thus exemplify most of the less central types in Kaplan's typology.

The general spirit of the change of attitude toward Thai culture, which occurred in the churches in recent years, can be seen as one of "acculturation" in Kaplan's sense of a "stress [by the Church] upon the inherent value of the traditional social [and cultural] system and the desire to work within its framework" (p. 20). This, in turn, derives from the missionaries' intention to "preserve features of traditional culture which they feel to be valuable and compatible with the development of Christian spirituality." A principal expression of this spirit is the emphasis by some churches, and especially the CCT, upon the fact that Thai Christians are and remain culturally Thais and that their religion should not infringe upon their allegiance to the Thai nation and monarchy. One way to symbolize this allegiance are prayers for the king common in both Protestant and Catholic churches, as well as special services on the king's and queen's birthdays[3]—although one informant stated that even Christian Thais prefer to visit the Buddhist *wat* (temple), rather than their church, on such occasions.

The growingly benign disposition toward Thai culture, however, often links up with attempts to adapt it to Christian purposes, or endow it with a new, Christian meaning, in a broadened sense of Kaplan's definition of the type of "Christianization" as "cases in which missionaries seek to create Christian versions of traditional [local] rites and practices" (p. 16). No systematic policy of "Christianization" has, however, been formulated by any of the major Christian denominations in Thailand: such cases of "Christianization" as have occurred resulted, in many instances, from the initiative of individual clergymen or missionaries rather than from that of the central church organs—even though the latter may have eventually endorsed and legitimized them.

An extreme case in point relates to the endowment of traditional Thai festivals with a new Christian meaning. Thus, many Thai Christians continued even after their conversion to celebrate the festival of Loi Krathong, on which lit candles are floated on rivers and waterways in containers made of leaves and decorated with flowers (Rajadhon n.d.). Some Christian clerics tolerate that festival, arguing that at the present time it is a cultural custom without religious meaning (even though it probably originated as an offering to the water spirits; cf. ibid., 43). One informant, however, went further and reinterpreted the festival in Christian terms. In his view, the candles can be seen as symbolizing the light of Christianity—originally arriving into the interior of Thailand on rivers and waterways (which at the time were the main means of communication) and dispersing the darkness of ignorance of the inhabitants. This is the most explicit and comprehensive example of an effort to endow a Thai festival with Christian meaning which I have come across; it is doubtful, however, that this interpretation is widely accepted—or even known—among rank-and-file Thai Christians.

Another major example of deliberate and ingenuous "Christianization" comes from the field of popular arts: it consists of the attempt by the Christian Communication Institute (CCI) at the Payap University in Chiang Mai (a Protestant institution) to utilize popular Thai theatrical genres for the dissemination of the Christian message.

One of the most popular traditional forms of the Thai folk-theater, the *likay* (Smithies 1971; Hiranburana 1975; Viralrak 1980; Carkin 1984) was adapted as the primary medium for that purpose. The *likay* was expressly chosen because, in the eyes of the missionary heading the institute, it is, unlike the classical *khon* and *lakhon* plays (Nicholas 1975), devoid of express Buddhist religious content. The traditional *likay* resembles the European operetta: it mixes dialogue with song, comedy and buffooning with romance, and the traditional story with improvisation on contemporary themes (cf. Smithies 1971). In recent times the *likay*, which was traditionally performed mainly on popular festivals, declined into cheap clowning, while "classic" *likay* plays are rarely, if ever, performed anymore.

The missionary revived the "classic" *likay* tradition, and already in 1977 formed a *likay*-troupe composed of individuals with some background in the performing arts. With the help of traditional *likay* artists he created plots which convey a novel Christian message, even as they preserve or conserve the traditional form. Some plots are, in fact, taken from biblical stories, but have been adapted to contemporary Thai circumstances. A brochure from the late 1970s, significantly entitled, "Using Thai Cultural Forms," explains that "Ligay stories we adapt from the bible are couched in Thai terms and have Thai appeal." Thus, the biblical story of the "Prodigal Son" is transformed into the

"Prodigal Daughter": The story of a provincial girl from a "good" house who is lured into the big city, Bangkok, with false promises by her Casanova-like lover. Though the plot does not expressly refer to it, Thais viewing the play will inevitably be reminded of the problem of young local girls being lured to Bangkok into prostitution. The plots of other *likay* plays, such as *Lazarus*, *Esther*, or the *Good Samaritan*, deal similarly with contemporary social problems in Thailand in a Christian spirit.

The *likay* plays produced by the CCI are distinguished by a very high technical level of performance; this is combined with a subtle, unobtrusive insertion of the Christian message; the *likay* of CCI is the very opposite of the crude and direct approach to proselytization practiced by some extreme fundamentalist Christian sects. It is the most comprehensive and conscious effort to clothe the Christian message in indigenous garments.

The *likay* plays of the CCI, some of them shown on the local TV station of Chiang Mai, reach a very broad audience, which generally responds enthusiastically to the well-produced shows. It is, however, hard to estimate the effectiveness of these shows in conveying the Christian message to the broad public. In a few instances viewers have been so impressed by the performances, that they afterwards expressed belief in the Christian message. It appears, however, that a more important effect of the plays is the fact that they engender a certain openness, sympathy, and receptivity to Christianity on the part of the local Thai public; and even more, since the plays are produced in a Thai style, that they convey the important meta-message that one can become a Christian without uprooting oneself from Thai culture, or losing one's national identity.

"Assimilation," in Kaplan's sense of "cases in which elements from a non-Christian setting have been introduced into essentially Christian ritual" (p. 15) is also a quite common type of Christianization of popular Thai culture and religion. Many instances could be cited, but a few salient examples will suffice. One instance is found in church architecture. Protestant churches in Thailand were initially built in the style of the time that prevailed in the missionaries' countries of origin. However, the style of recently constructed churches has been partially assimilated to that of the Buddhist *wat* (temple); in particular, the multiple-gabled roof (Kennedy 1979) has often been adopted. Still, care was taken for these churches not to resemble the *wat* too closely, so that the symbolic differences between the two religious edifices would not be obliterated.

The Catholics—whose early churches were utterly European in style—went even further: Some of their recently built churches, designed by "progressive" Catholic foreigners, entirely resemble a Buddhist *wat*. In one case, the architect even asked the members of the congregation to paint pictures with themes from the life of Jesus on the inner walls of the church, just as mural paintings, depicting the life of Buddha, adorn the walls of Buddhist *wats* (e.g., Krug 1979).

The interior of Christian churches generally remains Western in style: pews and chairs are commonly used to seat the congregation and a table serves as an altar. Some informants advocated instead the use of mats, on which worshipers could sit in the customary Thai manner. One foreign nun even suggested that low tables, as used in Buddhist temples, could be substituted for the present altars in the Catholic churches. Such changes, however, would bring Christian bodily postures at worship much closer than is presently the case to the Buddhist ones, and will therefore probably run into opposition from some members of the clergy, whether Protestant or Catholic.

Some of the most interesting instances of "assimilation" can be found in the area of church music. In the past, only Western musical instruments, such as the organ, and Western liturgical tunes, were permitted in church. Opposition to Thai instruments and music was deep-seated not only among foreign missionaries, but also among the Thai converts to Christianity. Thus, when, in the 1960s, a Protestant missionary in the province of Nakhon Pathom introduced into worship for the first time a Thai instrument, the *ranad*,[4] some of the local members of the congregation expressed fierce opposition, claiming that the instrument reminds them of the spirits (*phii*). The *ranad*, and later on other Thai musical instruments, were nevertheless gradually admitted into the churches. Presently, both Thai instruments and Thai tunes are routinely used in worship in many Protestant churches in Thailand.

The Second Vatican Council of the Catholic church formally permitted the use of profane music, and even of the music of other religions, in Catholic worship. However, conservative Thai Catholic priests have long opposed the use of tunes based on Buddhist chants in church, insistently seeking to mark themselves off from the Buddhists and declining to draw closer to Buddhist forms of worship. Gradually, however, Thai tunes nevertheless became accepted as a basis for an indigenous Thai liturgic music, for which new Christian texts have been provided. At present, Thai instruments and tunes are also commonly used in worship in Catholic churches.

Some indigenous forms of worship and obeisance were also assimilated, or are in the process of assimilation, by the Christian churches. Thus, in the Catholic church the use of jos sticks instead of incense has been permitted, as was the use of the Thai *puangmalai* (flower garlands) instead of the Western flower bouquet as an offering to saints.

The customary Thai sign of respect, the *wai* (clasping of hands on the breast, accompanied by a bow) has been substituted for the traditional Catholic curtsy. Most of these changes have not been initiated by the church, but have been at first spontaneously introduced into worship by the rank-and-file members of the congregation, and only subsequently officially recognized as accepted forms of Catholic practice. Cases were even reported of Catholic worshipers sticking gold leaves onto the pictures of Catholic saints, just as Buddhists stick them onto Buddha images. This custom appears to be a border case between "assimilation" and "toleration" in Kaplan's typology, since the church has not yet taken an official position on it.

Some of the customs adopted by the Catholics are frowned upon by the Protestants, since in their view they resemble "idol worship," and are therefore not permitted in most Protestant churches. Protestants are in general more selective and apprehensive in assimilating local customs than the Catholics have been in recent years.

Instances of "translation," in Kaplan's usage, as an "attempt to express Christian ideas and concepts in an [indigenous] idiom" (p. 13) are common in Thailand; only a few examples will suffice. The most readily available cases can obviously be found in the translation of Christian concepts, particularly in the use of Buddhist terms to render Christian ideas—such as addressing "God" as *phra chao*, a traditional address of Buddha (cf. Hughes 1984, 330), or using the word *bap* (demerit in the *karmatic* sense) as an equivalent of "sin" in the Christian sense (cf. Seely 1957, 49–50). "Translation" in a wider, ideologically significant sense can be found in the recent decision in the Catholic church to use terms borrowed from the hierarchy of ranks of Buddhist monks to designate positions in the Catholic hierarchy (e.g., *phra song* for a priest, *phra sankara* for a bishop). In a wider, less formal sense, "translation" is often used as a means of popularization of Christian ideas, which are foreign to local audiences. One of the most common instances is the reference to God or Jesus as the "Great Spirit," whose power is greater than that of the spirits of both popular Buddhism and tribal animism.

Finally, as a border case of Christianization of popular religion, examples of "toleration," as an acceptance by the churches of a "continued existence of [local] social customs, while at the same time maintaining that they [are] essentially incompatible with a true Christian life" (p. 10), could also be cited.

Perhaps the most important example is the permission, on the part of some churches, granted to the family of a deceased Christian to conduct a traditional popular funerary ceremony, instead of (or in addition to) a Christian one. The reason given is that non-Christian relatives often put considerable pressure upon the family, and refusal would create serious tensions within the kinship group. A more extreme case of toleration is the tacit consent of some Catholic priests for young Christians of religiously mixed parentage to enter a Buddhist monastery (*buat*) for the customary period of several months, an act for which they would have been excommunicated in earlier times. "Toleration" is a border case in both Kaplan's and our typologies: here the boundaries between

Christianization and indigenization appear to blur and an implicit and unintegrated religious syncretism seems to emerge.

Buddhification of Christianity

The processes of Christianization and indigenization are not completely symmetrical in Thailand; Christianization, in its various manifestations, resulted from an effort of foreign Christian missionaries to convert the Thais in their own country. No such effort in an opposite direction, namely to convert the Christians, was ever undertaken by the Thais. In fact, Christianity has aroused relatively little interest among Thai intellectuals or Buddhist monks; and since, owing to its limited success, it did not pose a real threat to Buddhism, there was little incentive among Buddhist theologians in Thailand to interpret Christianity in Buddhist terms or to evolve a "Buddhist theology of Christianity." If there were only few attempts among Christian missionaries and clergymen to interpret the concepts and beliefs of doctrinal Buddhism in Christian terms, there were until recently virtually no attempts by Thai intellectuals or monks to interpret doctrinal Christianity in Buddhist terms. In the last few years the venerable Buddhist sage Phra Bhuddhadasa published several treatises in which he pointed out similarities and overlaps between Christianity and Buddhism; his project, however, was expressly not to "Buddhify" Christianity, but rather to reduce the distance between the two religions.

Whatever Buddhification of Christianity has taken place in Thailand, therefore, has been diffuse and mostly unreflexive—an adaptation by rank-and-file Christians, and even by Buddhists, of some Christian beliefs and practices to broad Thai Buddhist conceptions. I am unaware of any systematic adaptation of basic Christian ideas to Buddhist theology in terms of the more central types of Kaplan's typology, such as "incorporation." Although some of the adaptations which I did come across are remotely related to doctrinal issues, they were accomplished at a popular level, so that the distinction between indigenization on a theological and on a popular level could not be crisply drawn in the Thai case.

The principal form which the process of Buddhification of Christianity took in Thailand could be called "transposition": a Buddhist reinterpretation of Christian concepts, ideas, and beliefs, whose meaning has been originally anchored in a wider Christian "construction of reality" (Berger and Luckmann 1966), into Thai Buddhist terms. These concepts, ideas, and beliefs are thereby endowed with a completely new meaning, substantially differing from that given them in Christianity. This process of "transposition" does not wholly correspond to any of the types proposed by Kaplan, but comes closest to "translation" and "assimilation." Kaplan defines "translation" (as a type of Christianization) as an "attempt to express Christian ideas and concepts in an [indigenous] idiom" (p. 13). The reversal of this definition would yield "[an] attempt to express indigenous [in our case Buddhist] ideas in a Christian idiom." "Transposition," however, goes beyond mere "translation," in that it tears out these ideas and concepts from their Christian framework and adapts them to the Thai Buddhist one. Hughes (1984, 1985), who studies this process most comprehensively, refers to it as "assimilation." The process indeed to some extent resembles "assimilation" as used by Kaplan, even though the direction of the process described is obviously the reverse of that discussed by Kaplan: Hughes talks of the way Christianity is assimilated to Thai culture (i.e., indigenized), rather than the manner this culture is assimilated *by* Christianity (i.e., Christianized). The parallelism, however, is not complete: When indigenous customs are "assimilated" by Christianity, they are officially accepted and legitimized by the representatives or the authorities of the churches. When Thais—Christians or non-Christians—"transpose" popular Buddhist meanings upon Christian beliefs or customs, no such recognition is forthcoming from Buddhist authorities. "Transposition" is a diffuse, decentralized, and perhaps largely unconscious process—which "assimilation," in Kaplan's sense, is not.

"Transposition" is found primarily among nominal Thai Christians, who, perhaps unwittingly, perceive Christian ideas in terms of an essentially Buddhist construction of the world. This emerges clearly from Hughes's extensive study; his findings are in general confirmed by my own research. Hughes's principal finding is that "the central themes of Thai Christianity were not those [taught by] the missionaries, but those of Thai culture" (Hughes 1984, 331). Hence, in Hughes's view, "Christianity in Thailand comes to perform similar functions within Thai culture to those performed by Buddhism and animism" (ibid., 333).

Hughes found in his study of Christian students at Payap University, that they generally conceived of Christianity within a *karmatic* worldview, and that their attitudes and practices were shaped by this conception (Hughes 1985). (There are even Christians in Thailand who believe that God created *karma* in the act of Creation.)

Hughes argues that Thai Christians perceive Christianity in terms of the traditional Thai concepts of merit and power (cf. Hanks 1962). According to Hughes, they seek primarily merit in the performance of their religious obligations, rather than forgiveness of sin and salvation by the grace of God (Hughes 1984, 26–27). From this derives their overwhelming concern with a ritualistic performance of Christian practices, an attitude which is dominant in Thai Buddhism (Hughes 1985, 35–36). Indeed, some tend to view the Christian "way" as higher than the Buddhist, just as the way of the monk in Buddhism is higher than that of the layperson (ibid., 37).

My own study confirms Hughes's findings regarding the *karmatic* meaning of merit-making (*tham bun*) attributed by local Christians to Christian practices. This attitude does not differ substantially from that predominant in all forms of popular Buddhist activities, from the offering of food to monks, to entrance into monkhood (cf. Bunnag 1973), all of which are seen primarily as merit-making activities. Informants pointed out that merit-making is the dominant motive in the religious activities of both Catholics and Protestants in Thailand. Thus, according to a Catholic priest, following the decision of the Second Vatican Council that believers should make offerings to the poor, members of the local congregation started to bring quantities of food to the church, though these could not be used for the intended purpose. The priest stated that, in the eyes of the believers, these were "offerings to God," contributed by Thai Catholics in a spirit of *tham bun*. Similarly, a Protestant missionary claimed that local Protestants do not celebrate Christmas as a symbol of the "good tidings," but rather as a merit-making ceremony. They do not grasp, according to the missionary, that Jesus already did all the merit for them—and that their salvation depends on divine grace rather than on human merit.

In contrast to the generally tolerant attitude toward and even encouragement by many contemporary Christian clergymen and missionaries of the introduction of indigenous forms of worship into Christian ritual, the majority of them refuse to adopt the conceptions and beliefs which support these in popular Buddhism. However tolerant in other respects, such "transpositions" of Buddhist meanings upon Christian practices are unacceptable to the churches and the great majority of their representatives, since such a process is seen essentially as the opposite of Christianization—it indigenizes Christianity, rather than Christianizes Thai culture; such indigenization is rejected by the churches, and by the majority of the members of the clergy.

Thus, clerics and missionaries generally complained in interviews about the tendency of local Christians to worship in the spirit of Buddhist merit-making; only one informant, an old-timer foreign Catholic nun deeply engaged in the dialogue with Buddhism, saw nothing wrong in praying in the spirit of *tham bun*, and pointed out that many non-Thai Christians also pray in the same spirit (i.e., ask God for a benefit in return for their prayer).

The *karmatic* exposition of Christianity in terms of merit-making is the principal example of the process of "transposition," as defined above. This is also the most common example of Buddhification of Christianity in Thailand: Even though it is accomplished on a popular and pragmatic level, rather than on a theological or philosophical one, it is deeply rooted in the Buddhist cosmology, according to which *karma* is an underlying principle of existence; merit-making as a means of achieving positive *karma*, is therefore a legitimate endeavor for a Buddhist, even though it does not lead to the ultimate release (*nirvana*).

Animization of Christianity

Animization is the process by which principal Christian ideas of divinity, God, Jesus, or the Holy Spirit come to be perceived in terms of power; the power of these beings is considered greater than that of the local spirits (Hughes 1985, 32). Many Christians in Thailand tend to see God Himself as an animistic power; in Hughes's words: "God continues to be understood as a powerful and beneficent spirit patron" (Hughes 1984, 329), and this in a situation in which "the spirits are just as much a part of the world for the Christians as for the Buddhists" (Hughes 1985, 32). Indeed, as Christian ideas spill over into the world of animistic religion, "Even many Buddhists believe that there is greater power in the Holy Spirit than in the local spirits" (ibid., 32). Hence, as Hughes points out, "It seems that most of the people who turned to Christianity did so because they saw God as having great power, greater than that of the local spirits" (Hughes 1984, 328); many Christians apparently persist in this belief to the present day. Indeed, some even see God in the image of a [Thai Buddhist] king, who combines infinite merit (ibid., 329) with supreme power over the world. The power of God—and particularly his supremacy over the spirits and his healing-power—is reported to have constituted a major inducement for the conversion of northern Thais to Christianity (Swanson 1984, 139). The missionaries emphasized this supremacy in their strategy of "contest of power," by pitching the power of God against the power of the spirits (Cohen 1991).

The perception of Christianity in terms of power is, on a different level, also an example of "transposition"; but it comes closer to the type of process of adaptation which Kaplan terms "assimilation" than to "translation." In its most concrete manifestation, this perception of Christianity turns it into magic, more powerful than that of local magicians, but of the same character (cf. Hughes 1985, 36). Christian practices are thereby assimilated to the magical interests of the local Thai worshipers. However, magical conceptions and practices are so strong in popular religion that they deeply affect even the community of monks (Terwiel 1975) and not merely the Buddhist laity. Interestingly, at least according to one informant, the local Catholic clergy appears to be similarly penetrated by the magical spirit of popular Buddhism, despite all efforts to make it adhere strictly to orthodox Catholic precepts.

Though Christian practices are perceived in terms of magical power, Christian symbols appear to be only rarely used in a manner analogous to the use of charms in popular Buddhism (Hughes 1985, 31). There seems to be little one-to-one "translation" of the Christian religious vocabulary into terms of popular Thai magic. This subject, however, deserves further study, beyond the confines of Hughes's or my own research.

The animization of Christianity proceeds on the level of popular religiosity, among both Thai Christians and even Thai Buddhists, in whose beliefs and practices "pre-axial" conceptions predominate, even though they are nominally members of "axial" religions. The process is even more prominent among the hill tribes, who often see in Christianity merely a means which is more efficient than their animistic religion in overcoming the threat of the spirits which populate their world (cf. Cohen 1991).

Conclusions

The principal purpose of this chapter was to distinguish and conceptualize two contrary processes of adaptation between Christianity and indigenous religions, namely Christianization and indigenization, and to examine the viability of this distinction on the example of Christianity in Thailand.

Various specific processes of adaptation were arranged, *within* each of these major contrary processes, in terms of Kaplan's typology of types of adaptation; this typology was conceived as loosely ordered from types which are more peripheral to the adapting religion (e.g., "toleration") to those which are more central to it (e.g., "incorporation"). A further distinction was made in terms of the kind of indigenous environment into which Christianity penetrated. We distinguished between "axial" and "non-axial" local religious orientations, and asked whether the processes of adaptation proceed at different degrees of intensity, or in terms of different specific types of Kaplan's typology, on each of these levels of encounter between Christianity and local religions.

The existence of both major contrary processes of adaptation, Christianization and indigenization, was confirmed by our data.[5] However, the two processes were found not to be symmetrical: the intensity and variety of the process of Christianization turned out to be much greater than that of the opposite process of indigenization. This should not come as a surprise in view of the fact that Christianity in Thailand played the role of an actively proselytizing religion, while Buddhism, and even Thai folk religion, remained on the whole impassive and unconcerned with Christianity. Indeed, no parallel contrary effort to "Buddhify" the Christians was made by the Buddhist hierarchy—an effort which could presumably involve an attempt to adapt Buddhism to Christianity, in order to make it more palatable to Westerners; such an effort could then involve some of the more central of Kaplan's types of adaptation, such as an "incorporation" of Christian precepts into Buddhism. It would be instructive to examine this question in situations where Buddhism is a proselytizing religion, e.g., in the contemporary West.

It follows from the above that a full symmetry between Christianization and indigenization could be expected only in those hypothetical situations in which each of two opposed religions seeks to proselytize the adherents of the other.

Though the distinction between the two principal contrary processes of Christianization and indigenization has been given empirical support in our discussion, this distinction is not equally crisp and unequivocal throughout the range of the specific types of Kaplan's typology. The relationships between the two major processes could be schematically represented as in figure 1.

Figure 1

Relationship between the Principal Processes and Specific Types of Adaptation of Christianity and Indigenous Religions

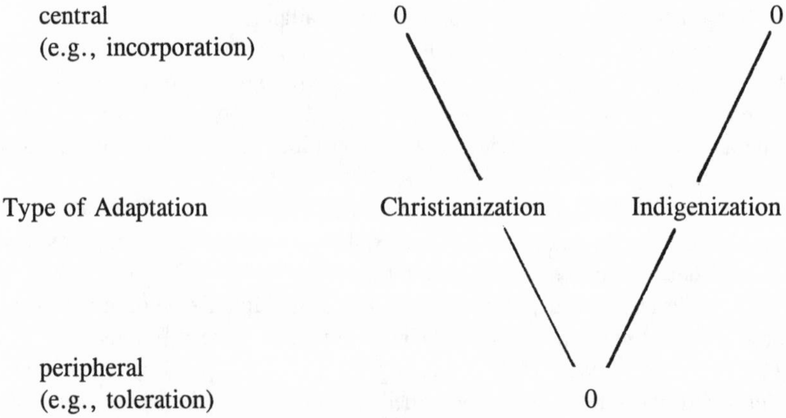

Figure 1 indicates that the lower, i.e., the more peripheral, a specific type of adaptation in Kaplan's typology, the less clearly the two principal processes can be distinguished from each other: Thus, in the case of "toleration" and even "translation" it is often difficult to decide whether in a specific instance indigenous beliefs and practices have been Christianized or, contrariwise, Christian ones have been indigenized. The higher, i.e., the more central, a specific type of adaptation, the clearer the distinction between the two principal contrary processes becomes: thus, an "incorporation" of basic Buddhist ideas into Christian theology would be an unequivocal opposite to the contrary "incorporation" of Christian ideas into doctrinal Buddhism. Such symmetrically opposed processes, however, could be found empirically only in the hypothetical situation indicated above, where each of the two religions seeks actively to proselytize members of the other.

Turning now to the difference between the penetration of "axial" and "non-axial" indigenous religions by Christianity, we find that significant processes of Christianization have taken place primarily on the "pre-axial" level of popular religion; this finding fits well an earlier one, namely that the missionary strategy of "contest of power," deployed on a mytho-magical "pre-axial" level, was much more effective in Thailand than the strategy of "battle of the axes," involving a direct confrontation of Christianity with doctrinal Buddhism (Cohen 1991). However, in those relatively few instances in which elements of doctrinal Buddhism have been adapted to Christianity, the more central types of Kaplan's typology, particularly "incorporation," were involved; whereas in the process of adaptation on the level of popular religion the more peripheral types, ranging between "Christianization" and "translation," predominated. The findings thus bear out, in a general way, our expectations, as formulated in the theoretical section of this chapter.

The same is basically true for the contrary process of indigenization, even though it proved to be much weaker and less distinctive than the process of Christianization. Those instances of indigenization which were uncovered were all outside the realm of philosophical Buddhism. Significant Buddhification was found in the realm of "kammatic" rather than "nibbanic" Buddhism. Animization was found among nominal Christians and even some Buddhists, who adhere to popular animistic beliefs.

The instances of indigenization which were observed lay predominantly within the range of some of the more peripheral types of Kaplan's typology, between "translation" and "assimilation." Since they differed subtly from both of these processes, I coined the term "transposition" to characterize them.

Returning now to the general process of Christianization, we find that, even as the Christian churches recently opened up to indigenous customs, in an effort to reduce the foreign character of Christianity and bring it closer to the local environment, they were deeply concerned lest they "contaminate" Christianity with local beliefs, and thereby engender an undesirable religious syncretism. To avoid such an occurrence, the churches generally agreed to adapt only those local customs which they declared to be merely "cultural" in character, i.e., devoid of any religious significance. However, as we have seen, such a declaration often involved a re-negotiation of the meaning of local customs; by declaring that they are devoid of a doctrinal basis in Buddhism, such customs have been, as it were, "neutralized," and thus made available for Christianization in one or another form. The consequence of this approach was that primarily customary indigenous *practices* were adopted or adapted to Christian worship. Indigenous *beliefs*, however, even those of popular religion, were unequivocally rejected by the great majority of Christian churches, and by their clergymen and missionaries. Local worshipers were thus permitted to transfer accustomed practices into Christian worship, but were asked to engage in worship—whatever its specific form—strictly in the spirit of Christianity.

Indigenization, however, works precisely in the opposite direction to Christianization: here Christian practices are endowed, through "transposition," with an indigenous meaning, and adapted to the local religious worldview. Since the Christian clergymen and missionaries are, on the whole, deeply concerned with the preservation of "correct" Christian beliefs, such indigenization on the part of nominal Christians was vigorously rejected by them.

The insistence on correct beliefs, even by the "liberal" Christian clergy and missionaries, accompanied by a readiness to adapt local practices, raises an interesting problem for comparative study: namely, whether this trait is peculiar to Christianity, and due to its emphasis on "belief" as the principal dimension of religiosity—so that in the case of another proselytizing religion, such as Judaism or Islam, which put a relatively stronger emphasis on practices than on beliefs, would one find an opposite readiness to adapt foreign beliefs, accompanied by an insistence on "correct" practices? Questions such as this will help to integrate the study of the processes of Christianization and indigenization, conducted here in a specific context, into the wider framework of the comparative sociology of religion, an integration which is at present virtually nonexistent.

Notes

1. This essay is based on data collected, within the framework of my study on "Social Change in Thailand," during the summer of 1986. The study has been conducted under a grant from the Harry S. Truman Research Institute for the Advancement of Peace at the Hebrew University of Jerusalem, whose support is hereby gratefully acknowledged. Thanks are also due to the National Research Council of Thailand for its kind assistance during field work and to D. Andrianoff, C. A. Kammerer, and E. Zehner for their comments on a earlier draft of this chapter. For related papers, see Cohen 1990 and 1991.
2. To avoid confusion, Kaplan's specific types will be kept in quotation marks throughout the text.

3. Thus, within the framework of the celebrations of the sixtieth birthday of the present Thai monarch King Bhumiphol in 1987, the Christians organized a huge concert in the king's honor, in which the choirs and orchestras of the various Christian schools performed.
4. The *ranad* is a Thai version of the xylophone; for the different types of *ranad* used in Thai music, see Duriyanga, 2516 B.E., 17ff.
5. Parallel processes have been revealed in the adaptation of Marxism to the Thai context. Thus, a recent study of radical thought in Thailand points out that "because Marx's theories were alien to the people of Thailand, it was useful to introduce Marxist philosophical arguments to the people in Buddhist terms...with which they were familiar. In doing so, the radicals had to alter some of the key concepts—to 'Marxianize' Buddhism. At the same time they had to 'Siamize' Marxism in bending the two systems of thought toward each other" (Wedel and Wedel 1987, 115).

References

Ansuchote, C. 1960. "The Vietnamese Refugees in Thailand: A Case Study in Decision Making," M.A. thesis, Thammasat University [Bangkok].

Beidelman, T. O. 1982. *Colonial Evangelism*. Bloomington: Indiana University Press.

Blanford, C. E. [1976]. *Chinese Churches in Thailand*. Bangkok: Suriyaban.

Boutilier, J., D. Hughes, and S. Tiffany, eds. 1978. *Mission, Church and Sect in Oceania*. Ann Arbor, Mich.: University of Michigan Press.

Bunnag, J. 1973. *Buddhist Monk, Buddhist Layman*. Cambridge: Cambridge University Press.

Carkin, G. B. 1984. "Likay: The Thai Popular Theatre Form and Its Function within Thai Society," Ph.D. diss., Michigan State University.

Catholic Plot. 1986. *The Catholic Plot against Buddhism*. Bangkok: Group of the Defenders of Security of Buddhism.

Chaiwan, S. 1975. *The Christian Approach to Buddhists in Thailand*. Bangkok: Suriyaban.

Chindarsi, N. 1983. *The Religion of the Hmong Njua*. Bangkok: Siam Society.

Cohen, E. 1991. "Christianity and Buddhism in Thailand: The 'Battle of the Axes and the Contest of Power.'" *Social Compass* 38(2): 115-40.

———. 1990. "The Missionary as Stranger: A Phenomenological Analysis of the Christian Missionaries' Encounter with the Folk Religions of Thailand." *Revue of Religious Research* 31(4):337-50.

Cooke, J. K. 1978. "The Gospel for Thai Ears." Unpublished manuscript. Payap University, Chiang Mai.

Déclaration. 1966. "Déclaration sur les relation de l'Eglise avec les religions non-chrétiennes." In *Les actes du Concile Vatican II*, Paris: Les Editions du Cerf, 3:159–66.

Duriyanga, P. C. 2516 B.E. *Thai Music*. Bangkok: Fine Arts Department, Thai Culture News Series 15.

Eakin, P. A. 1960. *Buddhism and the Christian Approach to Buddhists in Thailand*. Bangkok: Ruang Ratana.

Eisenstadt, S. N. 1982. "The Axial Age." *Archives Européennes de Sociologie* 23 (2):294–314.

———, ed. 1986. The Origins and Diversity of Axial Age Civilizations. New York: SUNY Press.

Gustafson, J. W. 1970. Syncretistic Rural Thai Buddhism. M.A. thesis, Fuller Theological Seminary.

Hanks, L. 1962. "Merit and Power in the Thai Social Order." *American Anthropologist* 64:1247–61.

Heinze, R. I. 1982. *Tham Khwam: How to Contain the Essence of Life*. Singapore: Singapore University Press.

Hiranburana, S. 1975. "Sociologie d'un théâtre populaire: Le Liké" Ph.D. diss., 3rd cycle, Univ. de Sciences Sociales de Grenoble.

Hughes, P. J. 1984. "The Assimilation of Christianity in Thai Culture." *Religion* 14(4):313–36.

——— 1985. Christianity and Buddhism in Thailand. *Journal of the Siam Society* 73(1/2):23-41.

Hvalkof, S., and P. Aaby, eds. 1981. *Is God an American? An Anthropological Perspective on the Missionary Work of the Summer Institute of Linguistics*, International Work Group for Indigenous Affairs (IWGIA) and Survival International.

Kennedy, V. 1979. "Monastery Roofs and Chofa Symbolism." In his *The Artistic Heritage of Thailand*. Bangkok: Sawadee Magazine and National Museum Volunteers, 165–69.

Koyama, K. 1974. "Will the Monsoon Rain Make God Wet? An Ascending Spiral View of History." In his *Waterbuffalo Theology*. Maryknoll, N.Y.: Orbis Books, 27–42.

———. 1976. "Is Christianity History-minded?" In his *No Handle on the Cross*. London: SCM Press, 98–109.

Krug, S. 1979. "The Development of Thai Mural Painting." In *The Artistic Heritage of Thailand*. Bangkok: Sawadee Magazine and The National Museum Volunteers, 170–84.

Lantern, Z. 1986. "The Missionaries: Why Have They Failed So Miserably?" *Bangkok Post*, May 25, 1986, 13.

Lewis, P., and E. Lewis. 1984. *People of the Golden Triangle: Six Tribes of Thailand*. London: Thames and Hudson.

McFarland, G. B., ed. 1928. *Historical Sketch of Protestant Missions in Siam, 1828-1928*. [Bangkok]: Bangkok Times Press.

McKinnon, J., and W. Bhruksasri, eds. 1983. *Highlanders of Thailand*. Kuala Lumpur: Oxford University Press.

Nicholas, R. 1975. "Le Lakhon Nora ou Lakhon Chatri et les origines du théâtre classique siamois." In M. Rutnin, ed., *The Siamese Theatre*. Bangkok: [Siam Society], 42–61.

Nontawasee, P. 1985. "Religious Minorities in Contemporary Thailand." Paper, Conference on Minorities in Buddhist Polities: Sri Lanka, Burma and Thailand, Regional Workshop, Chiang Mai, June 25–28, 1985.

Rajadhon, P.A. n.d. "Loi Krathong." In his *Essays on Thai Folklore*. Bangkok: Editions Duang Kamol, 37–44.

Schneider, J., and Sh. Lindenbaum, eds. 1987. "Frontiers of Christian Evangelism." *American Ethnologist* 14(1):1–185.

Seely, F. M. 1957. "Some Problems in Translating the Scriptures into Thai." *The Bible Translator* 8(2):49–61.

———. 1969. "Thai Buddhism in the Christian Faith." *Southwest Asian Journal of Theology* 10 (2/3):132–40.

Shapiro, J. 1987. "From Tupa to the Land without Evil: The Christianization of Tupi Guarani Cosmology." *American Ethnologist* 14(1):126–39.

Smithies, M. 1971. "Likay: A Note on the Origin, Form and Future of Siamese Folk Opera." *Journal of the Siam Society* 59(1):33–65.

Sobhon-Ganabhorn, V. P. 1984. *A Plot to Undermine Buddhism*. Bangkok: Siva Phorn.

Spiro, M. E. 1970. *Buddhism and Society*. New York: Harper and Row.

Swanson, H. R. 1984. *Khrischak Muang Nua: A Study in Northern Thai Church History*. Bangkok: Chuan Printing Press.

Terwiel, B. J. 1975. *Monks and Magic: An Analysis of Religious Ceremonies in Thailand*. London: Curzon Press.

Thapbing, J. E. 1974. "The Conversion of the Thai Buddhists: Are Christianity and Thai Culture Irreconcilable?" M.A. thesis, Ateneo de Manila University.

Thirty-three Points. 1962. *Thirty-three Points: Buddhist and Christian Teachings*. Bangkok: The Church of Christ in Bangkok, Office of Christian Education and Literature.

Thompson, V. 1967. *Thailand: The New Siam*. New York: Paragon Book Reprint Corporation.

Troeltsch, E. 1961. Church and Sect. In *Theories of Society*, ed. T. Parsons, E. Shils, K. D. Naegele, and J. R. Pitts. New York: Free Press of Glencoe, 664–70.

Ulliana, J. 1969. "Christians and Buddhists in Thailand." In *Modern Mission Dialogue*, ed. J. Kerkhofs. Shannon: Ecclesia Press, 13–28.

Viralrak, S. 1980. "Likay: A Popular Theatre in Thailand." Ph.D. diss., University of Hawaii at Manoa.

Walker, A. R. 1976. "Jaw-Te-Meh-Jaw-Ve—Lahu-Nyi (Red Lahu) Rites of Spirit Exorcism in North Thailand." *Anthropos* 71(3/4):377–422.

Wedel, Y., and P. Wedel. 1987. *Radical Thought, Thai Minds: The Development of Revolutionary Ideas in Thailand*. Bangkok: ABAC.

Whiteman, D. L., ed. 1983. "Missionaries, Anthropologists and Culture Change." *Studies in Third World Societies*, no. 25.

Winship, M. 1986. "Early Thai Printing: The Beginning to 1851." *Crossroads* 1:45–61.

Wyatt, D. K. 1984. *Thailand: A Short History*. Bangkok: Thai Watana Panich.

CHAPTER 3

From Inca Gods to Spanish Saints and Demons

JAN SZEMIŃSKI

Introduction

According to the testimonies of Peruvian Christians, the Peruvian Indians' conversion to Catholicism was very rapid. By the beginning of the eighteenth century Peruvians considered themselves Catholics, even better Catholics than the Spaniards. The process took less than a hundred and fifty years. In fact, the intensive campaigns of Christianization lasted less than eighty years, from around 1580 to 1660.

When the Spaniards came in 1532 there existed in Peru a highly organized Inca state church, with a hierarchy of priests and an elaborate mythology, more elaborate in the capital Cuzco and simpler in the provinces. Peruvian Indians understood and evaluated the new Spanish teachings through the concepts and images furnished by the truths of Inca religion, and they formed their image of Catholicism accordingly. Somewhat later the images of Andean pre-Christian religion developed. An analysis of these images can explain to some extent how the change of religion in a conquered and resisting society was accomplished so quickly.

In order to analyze these three images—that of Inca religion among Peruvian Catholics, of Catholicism among Peruvian Catholics, and of Catholicism among Peruvian non-Catholics—it is necessary to cope with the problem of sources.

Spanish sources are obviously biased simply because good Spanish Catholic authors knew beforehand what they should find in the Inca religion: the Devil. Inca sources on religion, whether written in Spanish or Quechua, whether Catholic or preconquest, have a different bias: they were all written by Catholics. However, these Catholics were familiar with both the Peruvian Inca religion, and the people who practiced it. Andean (Peruvian) Catholics were, moreover, viewed by other Indians as members of their own group, as opposed to the Spaniards.

Among all Peruvians the Inca religion served as the point of reference for understanding the Catholicism that the Spaniards taught. Neither Indians nor Spaniards conversed directly. Spaniards, when preaching or asking for information on Andean religion, operated according to what they expected the Inca religion to be. Indians understood what they heard through the truth of Andean religion. So when Catholicism was accepted and received, it was received through the filter of Andean religion. Such filtered Catholicism became Andean Catholic religion. Thus testimonies left by Andean Catholics can show how this filter worked.

I shall use two such testimonies left by two educated provincial Indian noblemen from southern Peru: Don Felipe Guaman Poma de Ayala,[1] from the southern part of what is today the department of Ayacucho in modern Peru, and Don Joan de Santa Cruz Pacha Cuti yamqui Salca Maygua, from the province of Canchis, today in the department of Cuzco, also in the modern Republic of Peru. Both of them worked for the clergy, probably as interpreters. Thus they were considered by Spanish authorities to be reliable Catholics. They were not afraid, however, of speaking positively about the Incas and about ancient religion, or of criticizing the clergy and other Spanish authorities for whom they worked.

These testimonies, together with other sources of Indian and Spanish origin, demonstrate how phenomena belonging to Andean religion became part of Andean Catholicism, even to the extent of being incorporated into official structures of the Catholic church in the Andes.

Andean Understanding of Catholic Teachings: Guaman Poma

Don Felipe Guaman Poma de Ayala's monumental *Nueva Coronica y Buen Gobierno* contains, among much other material, a description of the history of the world starting from Adam and Eve and divided into five epochs. This same scheme of five epochs was used by the author to describe the history of the Andeans before the Spanish conquest. Since the chronicle is illustrated, the drawings show which characteristics the author attributed to each epoch. The first epoch he called "El primer mundo [The first world] Adan: Eva" (see figures 1 and 2). He drew Adam and Eve in exactly the same way as he drew "the first generation of the Indians, Wari Wira Qucha Runa": living in a mountainous world, and working the land with Andean foot ploughs. His description of the world of Adam and Eve contains, moreover, some clearly nonbiblical elements:

> These said people, all of them, and their descendants, lived very many years, just Adam and Eve lived two or three thousand years—they probably bore two children at each childbirth, and so inevitably filled the world with people...the world became so full...that there was no place for them and they did not know the creator and maker of men and so because of that God ordered the world punished. All creation was punished for its sins with the waters of the Flood, and it was decided by God that Noah should be spared. (Guaman Poma 1936, 23)

Elsewhere Guaman Poma claimed that after the creation of the world God planted the seeds of every human group in its land: the Spanish in Castile, the Indian in the Indies, and the Negro in Guinea (Guaman Poma 1936, 915). The idea corresponds to the Andean image of creation, according to which ancestors of every human group were created by God and sent underground to their proper places, from which they sprouted when called by God or his envoy in sixteenth- and in twentieth-century Andean myths (cf. Urioste 1983; Yaranga Valderrama n.d.). The first humans, who were virtually immortal, multiplied by giving birth to two children with every pregnancy. Because they did not know their maker, meaning that they did not properly worship God, they were destroyed by the Flood (cf. Urioste 1983, 14–17; Molina 1575, fol. lv).

This last story reveals one of the basic elements of the reception of Christian teachings in the Andes. Don Felipe Guaman Poma belonged to the second generation of Andean Catholics; he received an excellent education, read many books in Spanish on the history of the world and the Indies, and even knew some Latin. His Catholic education was, in short, among the best for people educated in Spanish Peru in the second half of the sixteenth century (cf. Adorno 1986). Obviously he was taught Genesis and read the Bible, but chose what was important to the Andean vision of early humanity. For Guaman Poma it was important that for their good God created the world, created body and soul, and that these people lived for millennia. In his version of the creation, just as in the Andean version of history, sin is present: the world, all the world, is guilty and so it is punished by the Flood. The nature of this sin is lack of knowledge, which makes proper worship of God impossible. Yet this good Catholic, author of prayers written in Quechua for church use, neither mentioned nor considered important the story of the original sin of Adam and Eve, without which the orthodox Catholic history of the world is impossible, nor did he mention it at

Figure 1: The First World: Adam: Eva (Guaman Poma 1936, 22).

Figure 2: The First of the Generations, Indians *Wari Wira Qucha Runa* [The ancestors of animated stone] / The First Indian of this Kingdom. *Wari Wira Qucha Warmi* [The woman ancestor of animated stone] / In this Kingdom of the Indies. (Guaman Poma 1936, 48.)

all in his chronicle, in which he insists upon his own Christianity and names Jesus on nearly every page. According to the "Catecismo Mayor" published in 1584 in Lima in Spanish, Quechua, and Ayamara by the decision of the Peruvian episcopate (*Doctrina Christiana* 1584, fols. 33v.–34), the doctrine of original sin was universally taught. Don Felipe Guaman Poma de Ayala finished his chronicle in 1614 and so he must have known this teaching.

His description of the first age of humanity, from Adam and Eve to Noah, was structured according to Andean patterns: (1) Humankind was created (Adam and Eve); (2) Humankind multiplied; (3) Humankind sinned because of lack of proper knowledge (in the case of Adam and Eve, and their descendants, they did not know how to properly worship the Creator); (4) Humankind was punished for its sins by destruction (in this case by the Flood). Similar Andean elements appear in his description of other historical epochs as well.

The second age of humanity began with Noah and ended with Abraham. Don Felipe described the Flood as a cataclysm and God's punishment. Then he mentioned the story of the Tower of Babel and added: "In that age men lived 400 or 300 years. God ordered them to go away from this land, to disperse and multiply in all the world. From Noah's sons God took one to the Indies. Others say that this was one of Adam's sons. So the said Indians multiplied, and everything is known to God, because he, the powerful one, could keep these Indian people apart during the Flood" (Guaman Poma 1936, 25). This is followed by an enumeration of Noah's descendants up to Abraham, who went out of the land of the Chaldeans "and the Sodomites were destroyed because they started the first idols of the kingdom, and money was started. Abraham and his kin began to circumcize themselves and he offered his son to God in sacrifice" (ibid.).

The pattern recurs: (1) Humankind was created (Noah and family); (2) Humankind sinned (Sodomites, idols, money); (3) The sinners were destroyed.

There are, however, significant differences between the two types of human beings; people of the first age lived thousands of years and spoke one language, while those of the second lived only hundreds of years and spoke many languages. The first did not know their maker, while the second had idols, which implies that they knew something but falsely.

During the second age three important events are mentioned. First is the story of Noah and wine (Gen. 9:20–27). Its consequence, differentiation of blessings and status among the sons, is omitted. For the author only the fact that wine was cultivated and produced is important. In the story of the Tower of Babel (Gen. 11:1–9), the author is interested in two facts: the ability to construct and the differentiation of languages associated with the dispersion of humanity. The intent of reaching sky or heaven is omitted. And in portraying the story of Abraham's sacrifice (Gen. 22:1–18), the author even drew

Abraham sacrificing his son, but without any commentaries. Only obedience to God seemed important.

It is interesting to compare the story of Noah and his descendants with the depiction of the second age of the Andean world by the same author. This age is associated with the human search for God (the men pray: "A Pacha Kamaq! Maypim Kanki?"—Soul of the Universe! Where art Thou? [Guaman Poma 1936, 53]), agriculture and architecture, respect for parents and family, and the cult of Thunder represented as a family of three human males (Guaman Poma 1936, 54–55). The similarities are obvious. The writer, when he was writing about the second age of humanity from Noah to Abraham, chose elements which were also important in the image of the second age of Andean history: architecture, agriculture, and search for a proper cult. Elements which are the most important from a Christian point of view are mentioned, not because of their Catholic value, but only for the sake of their Andean counterparts:

1. Noah and the Flood because the story describes a cataclysm that ends an age, rather than because of the Lord's covenant with Noah and his descendants.
2. Noah and wine because the story describes agriculture, rather than because of the division of blessings and curses among Noah's descendants.
3. The Tower of Babel because it marks architecture, language diversification, and population growth, rather than because of the blasphemy of trying to reach the heavens.
4. Abraham and his son, as a proof of searching for God, and perhaps also as a proof of obedience, rather than because of the abolition of human sacrifice.

The description of the third age of the world, from Abraham to King David, consists of an enumeration of Abraham's descendants and of captains or judges, among whom Moses is mentioned as one among many. The Ten Commandments are omitted, and special attention is called to the genealogy of Jesus (Guaman Poma 1936, 27). In the third age of the Andean world (ibid., 57–62) the author mentioned some new technical abilities (weaving, metals) and the presence of captains, kings, and lords (ibid., 58). Moses appears with a commentary that the Indians are not descendants of the Jews because they are not similar racially and they do not know the laws of Moses, nor how to write (ibid., 60). This may be understood as a proof that the author did associate the third Andean age with the third "Christian" age.

Guaman Poma's description of the fourth age is reduced to an enumeration of kings, beginning with King David:

> In this age many became kings and lords, and they multiplied and there were many people in the world. Also at this time they entered into politics, not only in matters concerning justice but also in matters of government and in the use

> of the goods and arts of craftsmanship; and they tried to have many goods and riches so they went out in search of gold and silver. Also because of greed for riches, they abandoned good and embraced the evil of the world. (Guaman poma 1936, 29)

Since the next epoch starts with the birth of Jesus, the fourth epoch must have lasted up to Jesus' birth. Exactly the same characteristics were attributed to the fourth age of the Andean world, full of war and politics. In Quechua it was called *Awqa Runa* or *Awqa Runa Pacha*—The Warrior People or the World of Warrior People (Guaman Poma 1936, 63–78).

Lastly, Guaman Poma's description of the fifth age, starting with the birth of Jesus whom the author calls "our Lord and Savior," contains only an enumeration of emperors and kings up to Charles V, king of Spain and emperor of the Holy Roman Empire. The rule of Sinchi Ruqa Inka, second Inca king of Cuzco, is correlated, according to Guaman Poma's reckoning, with the birth of Jesus. The fifth age of the world corresponds exactly to the fifth age of the Andean world. Many chapters describe the kings, queens, and all aspects of Inca life and administration, up to the Spanish conquest. After the pages which contain the image and story of Sinchi Ruqa Inka (Guaman Poma 1936, 88–89), a special chapter is introduced. It describes the birth of Jesus and the mission of Saint Bartholomew in the Indies; in other words, in Peru (ibid., 90–95).

The story and activities of Jesus are not connected by the author with the original sin of Adam and Eve. Jesus' activities are associated with empire building; Roman and Spanish in the Old World, Incan in the Indies. Thus I tried to find out how Guaman Poma had understood Jesus' mission. At one point he wrote:

> [God] in order to redeem the world and men, suffered for thirty-three years and died and lost his life for the sake of the world and for men.... He created our father Adam and our mother Eve, the sky and the earth, water and wind, fish and animals, everything for man, and the sky [heaven] in order to breed us, men. So for the sake of these things our Lord Jesus Christ died and sent us the Holy Spirit in order to illuminate us with his grace. (Guaman Poma 1936, 13)[2]

This quotation allows us to understand some of the meanings of Jesus' deeds for the author, and to perceive their place in the traditional Andean worldview. In the Andean cosmology, the time–space continuum is divided into four parts:
The Upper Part of the World encompasses

Qaylla pacha—the world of limits and

Hanaq pacha—the Upperworld: sky and heaven.

In the Lower Part of the World are

Kay pacha—this world; the world we live in, Earth and

Hurin pacha (*Ukhu pacha*)—the Lowerworld; the interior of the Underworld.

In Hanaq pacha are the stars and constellations. Everything that exists, be it human, animal, plant, or rock, has its star or constellation. Such stars or constellations cause the existence of all the species in this, the lower part of the world. The normal existence of all is dependent on an equilibrium between the upper and lower parts of the world (cf. Hocquenghem 1984). Jesus, by his life and death in Kay pacha, this world, connected all the worlds and so created a basis for equilibrium and order. From the moment the Holy Spirit was sent to this world, humanity gained a special kind of knowledge which, it seems to me, consisted of an awareness of how to keep contact with the upper world, where according to the author's drawing (Guaman Poma 1936, 2), Jesus, the Holy Spirit, God-the-Father, and Mary abide. This explains to some extent how redemption was understood. Since God, with the holy family, stays in heaven, humankind lacked contact and knowledge of the upper world before Jesus' mediation. People were sinful because they did not know how to behave properly in the face of God in Heaven. Had the Andean religion known an image of original sin, it would have consisted of not having eaten from the forbidden tree.

In Guaman Poma's image of history, a new cycle of five epochs began with the Spanish rule in Peru (cf. Szemiński 1982–84). Both the Spanish and Andean fifth epochs of the earlier cycle (from Jesus in the Old World; from the first Inca in the Indies), should present similar characteristics. In the Andes this was the time of the order which was introduced by the Inca kings; later, because of lack of proper Christian knowledge, they lost power and thus control over order to Spanish Christians. In the Old World, the times following Christ were of emperors, kings, and popes, with these central powers imposing order.

Additional information is contained in the chapter on Christian Indians. According to Guaman Poma, the Indians would have been holy or at least very learned and very Christian men, if the Spanish clergy, governors, landlords, and the like had only permitted it (Guaman Poma 1936, 820). He also explains that the baptism of children preserves them alive and protects them from going to limbo in case of death (ibid., 824). So, after all, for Guaman Poma to be a good Christian is to be an Andean Indian, baptized but without Spanish rule.

Andean Understanding of Catholic Teachings: Pacha Cuti yamqui Salca Maygua

More or less at the same time that Don Felipe Guaman Poma de Ayala was writing his enormous encyclopedia (completed by 1615) another educated Indian nobleman, Don Joan de Santa Cruz Pacha Cuti yamqui Salca Maygua, probably much younger than Don Felipe (he belonged to the fifth or even the sixth generation of Catholics) wrote a short text, illustrated with drawings. The text, called *Relación de antiguedades deste reyno del Piru*, describes the history of the Andeans from the creation of the world to the moment when the Quri Kancha, the principal Inca shrine in Cuzco, was turned into a church. After introducing himself, the author makes his confession of faith:

> I believe in God triune but one, who is a powerful god, who created the sky [heaven] and earth, and all the things which exist in them, such as the Sun, the Moon, the Evening and Morning Stars, Thunderbolts, Lightenings, Thunders and all the Elements, and so forth, and then created the first men, *adaneba*, according to his own figure and likeness, forefather of the human species, and so forth, whose descendants we, the natives of Tawantin Suyu [Peru] are, just as are the other nations which inhabit all the universe of the world, the same way as the Whites and Negroes. For their help and health the son of the living God, that is, Jesus Christ, our Lord, incarnated through the deeds of the Holy Spirit in the entrails of the Virgin, Holy Mary, descending from heaven and glory only in order to free the human species from the hellish slavery of demons, to which they were subjected. So Christ our Lord lived among men thirty-three years, and because he was God and man, he suffered as a man death on the Cross in Jerusalem in order to redeem the human species. He died and was buried, and entered hell and took away the souls of the Holy fathers and from the dead he returned to life on the third day and during forty days he was in body and soul. And then he ascended to heaven and sat in the great power of God Almighty. From there he sent unto the apostles and disciples that gift of the Holy Spirit in order that the apostles and disciples should be stronger and more expert in reaching the spiritual things of God, and so forth. God is a true god over all the gods, He is powerful god, our creator, he is the one who governs in proper order the glory of heaven, and all the skies and all the ages as the supreme lord and just and merciful lord. (Pacha Cuti yamqui Salca Maygua 1613? fols. 2r.–2v.)

This credo is composed of two basic parts: a description of the creation of the world, and a description of Jesus' deeds. The description of the creation enumerates beings created by God, beginning with celestial bodies and ending with the first human being *Adaneba*; not Adam and Eve, but a combination Adaneba, bearer of the human species. The order of enumeration does not correspond to Genesis, but it does correspond to the Andean description of world order, which begins from the borders of the world and from heaven-sky and ends with humanity on earth. In the Andean descriptions Venus always appears in third place after the sun and moon, and so it does in Pacha Cuti yamqui Salca Maygua's Christian description.

The forebear of humanity, Adaneba, is described exactly as are the Andean forebears of every ethnic group. According to Andean legends (cf. Betanzos 1968, 9–10), the first ancestors of every group sprang from the earth. Both these ancestors themselves and the place from which they sprang were called *waka*. An Andean word, *waka* means something that is one but subdivided into two parts: the ancestor inside the earth is one, but subdivided into male and female (Szemiński 1987; 79–85). The concept of *waka* explains why the author consolidated the figures of Adam and Eve into one being, the forerunner of the human species. In the account of Adaneba and his descendants—whites, Negroes, and Indians—as in Guaman Poma's version of creation discussed above, the story of original sin is completely omitted.

The existence of the people who populated the world and the condition in which they found themselves is considered a sufficient cause for Jesus' redeeming act. They were in need of help, healing, and also redemption. What precisely was meant by this redemption? Its meaning can be detected by analyzing the development of action as the author describes it. Since he declares himself a Catholic, everybody has assumed that his description is what it claims to be: a declaration of Christianity. I do not doubt the sincerity of the author's credo, but can it not have additional meaning?

In order to reveal these additional meanings I shall use the Andean scheme of time and space continuum, and divide the action into stages. Since the text does not contain any information on *qaylla pacha* [the world of limits] and the information on the contacts among the various parts of the time–space continuum is particularly important, I present it below in the form of two tables.

Existence of the world changes according to relationships between its parts. Kay pacha, this world, is a result of the interaction between Hanaq pacha and Hurin pacha. Existence in Kay pacha is interpreted as life; absence from this world is interpreted as death. Persons and things in Kay pacha can be representatives and agents of other worlds. Obviously the situation before Jesus' intervention was one of lack of equilibrium between life and death, and thus between the worlds. When only the Underworld gave and took life, overpopulation and a miserable life for all was to be expected.

Indirect confirmation of such an interpretation is found in sixteenth- and twentieth-century myths. According to these, in the first age of humanity, when immortal or nearly immortal ancestors emerged from the earth, they lived miserably because of lack of food. They even became cannibals (cf. Urioste 1983, 2–5, 50–59; Yaranga Valderrama n.d.). But Jesus' intervention created a complete equilibrium between death and life in this world, through proper two-way contacts between Above and Below.

Thus an Andean Catholic's Christian confession of faith ultimately encompasses a very Andean confession. While this educated Andean nobleman is familiar with Christian teachings which provide some of the elements of the confession—Jesus, Mary, Jerusalem, the Holy Spirit—the relationships among these are Andean. Don Joan de Santa Cruz Pacha Cuti yamqui Salca Maygua's

Table 1: Jesus' Intervention in Human History

Stage No.	*Hanaq pacha* (Cielo-Heaven)	<Contact>	*Kay pacha* (This world)	<Contact>	*Hurin pacha* (Hell)
1	God, God's power, Jesus, Holy Spirit	No	Adaneba's descendants, Virgin Mary	Yes, demons enslave inhabitants of Kay pacha	Demons, souls of Holy Fathers
2	God, God's power	Yes, Holy Spirit intervenes	Adaneba's descendants, Virgin Mary, Jesus incarnated in her entrails	Yes, demons snatch humans	Demons, souls of Holy Fathers
3	God, God's power	Yes, Holy Spirit intervenes	Adaneba's descendants, Virgin Mary, Jesus as man	No, demons do not rule humanity	Demons, souls of Holy Fathers
4	God, God's power	Yes, Holy Spirit intervenes	Adaneba's descendants, Virgin Mary	Yes, contact re-established through Jesus' death	Demons, souls of Holy Fathers, Jesus
5	God, God's power	Yes, Holy Spirit intervenes	Adaneba's descendants, Virgin Mary, Jesus, Souls of Holy Fathers	Yes, double contact through demons and Jesus' death	Demons
6	God, God's power, Jesus, Souls of holy fathers	Yes, through Holy Spirit and Jesus' mission	Adaneba's descendants, Virgin Mary, apostles, demons, disciples	Yes, double contact through demons and Jesus' death	Demons

Table 2: Results of Jesus' Intervention

	First Stage	Last Stage
Hanaq pacha	God, Jesus, God's power, Holy Spirit	God, Jesus, God's Power, Souls of the Holy Fathers
	No Contact	Double contact: downward: Holy Spirit (life) upward: souls (death)
Kay pacha	humanity, Mary, agents of the demons	Humanity, Mary, demons' agents, apostles, and disciples (Jesus' agents)
	Double contact: demons govern and snatch people	Double contact: demons still have their agents (death) but the dead can come back (life)
Hurin pacha	Demons, souls of holy fathers	Demons

story also enables us to better understand some characteristics of the history of the world as told by Don Felipe Guaman Poma de Ayala, for example, the association of Jesus with the Inca kings. Both have similar functions. Jesus established cosmic equilibrium between life and death, while the Inca kings established social equilibrium among human beings.

Gods and Space

Pacha Cuti yamqui Salca Maygua recorded another consequence of Jesus' death: at this moment the demons that attacked people at night or in the evenings snatched them away, lost their power, and were conquered (Pacha Cuti yamqui Salca Maygua 1613?; fol. 3v.). Although the reason for kidnapping is not explicit in the text, it is found in the meanings of their names: *achakalla*—one that stings or punches, and *hapi ñuñu*—one that catches and sucks. Obviously the demons fed on human blood.

Both of the Indian intellectuals considered in this chapter identified the Andean deities of Hurin pacha with Christian-Spanish devils, demons, and the like. The initiative for such an identification probably came from the Spaniards, for whom anything associated with the Underworld meant hellish, and evil.

Andean deities, however, were not wholly evil even when represented in the Underworld, just as the beings inhabiting the sky (heaven) were not invariably good.

In Andean theology there existed, as is probably still the case, several parallel images of God, situationally conditioned, associated with different functions in the process of creation. Thus, a hermaphroditic god initiated the beginning of creation, while a pair composed of divinities consisting of a male and a female corresponding to different parts of the universe can be deduced from the oppositions between the ideas associated with Upper- and Underworld.

Hurin pacha (Underworld)	*Hanaq pacha (Upperworld)*
Underworld	Heaven, sky
Change, earthquake	Stability, permanent order
Future	Past
Invisible, inside	Visible, outside
At the back	In front
Night	Day
Moon	Sun
Earth	Air
Fertility, creation of	Duration, existence of
Phenotypes	Genotypes
Female	Male
Left	Right

Association of a given characteristic with Above or with Below does not mean that in either of the worlds characteristics of the other were excluded. It only means that normally they predominated in one realm (cf. Hocquenghem 1984; Szemiński 1987, 1986). The Spanish condemnation of all images associated with the Underworld (Hurin pacha) at once caused the images attributed to the Upperworld to be identified by the Indian and Spanish gods of sky and heaven. Thus Thunder (Illapa) became Santiago, Saint James, the Spanish war god (Arriaga 1968, 215; Guaman Poma 1936, 265, 276, 641–42, 885; Duviols 1971, 366).

One image of God represents him as a lineage of five generations, in which the members of the fifth generation appeared in the form of human beings intervening in Kay pacha, introducing changes or establishing order in this world. These members of the fifth generation were either seen as incarnations of God himself, or as his servants, called by his names of their own (cf. Szemiński 1987, 10–78, 1986, 122–24). For the process of assigning every Andean image a Catholic equivalent, divine envoys posed a special problem. Pablo José de Arriaga, a Jesuit expert on combatting idolatry, enumerated all the things and beings whose adoration he considered idolatry. The list included all beings of the Underworld, and much of the Upperworld including sun, moon, and stars, but it did not mention any general name for the Andean Creator-God. It did mention, however, an image of god corresponding to Hurin pacha, the Underworld, called Wari (Arriaga 1968, 201–5). His standing was obvious: beings of the Underworld are devils and demons. The list's omission of a general cult and of an image of God is understandable because that was not considered idolatry. The list reveals that the Jesuit expert accepted that part of Andean religion which he could identify with something undoubtedly Catholic.

The list also omits representations of God occurring in Kay pacha, when not symbolized by a shrine. Such images could be rather easily identified with Spanish saints. Thus, Guaman Poma, though condemning the identification of Thunder with Saint James, had no doubt that Saint James himself had intervened in the form of thunder on behalf of the Spaniards and against the Incas during the siege of the Spaniards at Cuzco by Manqu Inca in 1536 (Guaman Poma 1936, 406, 640).

The Story of the Miracle in Kacha

In Andean tradition there exists to this day a standard story type about God's intervention in the life of one human group. The story includes the following elements:

1. The people of a village congregate in their ceremonial center for a feast or rite of passage.
2. They eat and get drunk—appropriately.
3. God appears in the form of a poor old man.
4. God (usually) preaches.
5. God is not received by the people; no one serves him food, drink or coca leaves, so he does not participate in the celebration. In some versions he is assaulted.
6. Sometimes an exceptional participant invites God to partake of food, drink, or coca, and is told to leave.
7. God abandons the place.
8. God returns and destroys the place, killing the people as punishment for their sins.

(Of course there exists the opposite story, in which God's teaching is accepted without ending in a general blood bath). Some such stories were written down in Quechua by 1609 in San Damian village, province of Huarochiri, Peru (Urioste 1983, 4–5, 38–41, 202–205). In these stories two deities appear: Quni Raya Wira Qucha and Parya Qaqa. Quni Raya Wira Qucha is a general name of God-the-Creator. In this particular case he appears in stories about the first inhabitants of the region. The other name, Parya Qaqa, describes a mountain, protector of a warlike people, to whom the mountain gave the force and power to conquer and dominate other groups, some of which were expelled, others incorporated into the new political entity.

Don Felipe Guaman Poma knows much about Parya Qaqa. He mentions him as a regional deity, and an oracle, and identifies him with the local representation of Pacha Kamaq (soul of the Universe), a name given to God when associated with Hurin pacha, the Underworld (Guaman Poma 1936, 113, 185, 264, 268, 269, 277, 282, 288, 1099). He observes that:

> The elder men and women say that God tempted the Indians of every village, and that he came in the form of a poor hermit and begged for God's sake clothing, food and drink. It is said that these poor more frequently appeared in villages in which there was a feast in a public place. When nobody gave him alms, he went away. That is why they say that there occurred great calamities and punishments from God, Pacha Kamaq Tiqsi Wira Qucha [Soul of the Universe, the Founder, the Seedbed of the Essence of Life] so those misers were swallowed up by the earth, or were covered by a mountain, or else became lakes on Parya Qaqa's slopes, or on the slopes of Iswa, Apqara, just like the village of Kacha, and so the Indians and this kingdom do love hermits and Franciscan brothers. (Guaman Poma 1936, 286)

It is significant that the author attributed to God what Waru Chiri myths attributed to Parya Qaqa. Parya Qaqa, or any other local divinity, is transformed into a hermit, a Franciscan brother, through whom God punishes villages for their improper behavior.

Among places in which such punishments took place, the story of the village of Kacha is repeated by various independent sources, from the early years of Spanish rule up to the beginnings of the seventeenth century. Comparison of the versions, written down by Spaniards, shows that over the years, the Andean divinity who had destroyed Kacha was accorded, gradually, a set of characteristics that transformed him into a Christian apostle. Already in the earliest description, the divinity kneels (Cieza de León 1985, 8–9); later he is dressed in white and has a breviary in hand (Betanzos 1968, 10–11).

By 1572 he still kept an Andean name, but was dressed in white, had a book in his left hand and a stick in his right (Sarmiento de Gamboa 1942, 31). By 1586 he had lost his Andean name and became a bearded disciple, one of the apostles (Cabello Valboa 1951, 237–59). The process happened not only in Spanish, but also in the Andean imagination,[3] as seen in Andean texts.

By 1614 when Don Felipe Guaman Poma de Ayala was finishing his chronicle, he had no doubts that Saint Bartholomew had indeed come to Peru, to the Indies, from Jerusalem by the order of Jesus at the time when Sinchi Ruqa Inka had been ruling Cuzco and a part of the Collao, today's southern Peru and Bolivia (Guaman Poma 1936, 368). In Guaman Poma's vocabulary every white man was a Spaniard, and every Spaniard was at that time called *wira qucha*, so that every *wira qucha* had to be a Spaniard. Saint Bartholomew was a *wira qucha* (cf. Szemiński 1987, 12–20). The reason why the Spaniards received the name of *wira qucha* during the sixteenth century—and fairly early at that, during the 1530s and 1540s—is not yet quite clear, but it seems that one of the groups fighting for power between 1531 and 1536 believed the Spaniards to be God's envoys sent to help them take power. Other possible causes indicate associations with death and with springing from the Underworld (cf. Szemiński 1987, 1989; Mróz 1987).

Guaman Poma identified the happenings in Kacha with the first miracle accomplished by God in "this kingdom" through his apostle Saint Bartholomew. The description follows the pattern:

The people congregated in Kacha and Saint Bartholomew appeared in Kacha.

Because he was an apostle, it is implicit that he preached.

The people began to stone him and shoot at him with slings, in order to kill him. God caused a miracle, and fire from heaven burned the people of Kacha to ashes. (A continuation of the apostle's wanderings is implied by a description of another miracle, associated with a location near Lake Titicaca where Saint Bartholomew defeated a devil and converted an Indian [Guaman Poma 1936, 93–94]).

Don Felipe was not quite sure with which saints or phenomena described by the priests he should identify the Andean originals. In one place, already cited, he suggested that the stories should be understood as God's punishments in defense of the Franciscan brothers. In the case of Kacha, he opted for Saint Bartholomew. The choice was made easier because the same personage renamed Saint Bartholomew had been connected with a miracle in Carabuco, near Lake Titicaca, where according to Guaman Poma, and other authorities as well, there was a preconquest cross. That these should be the signs of the presence of Saint Bartholomew, apostle of the Indies and thus of the Indians, seemed that much more probable.

Pacha Cuti yamqui Salca Maygua also set down a version of the miracle of Kacha. It is short but particularly informative, since it forms part of a larger story about a hero who is called Tunapa and identified by the author with Saint Thomas. During the Middle Ages Saint Thomas was believed to have been the apostle sent to the Indies, and therefore also to the Indians. In Don Joan's version the place is called Kacha Pukara, the fortress of Kacha. It begins with an idol in the shape of a woman on a very high mountain. No mention is made of a congregation; Tunapa appears in Kacha Pukara, and deplores the idol. Whether he preached is not mentioned specifically but, again, suggested by his identification as an apostle. That he was probably not accepted is suggested by his throwing fire at the idol. The mountain and the idol are burnt (Pacha Cuti yamqui Salca Maygua 1613, fol. 4v.). The story, then, is slightly different from the preceding version.[4]

Originally Tunapa was a representative of God acting among human beings in order to introduce a new religion. This also implies an ideological justification of a new political power. Such representations of God were either identified with God's servants or with his descendants in the fifth generation, responsible for a part of the world, and for a portion of time. They behaved as mortal Andean personages, eating, drinking, and carrying on to their hearts' content. This Tunapa did. But the chronicler, who tried to present him as a monk, did not mention his more earthly activities. He did mention a total of four Tunapas, one for every party of the area of Tawantin Suyu (Peru, the Andean civilization). While Tunapa received an additional name,[5] each did the same thing: fought local demons called *hapi ñuñu*. The description of the *hapi ñuñu* indicates that they were identified with the ancestors who had sprung from the earth, but also with local authorities, who represented and claimed descent from them later. The *hapi ñuñu*, whether ancestors or local authorities, were evil because they took too much from human beings. The author associated their fall from power with the mission of Jesus and he identified Tunapa as an envoy of Jesus: Saint Thomas the Apostle. Tunapa then introduced fresh knowledge, a new religion, giving power to those who accepted his teachings. Opponents were destroyed. His actions are similar to those of Parya Qaqa, who introduced a new cult and a new power in Waru Chiri.

Tunapa's actions in Kacha Pukara indicate that local people preferred their own deity, did not accept Tunapa's teachings, and consequently were destroyed by fire. The author was very cautious while identifying Tunapa with Saint Thomas (fol. 4r.). Only toward the end of his work does he suggest that Quri Kancha, the chief Inca shrine in Cuzco, was recovered for Christianity thanks to the Spanish conquest (fol. 43v.).

Conclusions

Primitive Andean stories served various objectives: they taught ethics and the mores of hospitality, of mutual service and of respect for the stranger. The same stories served to explain the origin of new political and religious entities (for example, Yawyu predominance in Waru Chiri, Inca rule in the south).

Some of these stories occupied a special place in the Andean view of history, which linked empire formation to the preaching of a new religion and the abolishing of former centers of power.

In developed Andean theology the function of the stories was to explain the necessity of maintaining order in the world; in other words, maintaining the equilibrium between the Under- and Upperworlds. The existence of such equilibrium was also associated with the existence of an empire and a central power regulating order in human society.

The same stories also explained that when people were guilty of sin they were castigated. God intervened directly or through his envoys.

The Spanish conquest created new ideological imperatives. The imposition of a new official religion, with its insistence on the equation of God with light and the devil with darkness, led to a redistribution of Andean deities into two categories: (1) legitimated through positive Spanish associations: Thunder and Saint James, Tunapa and Saint Thomas, Virgin Mary and Mother Earth (Pacha Mama); and (2) delegitimated, because of association with devils and demons. In some cases, there appeared a tendency, backed by local Inca aristocracy, to incorporate into the official church cult the founders of the Inca form of Andean religion, by identifying them with Jesus' apostles. Accordingly, the Incas could no longer be heathen; could demonstrate their ancient Christianity, and to a certain extent defend their own cultural expression as Christian, and thus as legitimate. The Christianization of these stories was dependent on the Andean doctrine of sin. Because it endured, the fundamental Catholic belief in original sin never took hold. Catholic history went native.

Notes

The research for this chapter was carried out with the support of the Science Absorption Center, Ministry of Absorption, State of Israel.

1. I keep the original orthography of names, and have not added accents as in modern Spanish.
2. The sequence of beings created suggests that the author believed that the creation of Adam and Eve (always a pair) took place before the creation of heaven and earth. I have tried to compare the sequence with the enumeration of attributes of God as they appear in Inca prayers of the sixteenth century (cf. Szemiński 1986); there, names frequently appear describing God as the one who creates beings and things in complementary pairs.
3. Cieza de León 1984, 214, gives a good example of Pacha Kamaq, soul of the Universe, identified with God the Father.
4. Elsewhere (Szemiński 1987, 47–59), I have analyzed all the data of the chronicle which describe Tunapa's activities, so here I simply present my conclusions.

5. Even if the chronicle does not mention Pachakayuq as the name of the Tunapa who intervened in Anti suyu, Pachakayuq appears to be a general name—title of all the Tunapas (cf. Szemiński 1987; 47–59, 64–74, 101–102). By analogy with Andean villages where the second of four quarters usually received the same name as the village, I assume that Pachakayuq corresponds to Anti suyu. The meanings of all the names should be analyzed separately.

Quarter of the Tawantin Suyu	Tunapa's name
Chinchay suyu	Wari Willka
Anti suyu	Pachakayuq
Qulla suyu	Wihin Kira
Kunti suyu	Tara Paka

References

Adorno, Rolena. 1986. Guaman Poma. Writing and resistance in colonial Peru. Institute of Latin American Studies. *Latin American Monograph*, no. 68. Austin: University of Texas Press.

Arriaga, Pablo José de. 1968. Extirpación de la Idolatría del Pirú. In *Biblioteca de Autores Españoles, Crónicas Peruanas de interés indígena*. Edited and with an introduction by Francisco Esteve Barba. Madrid.

Betanzos, Juan de. 1968. Suma y narración de los Incas. In *Biblioteca de Autores Españoles, Crónicas Peruanas de interés indígena*. Edited and with an introduction by Francisco Esteve Barba. Madrid.

Cabello Valboa, Miguel. 1951. Miscelanea Antárctica. Una historia del Peru Antiquo. Universidad Nacional Mayor de San Marcos, Facultad de Letras. Instituto de Etnología, Lima.

Cieza de León, Pedro de. 1984. *Crónica del Peru, Primera Parte*.

———. 1985. *Crónica del Peru, Segunda Parte*. Pontificia Universidad Católica del Perú, Fondo Editorial, Lima.

Doctrina Christiana. 1584. Lima.

Duviols, Pierre. 1971. *Ethnohistoire religieuse du Perou colonial*. Documents edited by Paris: Ophrys.

Guaman Poma de Ayala, Don Felipe. 1936. *Nueva Coronica y Buen Gobierno*. Institut d'Ethnologie, Paris.

Hocquenghem, Anne Marie. 1984. Hanan y Hurin. Chantiers Amerindia. A.E.A. Supplement 1 to no. 9 on Amerindia. Paris.

Jesuita Anonimo. 1968. Relación de las costumbres antiguas de los naturales del Pirú. In *Biblioteca de Autores Españoles, Crónicas Peruanas de interés indígena*. Edited and with an introduction by Francisco Esteve Barba. Madrid.

Molina, Christoual de. 1575. Relación de las fabvias i ritos de los Ingas. Unpublished manuscript, Cuzco, kept in Biblioteca Nacional, Madrid.

Mróz, Marcín. 1987. Los Viracochas de la conquista: Entre un mito andino y un prejuicio christiano. Unpublished manuscript.

Pacha Cuti yamqui Salca Maygua, Don Joan de Santa Cruz. 1613? Relacion de antiguedades deste reyno del Piru. Manuscript, No. 3169, Biblioteca Nacional, Madrid.

Sarmiento de Gamboa, Pedro. 1942. *Historia de los Incas*. Buenos Aires.

Szemiński, Jan. 1982–84. Las generaciones del mundo según don Felipe Guaman Poma de Ayala. Estudios Latinoamericanos, Ossolineum 9:89–124.

———. 1986. Anatomía del Wira Qučan. Los himnos quechuas de la "Relacion de las Fabvias i Ritos de los Ingas hecha por Christoual de Molina" y las trampas de la traducción. Unpublished manuscript.

———. 1987. Un kuraka, un Dios y una historia: "Relacion de antiguedades deste reyno del Piru" por don Joan de Santa Cruz Pacha cuti yamqui Saca Maygua. Unpublished manuscript.

———. 1989. Revitalización, mesianismo y nacionalismo: el movimiento tupamarista. Unpublished manuscript.

Urioste, George L. 1983. Hijos de Pariya Qaqa: La Tradicion Oral de Waru Chiri (Mitologia, Ritual y Costumbres). Foreign and Comparative Studies Program. Latin American Series, no. 6, vol. 1–11. Maxwell School of Citizenship and Public Affairs, Syracuse, New York.

Yaranga, Valderrama, Abdon. n.d. La concepción del tiempo y de la historia en la crónica de Guaman Poma de Ayala y su supervivencia actual en la región andina. Unpublished manuscript.

CHAPTER 4

Japanese Christianity and the State: From Jesuit Confrontation/Competition to Uchimura's Noninstitutional Movement/Protestantism

JOHN F. HOWES

Christianity in Japan should be viewed as one part of the study of Christianity's spread as a result of the evangelical zeal which so shaped modern history in Europe and North America. A great deal of attention has been paid to the matrix of evangelization in these two continents, the missionaries who took the message, and how they spread it. The academic discipline of missiology has examined this record, and its efforts contribute in part to making missionary evangelization more effective.

To my knowledge, however, very few scholars independent of the evangelical system have looked at the results of the missionary labors apart from their origins. The Christian faith now has more than a century of local history in almost every part of the world. At least three generations of children have grown up in Christian homes, and accepted the faith or fought it as part of their spiritual development. Some have passed it on to their children. In each country the communities of believers have developed in constant contact with the various traditions of their own societies. Individual Christians have had to ask themselves how they differ from others of good will around them and how their own beliefs could leaven the society which formed them and their nonbelieving fellows alike. This new Christianity now rejuvenates the faith in the countries where it originated, yet its nature remains little understood there. This volume rests, it seems to me, on the assumption that the experiences of the various young churches throughout the world share something in common. Is this unstated assumption true, and if so, how can we best understand the factors which go together to make up this new Christianity?

The study of the missionary movement, however important in its own right, can tell us increasingly less about the contemporary church in these lands. As the historian of Japan considers Christian development outside what is sometimes called "Christendom," he will start with the assumption that Japanese developments bear little resemblance to what happened elsewhere. Whether this idea results merely from the assumptions of uniqueness, to which Japanese and students of their culture alike are prone, can be determined only after brief reference to the meaning of Christianity in Japanese history. In some senses it is probably unique, whereas in other senses Japan's experience will be found to resemble that of numerous other young churches. The other essays in this volume give a number of perspectives from which to develop comparisons.

My essay consists of four sections: a description of Japan's first encounter with Christianity, which led to two-and-a-half centuries of hatred and mistrust; a new vision of Christianity as a seminal part of the attractive life introduced by the Industrial Revolution to the West; the single individual who best worked through for himself the implications of this compelling faith within a society whose members were bred to distrust it; and, finally, how this individual interpreted passages in the Hebrew Scriptures which deal with the subject of nations and God's relationship with his people.

Catholicism and Colonialism

Christianity first came to Japan in the middle of the sixteenth century. Though no one then could have forecast its success, the faith spread rapidly, in part because various contending political leaders wanted to use it for their own ends.[1] When in 1600 one faction won and established a new national government, its leaders could not tolerate the possibility that Christianity might give aid and comfort to its enemies. They therefore ruthlessly suppressed it. The initial success of Christianity and its subsequent difficulties are usually described together.

The Jesuits first brought the faith to Japan as part of their attempt to win new believers to compensate for those lost to the Protestant Reformation.[2] They came aboard Portuguese ships whose masters sought trade and brought the padres as chaplains. Portugal established a base in Macao, from where ships sailed to the islands off the south of Kyushu and then to Kyushu itself. There, a number of local feudal rulers were jousting for political supremacy.

The missionaries followed a strategy that had worked elsewhere. They sought out those in authority, expecting that a conversion there would facilitate their work with the common people. One of the missionaries soon met Oda Nobunaga, the first of the three great unifiers who, by 1600, would end a century of incessant warfare. The missionary's letter tells of a visit to Oda on the walls of the Kyoto Nijo Castle, which was being built at his behest. In a flamboyant gesture of rulership, Oda wore a tiger skin for the interview. Other missionaries spent much time with Toyotomi Hideyoshi, the second of the three great unifiers. The missionaries' letters, quoted at length in many histories, give us our most intimate glimpses of these two men.

The monks commanded respect, perhaps just because they dared to walk about unarmed in a society where other men of their social standing carried swords. Whatever the cause, they succeeded beyond everyone's most enthusiastic expectations. Within fifty years of the arrival of the first missionaries, a higher percentage of Japanese appears to have been Christian than at any subsequent time.

The advent of these strangely dressed but impressive "barbarians" attracted the attention of everyone who saw them and inspired a genre of painting called "Southern Barbarian Art."[3] Best known among these works are screens painted in brilliant colors, often on backgrounds of gold, to highlight the differences in the newcomers' appearance. The brilliant colors represented current European tastes, very different from the restrained Zen-inspired art which otherwise dominated Japanese aesthetics. The scenes depict the strangely dressed foreigners, the exotic animals like elephants they brought with them, and their dark-skinned servants.

While the missionaries, by their very presence, attracted attention, they themselves tried to bring change to the community in which they worked. They devised a system of romanization for the Japanese language. Their dictionaries, printed at presses which they set up and taught converts to operate, give us the best indication of Japanese pronunciation at the time. The missionaries' explication of the gospel also introduced a new dignity and sense of self-worth to the individual believer. Anything which could motivate such developments seemed to secular officials to possess great strength.

By the end of the sixteenth century, however, increasing consolidation of power lessened the number of contestants for it and those in control began to fear the potential of the new faith. Converts were accepting a foreign faith. If, in addition, they accepted political direction from Europeans, they might facilitate the entry of Europeans as a competing political force in Japan. As a result of these suspicions, the missionaries were ordered home, but a disturbing number simply went underground with their converts protecting them. Public mass crucifixions only fed the determination of the converts. Finally, in 1638, about forty thousand peasants rebelled in desperation and barricaded themselves in an abandoned castle a few miles from Nagasaki. The new central government which, since 1600, had enjoyed a precarious hegemony, put down the rebellion, but only with the assistance of offshore fusillades from Dutch ships. The Dutch assisted the Japanese rulers to prove that they were not Catholics and thus to curry favor with the new government; consequently, they became the only Europeans with whom the Japanese had regular contact until the Meiji Restoration of 1868.[4]

Convinced that Christianity would subvert its people's loyalties, the new central government outlawed Christianity in all forms and tried to eradicate it. Because believers had demonstrated that they could retain their faith despite great pain and hideous tortures, the authorities began to use psychological pressure instead. It was reasoned, with justification, that a sure way to identify Christians was to make everyone periodically trample on a sacred image. To this end, officials devised bronze plaques which bore images of the crucifixion or a madonna. They then ordered everyone to trample on the image; those who refused revealed themselves as being Christian. Lists were made of all the family members of such people and the dates they had trampled on the image were also recorded. These lists, kept carefully by local Buddhist temples, became population registers and provide the most reliable demographic information about Japan before the middle of the nineteenth century. Their titles—"Records of Conversion [away from Christianity]"—served to remind members of succeeding generations of the dreadful first purpose for which they were designed.[5]

The government erected signs at crossroads to warn passersby that the "devilish religion" was forbidden. About thirty by seventy centimeters in size, the signs also listed other regulations. However, the notices contained nothing about the penalty for disobedience; the government considered warning sufficient, and magistrates could choose what punishment they considered fitting. No one who read them would suppose that disobedience would result in anything other than death. (In 1873, when the new Meiji government decided to stop enforcing the prohibition, it simply had the signs removed.)[6]

Despite the fact that two centuries after the origin of the ban, age had weathered the notice boards and the repeated trampling of the holy image had become routine, government officials renewed their concern over the possible evil effects of the proscribed faith. This was due to a new threat: the coming of a second wave of Europeans to Japan's shores. The Russians extended their control over Siberia and the East coast of Asia. They established bases in Sakhalin and Alaska and tried to endear themselves to the Ainu of Hokkaido and southern Sakhalin.[7] The British conquered India and meddled in China. The Americans sought safe haven in Japan's closed ports as part of their new trade routes to Canton and Shanghai.[8] In all these places, Christianity was seen to exert great influence.

Aizawa Seishisai, an influential thinker who tried to develop a defensive strategy against this political threat, considered the Westerners' faith one of their main strengths. As he saw it, Westerners used Christianity to wean the common people away from their national allegiance. Japanese commoners would be easy prey. They "are attracted to pernicious doctrines from abroad because they need a basis of spiritual reliance within. It is no surprise that...[the Christian barbarians] take advantage of this spiritual void and this fear of the hereafter to deceive our commoners into embracing their notions of paradise and hell....[They] embrace the foreigners' words of religion as they long for a mother's compassion; they are attracted to any pernicious doctrine from abroad."[9]

Aizawa recognized the threat of political subversion by the forbidden faith and intuitively recognized the power of the Christian message, considering the religion a greater threat to Japan's independence than armed strength. Aizawa was writing in 1825; thirty years later, the most influential thinker among those who would lead the Meiji Restoration knew the distinction between Catholicism and Protestantism. "It differs from the Christianity brought [to Japan] in the Tembun era [1532–54] as night differs from day. It is a religion that combines government and edification. From sovereign to commoners—all are true to its commandments,"[10] and so easily united into strong national units.

These examples will demonstrate that the nineteenth-century evangelical drive of Protestantism arrived in Japan to face both a populace that with good reason feared Christianity and a ruling class with imperfect but essentially correct notions of the strength that Christianity gave to Western society. Taken together, these antagonistic official attitudes constituted a formidable barrier to evangelism. But the way that Christianity was seen to reflect Western political and military strength made it attractive to those who wanted to appropriate that strength for themselves or their nation.

Protestantism and Enlightenment

Early in 1868, a new government brought an end to the two-and-a-half centuries of rule by the Tokugawa family. This event, known to history as the "Meiji Restoration," after the emperor who saw it accomplished, enabled the government to alter a number of policies and to enter into diplomatic relations with Western powers. In the next few years, new institutions based on Western examples superseded the discredited feudal framework of the old government.[11]

In their first few months, the new rulers faced a painful dilemma.[12] A few weeks after the Restoration had been announced, peasants approached the Catholic chaplain who ministered to the members of the foreign community in Nagasaki. The farmers identified themselves as Christian and introduced the chaplain to numerous others who shared their faith. Thus the new government learned that centuries of oppression had not eradicated Christianity. This occurred before the new government had complete control of the country and while it was still seeking to persuade the Western powers to support it against the remnants of the Tokugawa forces. Consequently, young Meiji officials could not simply do away with the Christians. Only a few were executed, but the rest were uprooted and sent in small groups to distant cities. Until the signboards were removed in 1873, the young leaders of the new government felt the need for constant defense of their policies toward Christians before the Western consular representatives. The appearance of "hidden" Christians, centuries after all traces of Christianity had otherwise vanished, reinforced in the minds of apprehensive officials the "insidious" nature of the faith.

In the meantime, the appearance of Westerners in the new "concessions," as the areas in which the foreigners lived were called, attracted widespread attention. Once again, artists, this time printing thousands of copies of their works by the woodblock process, carefully recorded the exotic ways of these strange people.[13] Everything Western conjured up exotic vistas:

> On Christmas, the church music sounded even more refreshing than usual, and beautifully dressed Western children ran about happily. Grand ladies in warm-looking fur coats passed in groups of three or five on their way to church. Everyone's face looked serene and peaceful strains of piano music echoed through the air. One step outside of the concession and people looked as if they were going to bite you as they went about in the busy bustle of dusk.[14]

Another observer recalled the actions of a street-corner evangelist: "One Sunday morning a school-mate of mine asked me whether I would not go with him to 'a certain place in the foreigners' quarter, where we can hear pretty women sing, and a tall big man with long beard shout and howl upon an elevated place, flinging his arms and twisting his body in all fantastic manners, to all which admittance is entirely free.'"[15] The historian sees in this attraction of outlandishly different folk customs an attitude quite similar to that which greeted the appearance of the first Catholics three centuries earlier.

Although it had been a Catholic priest who had first met the Nagasaki Christians, the faith that would become well known in modern Japan was Protestantism, and predominantly Anglo-Saxon. All those who earned themselves niches in secular histories as effective evangelists are Americans who came within a few decades of the reopening of the country in 1854. One was an eye doctor who started a tradition of Western-style ophthalmology and who also developed the romanization of the Japanese language which, with a few modifications, is still in use.[16] Two others had served with the Northern forces in the American Civil War.[17] They were invited to Japan by the government as secular educators and only discussed Christianity when their students demanded it. All three were well educated for their generation and shared the general optimism characteristic of their nation. By the time they departed, they left behind them a generation of converts hard at work in establishing a vigorous Christian church. For the rest of the century, individual missionaries would strongly influence the lives of numerous Japanese leaders, but the Church itself developed independently and, increasingly, missionaries served under Japanese leaders.

Though membership in these churches never exceeded 1 percent of the population, individual Christians exerted an influence out of all proportion to their numbers. Many of Japan's promising young writers became Christians.[18] Most did not continue their church activities as they matured, but a surprising number returned to their early faith in old age or at least expressed a continuing sympathy for Christian ideals. Those who had a knowledge of Western languages and cultures also included a high proportion of Christians. Since these tongues and lands were generally held in high regard, these few individuals enjoyed the respect of others in the community.

Christianity also helped mold education and social reforms. Under the Tokugawa government, official policy strictly separated various social classes in a manner similar to that prevalent in Europe at the time. Upper-class male samurai were expected to lead society. Even before the reentry of Westerners and the official adoption of Western education, a large proportion of them could read and write. As a result, they had the responsibility of thinking about broader issues. Members of other classes became literate to the extent that their jobs required it, but they suffered the restraints of their subordinate positions. The Christian message, brought for the most part by Americans, taught the equality of all individuals; women like men. This view of life, which was totally new in such a strictly controlled hierarchical society, gave a refreshing sense of worth to individuals who may have been otherwise indifferent to the specifics of Christian doctrine.

A national consensus that education must be improved led to the formation of a centralized national school system with an acknowledged role for Christian missionary schools. The main aim of the Japanese leaders was to make the secret of Western strength their own. This strength seemed partly to rest on the superior education Westerners offered their children. Within a few years of the Meiji Restoration, officials had mapped out ambitious plans for mass education, but the number of schools never matched the demand. At the same time, planners found that the Western curricula they emulated were founded on

Christian principles. The Western secular educators who became effective evangelists impressed Japanese on an individual basis. The authorities in charge of education wanted to know the basis of the teachers' perceived moral strength. Schools founded by missionaries could hardly be closed since they met a need which all acknowledged, nor could the teachers who came at no expense to the Japanese be forbidden to teach Christianity, lest they simply go home. The parents of girls could hardly object to the mission schools since their daughters could obtain there an education far superior to that afforded females in the government schools. In short, for many reasons, by no means all directly related to the nature of the faith, Christian teachers contributed much to education.

Christians also demonstrated a new effective concern for the amelioration of various social ills. Caroline Macdonald, a heroic Canadian missionary, first demonstrated a concern for the spiritual and psychological state of prisoners.[19] Other women founded organizations modeled on those in the West against prostitution and alcohol abuse. Salvation Army workers who sang and preached on the street became an accepted part of urban life. Even those who did not populate the modest churches, which were growing steadily in number, came to accept Christianity as a normal part of religious expression in Japan.

Though many Japanese in responsible positions themselves accepted the Christian faith, the new national institutions established after the promulgation of the Constitution in 1889 discriminated against it. The Constitution guaranteed freedom of religion but, as with the other freedoms it promised, "within limits not prejudicial to peace and order, and not antagonistic to [the people's] duties as subjects."[20] And in the closing years of the nineteenth century and the first years of the twentieth, government laws increasingly prescribed a kind of nationalism which opposed the traditional Japanese attitudes to Christian ones. Christians continued to enjoy freedom of faith, but they grew up in schools which taught an attitude toward their own nation and others that was at variance with Christian belief.

In retrospect, it appears that once again the Japanese leaders feared that individual converts would lose their allegiance to the Japanese state. They might support one of the Western powers against their homeland. The concern became greater as, with the passage of time, the Western powers competed with Japan to control the Western Pacific. The resulting uneasy truce between Christianity and nationalism continued until the defeat of Japan in 1945. Christians could practice their faith, but they had to take particular care to make clear their loyalty to the state.[21]

The career of one Christian leader demonstrates the uneasy balance these conditions introduced. Kagawa Toyohiko (1888–1960) was orphaned as a young boy.[22] Denied the love he craved in the home of relatives who raised him, he found affectionate surrogate parents in a missionary couple. Precocious and introspective, he avidly read all the books in the libraries of the mission schools where he studied. His achievements led to study in Princeton Theological Seminary, followed by his return to Japan where he inaugurated Christian social work in the slums. His battles there against ignorance, poverty, and disease gained him worldwide recognition. He wrote novels which, though not great literature, disseminated a Christian view of life through society. He used the profits from their sales—hundreds of thousands of copies—to support Christian cooperatives and Japan's first medical insurance scheme.[23] In the 1930s Americans acclaimed him as an example of the Christian conscience at work in a nation racing into hostilities. He could have remained in the United States during the war but elected to return to Japan. There he found himself isolated. In the end he consented to army requests to make propaganda broadcasts intended to persuade American soldiers to give up their fight against Japan. In the postwar disillusion with Japanese institutions, Kagawa's countrymen could not countenance the memory of this cooperation with the army, the agent which had come to represent government oppression. Though he continued to be active with his Christian concerns in the new liberal environment after 1945, he could not live down his apparent compromising of his Christian ideals. He commands our respect, for his dilemma demonstrates how official fear of Christianity affected even the most dedicated Christians before Japan's surrender in 1945.

In contrast to Kagawa Toyohiko, Uchimura Kanzo's consistent disavowal of the Japanese state provides the model for what has become popularly accepted as the ideal Japanese Christian in modern Japan.

The Lonely Prophet

The secular concerns outlined here which affected the fortunes of Christianity in Japan permit a number of generalizations. First, Christianity always commanded attention out of all proportion to the number of its adherents. Second, those who embraced Christianity became exceptionally loyal to and effective in their faith. Finally, government authorities worried that the moral authority of Christianity might lead converts to abandon their political loyalty to their homeland.

Kagawa suffered in the dark days of World War II because of this official conviction that one could not be at the same time a loyal Christian and a loyal Japanese. However, the individual who, since 1945, exemplifies the correct handling of this problem is Uchimura Kanzo. He is also interesting because he inspired an indigenous Japanese-Christian group which eschews formal organization and because he remains Japan's greatest student of the Bible. A glance at his life and works will show how Christianity has found a lasting home in Japan.

Uchimura was born in 1861 into the home of a low-ranking samurai family. His father, a scholarly gentleman, served as a private secretary to his feudal lord. Shortly after the Restoration, Uchimura's family decided that he should use his superior intelligence in the study of English. He learned rapidly and soon found himself among the nation's best students of the language. Together with a number of the others, he enrolled in the new Sapporo Agricultural College. There he received training modeled on that of the American land-grant colleges, designed to produce engineers with commissions in the army reserve. The government hoped that young men with such training would remain in Hokkaido and help develop it as a bastion against Russian colonial expansion. In fact, Uchimura, like most of the students, returned to Tokyo and found quick employment because of his superior training.

Uchimura had formed a small Christian church in Hokkaido with a number of the other young men converted to Christianity by the charismatic American who had developed the college's educational program. After returning to Tokyo, he worked enthusiastically with other converts of his age. Then, suddenly, after a short and disastrous marriage that ended in divorce, he went to the United States for further training. Here he discovered that his new faith had not made him as international a man as he had anticipated. Instead, he remained painfully conscious of himself as Japanese. He finished a second bachelor's degree at Amherst College and then, after a few months in theological school, returned to Japan.

Uchimura's life up to this point is described in his English-language book *How I Became a Christian: Out of My Diary* (1895), a piece of confessional literature that deserves inclusion in every reading list about Third World Christianity.[24] Reading it carefully, one is aware of an unrelieved sense of tension. One source of this appears to be the lack of any mention of the divorce and its relation to his trip abroad in a work otherwise greatly concerned with motivation. Uchimura appears to have sided with his mother rather than his wife in the altercations which broke out between them in the small Uchimura home that he, as the eldest son, and his bride shared with his parents. When he sent his pregnant bride home and refused to accept her back, his Christian friends criticized his lack of charity. In none of his subsequent writings did he ever allude to the divorce, but one judges that from this experience he came to recognize in a very personal way the conflicting demands that his new religion and the ethical precepts of his society placed on him. By Confucian standards, he would have had no choice but to back his mother in a situation of this sort. Whatever the cause, the awareness of an almost unbridgeable chasm between the two ethical systems characterized all his subsequent work.

Back in Japan, with the best education both his society and the United States could offer, Uchimura quickly alienated those who wanted to employ his great talents. He took employment as the headmaster of a Christian school established by Japanese converts, but left in anger. Missionaries invited by the schools's founders assumed themselves to be in charge and disagreed with Uchimura's program to discuss Christianity only after he had introduced students to great religious leaders of their own Buddhist heritage.

A few years later, he also cut himself off from government employment in an incident that remains the prime example of action on behalf of individual conscience over group loyalty in modern Japan. The conservatism which would mark Japanese attitudes toward Christianity in the early twentieth century started with the Constitution of 1889 and a companion document, the Education Rescript of 1890. The Constitution set up the framework for the new modern Japanese state and the Education Rescript outlined a code of ethics to be taught in the nation's compulsory national schools.[25] The latter aimed to ensure that each child would be socialized in the Japanese version of the Confucian ethic. A hierarchy of values with unquestioned obedience to superiors ensured loyalty to the Emperor. To impress upon students the importance of the document, officials had the Emperor Meiji sign in his own hand a number of copies for distribution to leading schools. Uchimura taught history and English language at the most prestigious of these schools. At the ceremony staged for the presentation of the document, the official in charge ordered the faculty members and students to come up individually and bow before the document "*in the manner in which we used to bow before our ancestral relics as prescribed in Buddhist and Shinto ceremonies*....[H]esitating in the doubt, I took the safer course for my Christian conscience...took my stand and did *not* bow."[26] His action was reported in the press alongside articles that described the stubborn opposition to government policy among the elected members of the brand-new lower house of the legislature, where many of the opposition parliamentarians were also Christians. The parallel was unmistakable: Christians obeyed an authority above the state. In vain did Uchimura argue his higher loyalty to the emperor's intention; the emperor, he said, desired that the virtues outlined in the Rescript be implemented in daily life, and not that the paper which listed them become an object of worship. Uchimura lost his job and in disgrace became a symbol of unrepentant opposition.

Uchimura retired to Kyoto where a sympathetic bookstore proprietor staked him to a subsistence allowance as he began to write. The writing style that he developed throughout the 1890s, combining sophisticated vocabulary and English-style syntax, resulted in a Japanese which was unusually clear and forceful. His numerous books in English and Japanese pled the cause of the man of action. By the end of the decade, his undeniable stature led the publisher of Japan's largest newspaper to make Uchimura chief editor. Under his leadership, it became a crusading force that commanded respect. Then, at the height of his power, he resigned because the publisher of the newspaper, one suspects under pressure from the government, abandoned the newspaper's opposition, championed by Uchimura, to the forthcoming war with Russia. This dramatic act, once again in the interest of individual conviction over official policy, became the second great example of the independent Christian conscience in modern Japan.

Uchimura at this point concluded that he could no longer work with any of the secular institutions in his society and decided to support himself with a monthly magazine dedicated to the study of the Bible. He had begun the magazine in 1900, the beginning of what some believers thought would be the "Christian Century." He now had no alternative to supporting himself from this enterprise. He succeeded. By the time of his death, 357 issues had appeared, all on schedule. They averaged about sixty pages and he himself wrote about half the copy. In this magazine he published works which, more than half a century after his death, give him his standing as the leading Bible scholar in Japan. He, alone among his contemporaries, wrote widely on the Hebrew Scriptures as well as the New Testament.

Readers of his magazine gradually began to come to him for lectures on the Bible. The audiences grew until, at their largest, Uchimura regularly addressed groups of several hundred, all of whom paid admission fees. Those who attended included some of the brightest and most dedicated young Japanese of their generation. For a few years following World War I, Uchimura emphasized the imminent Second Coming of Christ, as did thousands in Europe and North America. Next, his young followers helped him as he delivered great lecture series on Job (twenty-one lectures), Romans (sixty lectures), the biography of Christ (seventy-six lectures), and a number of other subjects. These lectures, bound in book form, went on to become Japanese classics in their own right.

As Uchimura approached his seventieth birthday, it became apparent to him that upon his death, his followers would form a church in his memory around his ideas. He distrusted the Church as a Western organization which had corrupted the core meaning of the Gospels by its overly close association with secular authorities down through history. Because they represented one or another of the denominations and did not usually respect their converts, he also disliked missionaries as a group. When a retired American woman who had been a missionary gently informed him that she thought his followers would start a church in his name after his death even though he did not want it, he reacted with hysterical petulance. After a long literary debate over the essence of his ideas with the individual most likely to succeed him as leader, Uchimura left among his unpublished papers a manuscript which clearly disavowed the movement which became associated with his name. He died in 1930, one year before the Japanese army embarked on the adventures which led directly to the Japanese participation in World War II.

The movement attributed to Uchimura is *Mukyokai*, the "We-Need-No-Church Principle," to adopt a translation Uchimura used in his old age. This movement has excited considerable attention in Europe and was widely publicized by the Swiss theologian Emil Brunner. Carlo Caldarola's work *Christianity, the Japanese Way* (Brill, 1979) introduces the movement in terms similar to those used by Brunner. Both Brunner and Caldarola accepted the contention of Uchimura's followers that his presentation of Christianity had been uniquely suited to Japanese circumstances. There is much to what they say, but in fact the attempt to establish a Japanese type of Christianity independent of its Western origins runs through much of Japanese Christianity. To focus on the concept Mukyokai, which is never satisfactorily defined, detracts from what I see as Uchimura's main message: the need for complete and ultimate independence from all human forces and entire reliance on God.[27] To depend on the name of a movement, even one such as Mukyokai which denies religious affiliation, diverts man from his real loyalty to God himself. To act on this truth, of course, remains open to all, not only to Japanese. Uchimura realized that he was bringing up an idea which had appeared before in world history and he did not, at the time of his death, consider the "no church" idea to be particularly Japanese.

Accepting this attitude toward the institution usually attributed to Uchimura leads one to ask what it is about Uchimura that makes him special in the history of religion. This, one concludes, must be found in his actions and writings.

The Nation and the Hebrew Scriptures

To distinguish between Uchimura's actions and his writings is, in general, to discuss separately the earlier and later parts of his life. During the period between his refusal to bow and his resignation from his newspaper position due to disagreement on the issue of war, Uchimura remained much in the public eye. Most of the young men who attended his lectures on the Bible had been attracted in the first instance because of his reputation for vigorous dissent over matters of public morality. Though he wrote much during this early period, the great mass of his work appeared when he started to write almost exclusively on topics related to the Bible. His careful analysis introduced readers to the convictions that underlay his forceful personality.

The difference between the young Uchimura as a man of action and his later thoughtful works presents the scholar who wishes to understand his importance with a peculiar dilemma. To his students he represented a lonely voice of integrity in a wilderness of hypocrisy and falsehood. When, after his death, his students experienced the despondency induced by the war and its repercussions, he alone represented faith in the transcendent Christian God. Thus, as they began to patch together their own lives and the new postwar national culture, they defined his ideas as "Japanese Christianity." Uchimura himself, at points in his career, had given them justification for this assumption, and they were not alone. Uchimura's works were published and republished in multivolume series—six of which come to mind, including the recent *Complete Works*, in forty volumes of more than five hundred pages each.[28] A marathon court case, the official record of which occupies several feet of shelf space and has also been published, deals with the rights of a historian to publish the facts as he sees them without interference from the Ministry of Education. The textbook passages which brought on the controversy were written by the historian Ienaga Saburo. They include one in which Ienaga, in a high-school textbook, praised Uchimura's refusal to bow. Conservative officials considered the praise unmerited.

Ienaga, who has clearly risked his reputation by his interpretation of Uchimura's most famous act, once told me that he could not deal with Uchimura's later studies of the Bible because he was not himself a Christian. That an accomplished intellectual historian will risk his career over an interpretation of Uchimura's actions, but consider himself unqualified to deal with Uchimura's thought, demonstrates the nature of the problem.

It falls on those outside Japan to place Uchimura in the perspective of world Christian history. Paradoxically, this seems the best way to start the assessment of his later importance within Japan.

Uchimura's basic answer to the dilemma posed by the nationalists of loyalty to Japan or to Christianity was that, by being a true and loyal Christian, a Japanese serves the higher interests of his country. Japanese Christians would normally live up to the requirements of their native Confucian ethics which, at best, required the lay servant to rebuke the mistakes of his master. Uchimura found the prototype for this kind of individual in the prophets of the Hebrew Scriptures.

In their love of Israel he also found in the Jews the prototype of true Japanese patriotism. He was among the first Japanese to find great similarities between the Japanese and the Jews, and he pointed out the parallels in his works. This has led to a spate of recent writings in Japanese which expand on the original points made by Uchimura.[29]

In an attempt to compare Uchimura's treatment of texts which reveal aspects of the Jewish attitude toward the nations, I asked E. John Hamlin, an authority on the Hebrew Scriptures, to suggest relevant passages. In response to my request, he identified several passages,[30] and I examined Uchimura's commentaries on these passages.

Of the eleven passages which Hamlin identified, Uchimura made no reference to eight. Of the remaining three, he made significant reference to two. The first is Genesis 12:3: "and in you [Abraham] shall all the families of the earth be blessed."[31] Uchimura refers to this passage in a lecture he called "A Life Ordained by God" (Kami ni michibikaruru shogai). Briefly, he says that God often prescribes lives for us at variance with what we anticipate. Abraham seemed a failure in terms of his own ambitions, for he wandered most of his days through areas he disliked. He did not achieve his goals but did accomplish God's goals for him and thereby achieved much more than he had planned for himself. "He became the founder of a great people. He also came to be called the 'Father of Faith' and the model for all of those who believe in God. Enjoined that 'all the peoples would obtain blessing through you,' he became the foundation for the salvation of all peoples,"[32] because he followed the demands God made of him.

For most of the twenty-seven references listed in a comprehensive index, Uchimura takes the text literally in terms of individual faith. The individual who desires salvation for himself should turn to the one God of Christians and Jews alike. Late in his career and two years before the reference to Abraham mentioned above, Uchimura dedicated a whole lecture-commentary to this verse, Isaiah 45:22.

> Turn to me and be saved
> all the ends of the earth!
> For I am God and there is no other.

He delivered it in 1924, seven months after the United States had passed the act which prohibited further immigration from Japan and other Asian countries. To be lumped together with other Asians and forbidden entry to the United States had shocked Japanese who had counted the United States their friend.[33] Early in his lecture, Uchimura said of this passage, "It is God's word, and we cannot understand God's word apart from the light of our own experience.[34] Upon what can man depend? Not on other men, nor the state, not Japan nor even the United States. We felt a great shock when we realized that we could not depend on the one nation which seemed to embody God's will on earth. But we return: we can depend only on God and conclude, Japan is called a land of God[s]; it has had a faith since antiquity. Through the nurturing of faith in Jesus Christ in this country, will not this country be saved and at the same time the whole world be saved, so that man's despair over the United States will appear as faith in Japan?" (p. 500). Thus, Uchimura refers to nation-states in comments on a passage which he usually interprets in personal terms. Here it inspires a vision of national greatness not unlike that of the Hebrew prophet. In a time of great concern over his nation's future, he sees the sum total of the faith of individuals as the touchstone for national salvation and a role of world leadership for Japan.

In these two passages, we see a number of elements which characterize Uchimura's view of Christianity. In the first place, he sees himself and his fellow Japanese in direct historical descent from the beginnings of the faith described in the Hebrew Scriptures. Abraham "became the foundation for the salvation of all peoples," including the Japanese. Not included in this passage, but apparent in many others among Uchimura's works, is the conviction that the historical foundations of Christianity which begin in the Old Testament and end with the works of the apostles form the entire basis of the Christian faith. The accretions which have taken place in the name of "Christianity" after the events mentioned in the Bible distort the true faith. The core of the Christian belief can be discovered only in this book which so firmly roots its claims to salvation in the events it describes.

Secondly, Uchimura sees Christianity as a life of encounter for each individual. The encounter is induced by the faith. If one becomes Christian through contacts with other Christians, reading of the Bible, and prayer, he at once finds himself in opposition to the rest of society around him. As a result, "we cannot understand God's word apart from our own experience." Christian faith is existential; one understands it and grows in it as one attempts to meet the daily vicissitudes of life in the spirit of Christ. Thirdly, man is expected to have strong goals in life. Abraham's goals were completely frustrated by God's design. In a similar way, every Japanese would have clearly defined aims which he too must put aside if he wants to do God's will.

Finally, in his attempt to implement Christian principles in his life, the Japanese Christian also helps fulfill Japan's role in world history. The Japanese people of Uchimura's generation had found themselves obsessed with the psychic need to fit Japan into the larger world of international relations. Its two-and-a-half centuries of isolation had left it unprepared for relaxed relations with the powers who ruled the world of the late nineteenth century. Uchimura had dealt with the problem of Japan's place during this period in one of his first books.[35] By the end of his career, disillusioned like many of his countrymen with the United States, he saw that a Japan as a nation of Christians might become God's instrument to further God's plans for mankind.

Conclusion

At this point we can return to consider the Uchimura tradition in the context of its possible relation to newly developed Christianity in other parts of the world. Christian roots in Japan go back four-and-a-half centuries but had almost died out when Christianity returned in its Protestant form in the mid-nineteenth century. The Japanese demand for an independent Christian church, which began within fifteen years of the arrival of the first missionaries, meant that Westerners never ran it. Kagawa, for example, though bound by emotional ties to an individual missionary family, completely controlled every element of his work. He asked Western audiences for financial assistance to expand his many activities, but his works prospered on their own firm economic base.

Uchimura's experience confirmed his conviction that Japan needed a Christianity independent of Western churches or their representatives. He felt that their insistence on denominational loyalty led to the attempt to influence the faith of the Japanese in ways not consistent with the Japanese experience. Only with a return to the biblical Scriptures and their history of God's relation to man before the advent of the great mixture of secular history and religion that became known as "Christianity," could the Japanese find a faith suitable for their needs. It is the attempt by each individual believer to return to the Scriptures which forms the core of Japan's Mukyokai. Japanese individuals who come to Jerusalem to study the Old Testament languages and their world will, when asked, trace their interest to Uchimura and this understanding of Christianity in his own land.

What I have described closely resembles the Mukyokai which Uchimura disclaimed at his end. The difference between the loosely defined Mukyokai of the present and Uchimura's view at the time of his death is that he made provision for ongoing circumstances that would nurture youth in the faith. He felt, as he neared his death, that any organization would inhibit the individual's freedom to come to his own Christian understanding on the basis of his own experience. Organization leads logically to the need for creeds and sacraments which force the individual to alter the results of his experience to fit the common framework of the group or face expulsion from it. Though Uchimura recognized such group agreement as the necessary precondition of many ecclesiastical organizations, he did not himself feel such a need and did not want his name linked to an organization that did feel it. "If I have a church," he said at one point, "it is my writings."[36] Appropriately enough, his ideas have been, for the most part, spread by his books.

Critics have correctly foretold the problems that such an interpretation of Christianity invites. It depends for new members on candidates who come to it out of their own spiritual struggles. Meetings of believers formed around Uchimura's ideas are troubled by Christian education, by the need to care for the aged professional leaders who have retired from leadership of their own Bible-study groups. Even those direct descendants of the man who, as Uchimura's putative successor, tried to define Mukyokai, recognize the problems posed by lack of organization. Yet they feel that only in its absence can true Christianity grow.

The Uchimura tradition seems to have led to a Christianity of believers who are especially sophisticated in their knowledge of the faith in the tradition of nineteenth-century evangelical Protestantism. We can seek enlightenment regarding how this compares to developments in other countries in the other essays in this volume.

Notes

1. Neil F. McMullin, in *Buddhism and the State in Sixteenth-Century Japan* (Princeton: Princeton University Press, 1984), demonstrates how Buddhist intransigence motivated the first of the three great unifiers to ruthless military suppression of organized religion.
2. A large body of literature deals with Catholic Christianity in this period of Japanese history. These are some of the major works in English for a study of the material covered in the first section of this chapter. Anezaki Masaharu (all Japanese names are given Japanese order with the family name first) initiated the study with specialized works in Japanese and shared his broad conclusions with Western readers in his *History of Japanese Religion with Special Reference to the Social and Moral Life of the Nation* (London: Kegan, Paul, Trench, Trubner, 1930). George Sansom's *The Western World and Japan* (New York: Knopf, 1950) sets the advent of the Europeans in world context. Charles Boxer's *The Christian Century in Japan, 1549–1650* (Berkeley: University of California Press, 1967 [corrected version]) relies on missionary sources to make it the standard study. Michael Cooper's *They Came to Japan: An Anthology of European Reports on Japan, 1543–1640* (Berkeley: University of California Press, 1965) uses the same sources to introduce the reader to individual missionaries. George Elison's *Deus Destroyed: The Image of Christianity in Early Modern Japan* (Cambridge: Harvard University Press, 1973) deals with the anti-Christian writings of apostate Japanese priests. And two novels, Endo Shusaku's *Chimmoku* (Silence) (Tokyo: Sophia University Press, 1969) and Nagayo Yoshiro's *Seido no Kirisuto* (The Bronze Christ) (New York: Taplinger, 1959) deal with apostasy during the Christian century. A standard bibliography of works in Chinese and Japanese is available in the Committee on Asian Cultural Studies of International Christian University's *Christianity in Japan: A Bibliography of Japanese and Chinese Sources, 1 (1843–1858)* (Tokyo: International Christian University, 1960). A useful parallel study by the same organization is *Comparative Chronology of Protestantism in Asia, 1972–1945* (1984).
3. Okamoto Yoshitomo, in *The Namban Art of Japan* (Tokyo and New York: Weatherhill, 1972), depicts a number of these appealing works.
4. Grant Goodman, in *Japan: The Dutch Experience* (Dover, N.H.: Athlone, 1985) introduces the importance of the Dutch connection in Japanese history.

5. Thomas C. Smith, in *Nakahara: Family Farming and Population in a Japanese Village* (Stanford: Stanford University Press, 1977) demonstrates how the materials in these registers can be used to understand Tokugawa Japanese society.
6. Kishimoto Hideo, ed., *Japanese Religion in the Meiji Era*, translated by John F. Howes (Tokyo: Obunsha, 1956), p. 84.
7. George Alexander Lensen, in *The Russian Push Towards Japan: Russo-Japanese Relations, 1697–1875* (Princeton: Princeton University Press, 1959), chronicles the Russian movement across the continent.
8. Hugh Borton, *Japan's Modern Century* (New York: Ronald, 1955), pp. 10–11.
9. Aizawa Seishisai, *Shinron* (New Theses), as quoted in Bob Tadashi Wakabayashi's *Anti-foreignism and Western Learning in Early-Modern Japan: The New Theses of 1825* (Cambridge: Harvard University Press, 1986), pp. 122, 131.
10. *Yokoi Shonan iko*, pp. 242-43, as quoted in Wakahayashi, *Anti-foreignism*, p. 143.
11. John K. Fairbank, Edwin O. Reischauer, and Albert M. Craig, *East Asia: The Modern Transformation* (Boston: Houghton Mifflin, 1965), pp. 244–88.
12. The standard English-language works on Japanese religion which provide the framework for this section of the chapter begin with Kishimoto, *Japanese Religion*. Charles W. Iglehart's *A Century of Protestant Christianity in Japan* (Tokyo and Rutland, Vt.: Charles Tuttle, 1959) gives the standard missionary interpretation. Irwin Scheiner's *Christian Converts and Social Protest in Meiji Japan* (Berkeley: University of California Press, 1970) depicts the history of early Protestantism from Japanese sources. Fred J. Notehelfer's *American Samurai: Captain L. L. Janes and Japan* (Princeton: Princeton University Press, 1985) deals with one of the secular teachers whose students became leaders in many Christian endeavors. Cyril Powles's *Victorian Missionaries in Meiji Japan: The Shiba Sect, 1873–1900* (Toronto: University of Toronto–York University Joint Centre for Asia-Pacific Studies, 1987), analyzes the work of British and Canadian missionaries, which differed in several important ways from that of the more numerous American missionaries. Sansom, *The Western World and Japan*, sets out the cultural background. The standard bibliography is the Committee on Asian Cultural Studies of the International Christian University's *A Bibliography of Christianity in Japan—Protestantism in English Sources* (Tokyo: International Christian University, 1966).
13. Tamba Tsuneo's *Yokohama Ukiyoe* (Tokyo: Asahi Shimbun, 1962) gives many examples which demonstrate Japanese preoccupations.
14. Kishimoto, *Japanese Religion*, p. 199.
15. Uchimura Kanzo, *How I Became a Christian: Out of My Diary* (Tokyo: Keiseisha Shoten, 1895); as included in *Uchimura Kanzo Zenshu* (Tokyo: Iwanami Shoten, 1982), 3:13. Hereafter "*Zenshu.*"
16. See Edward R. Beauchamp, "James Curtis Hepburn," in the *Encyclopedia of Japan* (New York: Kodansha International, 1983), 3:127.
17. L. L. Janes, for whom see Notehelfer, *American Samurai*, and W.S. Clark, for whom see John M. Maki, "William Smith Clark," *Encyclopedia of Japan*, 1:321.

18. Nobuya Bamba and John F. Howes, in *Pacifism in Japan, the Christian and Socialist Tradition* (Vancouver: University of British Columbia Press, 1978), pp. 35–90, give two examples of this phenomenon.
19. Margaret Prang, "Caroline Macdonald and Prison Work in Japan," Working Paper Series no. 51 (Toronto: University of Toronto–York University Joint Centre for Asia-Pacific Studies, 1988).
20. Hugh Borton, *Japan's Modern Century*, 2d ed. (New York: Ronald, 1970), p. 574.
21. Aikawa Takaaki, *Unwilling Patriot* (Tokyo: Jordan Press, 1960) vividly portrays the dilemmas of an ordinary Japanese Christian at this time.
22. For two opposite views of Kagawa, see George B. Bickle, Jr., *The New Jerusalem: Aspects of Utopianism in the Thought of Kagawa Toyohiko (1888–1960)* and Yuzo Ota, "Kagawa Toyohiko (1888-1960)" in Bamba and Howes, *Pacifism in Japan*, pp. 169–98.
23. Uchikawa Eijiro, *The Twilight Years of Nitobe Inazo*, trans. Michael Newton (Tokyo: Kyobunkan, 1985), pp. 76–77.
24. See note 15 above.
25. See Borton, *Japan's Modern Century*: for the text of the Constitution, pp. 490–507, and for the Education Rescript, p. 178.
26. Letter to David C. Bell (emphasis in original), 6 March 1891; *Zenshu*, 36, 331-32.
27. Support for this statement is contained in my lengthy critical biography of Uchimura now in the final stages of preparation. I will be glad to share details of the argument with those who are interested.
28. (Tokyo: Iwanami Shoten, 1981–84).
29. Yamamoto Shichihei is generally considered the "Isaiah Ben-Dasan" who wrote *Nihonjin to Yudayajin* (the Japanese and the Jews) (Tokyo: Yamamoto Shoten, 1970). His love for the Old Testament also appears to be the motivation for his republication of Uchimura's works. The most famous book in this vein has been written by a man who also republished a number of Uchimura's works.
30. The passages included Genesis 12:3, Psalm 22:23, Isaiah 42, 6–7, Isaiah 44:5, Isaiah 45:6, Isaiah 45:22, Isaiah 49:6, Isaiah 49:8, Isaiah 51:4–5, Isaiah 53:11, Isaiah 55:5. Hamlin spent his career in the development of theological education in Southeast and East Asia. He taught the Hebrew Scriptures in China, Thailand, Singapore, and Burma. At the same time, he worked with the leaders of the churches, helping them graft their faith onto their cultural roots.
31. All biblical quotes are from the Revised Standard Version.
32. "Kami ni michibikaruru shogai," *Seisho no kenkyu* 313 (August 1926), p. 354; *Zenshu*, 30:33–34.
33. Yanaga Chitoshi, *Japan Since Perry* (New York: McGraw-Hill, 1949), pp. 442–46. Reprinted 1966 (Hamden: Archon Books).
34. "Sukui no iwa," *Seisho no kenkyu* 292 (November 1924), p. 497, *Zenshu*, 28:394.
35. *Chiri gakko* (On the study of geography), later retitled *Chijinron* (Of Earth and Man) (Tokyo: Keiseisha Shoten, 1894), as included in *Zenshu*, 2:352–480.
36. Diary, 18 April 1919; *Seisho no kenkyu*, 226 (May 1919), p. 235; *Zenshu*, 33:98.

CHAPTER 5

Tamil Hindu Responses to Protestants: Nineteenth-Century Literati in Jaffna and Tinnevelly

D. DENNIS HUDSON

The Tamil-speaking population of southern India and northern Sri Lanka today represents over fifty million people. Their cultural heritage is among the oldest in South Asia. Their poets have created subtle and complex literary works for at least two millennia. Tamils have participated in the major traditions of South Asia—Vedic, Buddhist, Jaina, Muslim—but by 1000 CE their dominant religious culture centered itself in Hindu temples patronized by vigorous and expansive Tamil dynasties.

The many temples built or expanded by these dynasties on both sides of the Palk Strait (situated between Sri Lanka's northern Jaffna peninsula and southeast India) were viewed as palaces of the gods. In return for the blessings of regular rains, personal and communal increase, and victory in war, the gods residing in those palaces received patronage from kings and merchants and controllers of land. Outside of the royal courts, these temples were the primary patrons of the arts and literature, and where they were displayed. They served the larger Hindu culture as multiple centers of a network of regional and caste subcultures and sectarian traditions that remained distinct while related. They were architectural expressions of the Hindu concept of a seamless order fusing cosmos, nature, and society into a multifaceted hierarchy. This seamless order is *Dharma*. Dharma, though not impenetrable, had proven highly resistant to the evangelism that Christian missionaries from Europe had launched among the

Tamils in the sixteenth century.[1] Not surprisingly, under Portuguese influence Christian congregations first emerged among the Tamils in those castes that by virtue of their nature lived on the outer boundaries of Dharma, proximate to the demonic realm of disorder and poverty. These castes were not admitted into the major temples. The earliest Tamil Catholics were fishermen and people who for economic reasons congregated around the newly established centers of Portuguese power. Over time, as French colonies appeared and as Jesuits experimented with modes of evangelism more consonant with Dharma, a small number of Catholics from the castes of high status Brāhmans and Veḷḷālas came into being.

Protestant congregations appeared where the Dutch, Danish, and British East India companies replaced the Portuguese. Only in the early eighteenth century, however, did Protestant missionaries appear, German Pietists sent by the king of Denmark. They created the first Tamil-speaking congregation and German missions developed others throughout the eighteenth century. But it was the British and American missionaries from the early nineteenth century who made a decisive difference in Tamil Protestantism. Their impact will be our concern here.

The fullest documentation of responses made by members of the Tamil Hindu literati to Protestant missionaries comes from their encounters in the nineteenth century with the missions of the Anglicans, the English Methodists, and the American Congregationalists. This study examines two of these responses, one negative and one positive, but both significant. Both responses came from members of the same high-status class of castes and at the same period, but on opposite sides of the Palk Strait. Both responses occurred within the framework of the Tamil language and thought, and produced a large body of Tamil literature. And both responses were creative acts of judgment by individual men about matters they considered sacred.

The Reponse of Nāvalar Āṟumuga Piḷḷai in Jaffna

Our first subject is Āṟumuga Piḷḷai of Jaffna (1822–79), commonly known by his later honorary title *Nāvalar*, The Learned. His activities are a major reason why Protestant conversions among the high castes in Sri Lanka decreased notably in the mid-nineteenth century.[2] In contrast to Sinhala-speaking Buddhist Sri Lanka, the northern peninsular of Jaffna was overwhelmingly Tamil and Hindu, and Āṟumuga Nāvalar's own class, the landed Veḷḷālas, dominated the society. Except for a small number of Brāhman temple priests, they held the highest status in the dharmic hierarchy. They provided the poets and theologians who expounded the devotion and theology of Śaiva Orthodoxy (*Śaiva Siddhān-*

ta), the major Hindu tradition on both sides of the Palk Strait whose cultic heart was the temple town of Chidambaram in Tamilnadu.

Āṟumuga Nāvalar was born to a Veḷḷala family that had been in Jaffna for centuries. One ancestor had fled the "barbaric" Portuguese and became an influential ascetic in Chidambaram. Nāvalar's father was a Śaiva poet and he gave his son a solid foundation in Tamil literature at an early age. Like many Veḷḷāla boys of the second generation to live under British rule, Nāvalar entered a Christian mission school at the age of twelve to learn English.

While Āṟumuga Nāvalar studied at the Wesleyan Mission School in Jaffna Town he gave serious attention to Protestant thought. The preaching of American missionaries, he later reported, persuaded him to read some of their books. Feeling sympathetic to what he read, he turned to reading the Bible regularly. But as he read, apparently on his own and without the interpretive guidance of a Protestant, the Bible posed more questions than it answered.

Āṟumuga Nāvalar did so well as a student at the Wesleyan Mission School that at nineteen he was invited to stay on to teach English and Tamil. At the same time the missionary principal, Peter Percival, hired him to help him write and edit treatises and hymns and, most imporantly, to translate the prayerbook and the Bible. He worked with Percival for eight years (1841–48) until he was twenty-six.

In this Protestant context Āṟumuga Nāvalar learned what it means to be a Śaiva. The nature of devotion to Śiva had been defined a thousand years before out of encounters with Tamil Buddhists and Jainas. The view of Śaiva Orthodoxy that emerged instructs our understanding of Āṟumuga Nāvalar's personal situation as a teacher and scholar in a Protestant context.

The view is that of a *maṇḍala*, a map whose sacred center expands outwards into peripheries bounded by a wilderness.[3] At the center of the maṇḍala stands Śaiva Orthodoxy and around it three circles expand concentrically to form the realm of Dharma. Outside of Dharma is the wilderness of delusion. All traditions that accept the body of scriptures called Veda are within Dharma. Only those that accept in addition the related sectarian body of scriptures called Agama that Śiva revealed are in or near the center. All traditions that reject the Veda are outside Dharma in the realm of darkness. By Āṟumuga Nāvalar's time the realm of darkness included not only the Buddhists and Jainas, but also the Muslims, Catholics, and Protestants.

Now since Āṟumuga Nāvalar was teaching in a school that belonged to this nondharmic domain of darkness, and was translating the liturgy and scripture of a religion in that domain, we can imagine the personal conceptual problem he faced. How was he to sustain personally the Śaivism that told him he stood at the center of the maṇḍala, while he confronted a rich and powerful Christian civilization whose religious spokesmen insisted that *they* stood at the center and that Śaivism stood in the uncivilized darkness?

This dark view of Śaivism was expressed openly and frequently by the Protestants, notably in the *Morning Star*, a Tamil and English journal founded in 1841 by Tamil Christians at the American Mission Seminary in Batticotta. Śaivas, Muslims, and Catholics live in the darkness of this wilderness, they proclaimed, but of the three, Śaivism is the most evil:

> There is nothing in the peculiar doctrines and precepts of the Siva religion that is adapted to improve a man's moral character or fit him to be useful to his fellow men.... If the world were to be converted to the Śiva faith no one would expect any improvement in the morals or the happiness of men. Every one might be as great a liar and cheat—as great an adulterer—as oppressive of the poor—as covetous—as proud, as he was before—without sullying the purity of his faith.[4]

Śaivism, they said, is merely a creation of Brāhmans and contains nothing of value and shares nothing with Christianity.

The *Morning Star* made an impact on the literati in Jaffna. In September of 1842 over two hundred men gathered at a monastery at a Śiva temple to hear five of the most eminent describe plans to counter such attacks and halt the conversions that were beginning to be made among young men of the high castes. Significantly, Āṟumuga Nāvalar served as the recording secretary of this meeting.[5] The speakers asserted that Christianity was merely the creation of the missionaries and that Tamils converted to it only because of their ignorance of Śaivism. Out of pity and compassion for Christian converts they should collect money and start a school for their youth based on the Śaiva scriptures, Veda and Āgama. Moreover, they should purchase a printing press and through small tracts "publish the absurdities of the Christian religion."

The school opened a month later and a former teacher at a Christian school taught grammar and literature, while a man from India qualified to teach Āgama was awaited. The printing press, a much more expensive enterprise, never materialized. The Śaiva school, however, soon dissolved.

Fruitless as the meeting proved to be, it provides our earliest glimpse of Āṟumuga Nāvalar's response to the Protestants. Some of the ideas expressed during the discussion may have been his, particularly the assertion that what the missionaries taught was their own creation. Three of his lifelong projects as a Śaiva activist found expression at this meeting: an aggressive intellectual attack on Protestant missionaries, the establishment of Śaiva schools based on Veda and Āgama, and the founding of a Śaiva printing press. Eventually, given his literary talent and his piety, these projects logically extended into others: the reform of Śaiva temple practices according to the Āgama texts, public lectures on Śaivism in temples, publications for instructing Śaivas in piety, the development of Śaiva prose literature, and the dissemination of printed Tamil classics.

Eleven days after the meeting, Āṟumuga Nāvalar wrote a letter to the *Morning Star*.[6] Signing it anonymously as "The son of a Śaiva and the lover of good doctrine," he made observations and posed questions that had arisen from his own reading of the Bible and that had been expressed at the meeting, perhaps at his own prompting. In the letter he admits that at one time he thought Christianity might be true and did as the Protestants urged and read the Bible. But in his reading the temple in Jerusalem loomed large. Its rites and liturgies looked to him very like those followed in Śiva's temples.

Now by the time Āṟumuga Nāvalar wrote this letter he had been working with Peter Percival for a year and had been reading the Bible in fine detail, translating it word by word. Being a Śaiva, his reading took seriously not only the domain of doctrine, which the Protestants cherished, but also liturgical behavior, which Śaivas cherished and Protestants largely ignored. His reading confirmed to him that a temple-centered cult with similar liturgies stood at the center of both the Bible and the Śaiva scriptures, and it convinced him that the Bible was not an authority Protestants could reasonably appeal to when they spoke of Śaivism as the work of the devil. Yet the missionaries and the editors of the *Morning Star* said that the worship of Śiva in the temple was devilish. The conclusion, he suggested, was that the missionaries had created a religion that their own scriptures did not support. They had done with Protestantism just what they say the Brāhmans had done with Śaivism.

The twenty-year-old Āṟumuga Nāvalar, it seems, had perceived the vulnerability of nineteenth-century evangelical Protestantism when it was viewed within the context of a sophisticated temple-centered religious culture. Protestants staked everything on doctrines they found in a book, a book that itself was centered in a temple cult, but which they had divorced almost completely from that cult. Āṟumuga Nāvalar probably thought that as a Śaiva he had greater feeling for the liturgical context of Jesus's life and worship than the Protestants. Biblical liturgies were so familiar that as he read, he said, he felt like the demon who came up from a well. Being afraid to go to the tiger's village, the demon went to the jackal's only to find that the jackal's village belonged to the tiger too.

Āṟumuga Nāvalar also hints in the letter at a theology of history:

> The eternal, joyful and holy Supreme Being who created, protects and rules all the worlds, is gracious to this land and sends gurus from the distant land of America where a prosperous order and the Christian path prevail, and in order to bring the people of this place to a high and full condition, he chastises them. May the Supreme Being be greatly praised for this boundless compassion.

Christian readers would have interpreted this statement to confirm that God, through the missionaries, was bringing the Tamils to the "high and full condition" of Christianity. Āṟumuga Nāvalar meant it differently. Following the theology of history taught by Śaiva Orthodoxy, he believed Śiva to be the one who was bringing the Christian missionaries to the Tamils. Śiva did this in order to chastise the Tamils and to awaken them to the path he had revealed to them in Veda and Āgama but which they had let fall into disrepair. The missionaries did not realize that they were Śiva's instruments, of course, and acted from their own self-created delusion. But as the simile of the tiger and the jackal suggested, it was Śiva who danced out the rhythms of history. Just as the royal tiger ruled both his own village and that of the wild jackal, so Śiva ruled both the realm of Dharma and the realm of dark demonic wilderness. And even though the poor demon with whom Āṟumuga Nāvalar identified fled to the Christians, he learned that nevertheless he could not escape from Śiva.

While working for Peter Percival, Āṟumuga Nāvalar studied Sanskrit and the scriptures (*Āgama*) that guide the liturgies of Śaiva Orthodoxy. He gained a reputation as a local expert in this field and at the age of twenty-four began to apply his knowledge locally. In 1846 he started free and informal classes in Śaiva literature for his friends, he talked two Veḷḷāla young men out of receiving baptism from Percival, and with a Śaiva school in mind he traveled to Madras to look at schools and to meet scholars.

In the following year he sought to reform Śaiva temple worship according to the scriptures. The Kaṇḍaswāmi Temple in his hometown of Nallūr had been built about a century earlier, but not in accord with the Āgama texts. During its major festival in July–August, Āṟumuga Nāvalar informed its trustees that they violated the scriptures in three ways: by the way the temple was constructed, by using a spear rather than an image as the primary icon of the deity, and by using as priests Brāhmans who had not been initiated into scriptural modes of worship. The trustees found him offensive. He had begun what turned out to be a life-long conflict with various Śaiva authorities.[7] At issue was the status of unwritten and immemorial local custom when it conflicted with the written and universally applicable canons of scripture (*Āgama*).

Revealed scripture (*Veda* and *Āgama*) as the universal authority for cultic practice had always been part of Śaiva Orthodoxy, but the aggressive Bible-centered tradition of the Protestants no doubt sharpened it in Nāvalar's mind. The Tamil and Sanskrit canon of Śaiva Orthodoxy did not sanction popular practices of Śaiva culture, such as animal sacrifices and the worship of malevolent deities and demons, which the missionaries attacked ceaselessly. It provided instead a sophisticated esoteric interpretation of temple worship and of the stories of the gods that placed them in a domain of symbolism beyond the derision of the missionaries. If enforced according to its own scriptures, Nāvalar believed, Śaiva Orthodoxy would purify popular religion, raise the ignorant to a higher level of culture, inspire the literati in their devotion, and defuse the ignorant criticisms of the missionaries. Education in Śaiva Orthodoxy, he concluded, would bring many to salvation from endless birth and death, to Eternal Freedom (*Mukti*), and would halt the spread of Christianity.

On the last day of 1847 Āṟumuga Nāvalar made a dramatic move to spread the "Splendor of Śiva" (*Śivaprakāśa*) and disperse "darkness" in Jaffna. At a time of tension between the Hindus and Christians, he took the methods of the Methodists into the Śaiva temple through weekly scripture-based sermons. Every Friday evening, inside the walls of the Vaidīśvaran Temple in Vaṇṇārpaṇṇai adjacent to Jaffna Town, he read sacred texts and preached from them to crowds of high-caste men and women. He was assisted over the months by a Brāhman friend and by his students. Eventually he launched a circuit of preachers who carried the weekly sermons into the villages of the Jaffna peninsula.

Sermons (*prasaṅga*) were not new to Śaivism, but Āṟumuga Nāvalar's systematic and scripturally based style was, as was his circuit of preachers. His goal was the education and moral reform of his largely Veḷḷāla and Brāhman audience. If they knew the rudiments of scriptural Śaivism and acted on them, he reasoned, they would strengthen Dharma and weaken the Christians. Though he threatened to sue the *Morning Star* if they published any unauthorized report of these meetings, his sermons basically articulated conventional Śaiva piety. Besides attacking the non-Orthodox practices of Śaiva temple priests and attacking the Christians, he preached on ethical, liturgical, and theological matters: the evils of adultery and drunkenness, for example, the value of nonkilling, the proper conduct of women, the worship of Śiva's symbol the *liṅga*, the initiations of Śaivism, the importance of giving alms and protecting cows, and the unity of God.[8]

It was inevitable, of course, that such public work on behalf of Śaivism would antagonize his missionary employers.[9] But that was not the reason Nāvalar left his work with Peter Percival eight months after he began his weekly sermons. Percival, in fact, ignored whatever offense he might have felt from Nāvalar's evangelism and urged him again and again to stay at the Wesleyan Mission School at a higher salary. Percival depended heavily on Nāvalar's exceptional learning as Tamil referee for the Bible translation he had been working on for years. Āṟumuga Nāvalar nevertheless gave up this his sole source of income. He chose instead to devote himself full time to the Śaiva school he had founded the month before.

Looking back on his life at age forty-six, Āṟumuga Nāvalar recalled his motivation at age twenty-six.[10] He had left Percival, he said, in order to satisfy an enormous desire to see Śaivism grow, a desire he had possessed from childhood. He knew he could easily have a career commensurate with his abilities and live prosperously, as had many of his students and friends, and he knew that without such a career he would not be respected. But an ordinary householder's career was not what he wanted. His desire to serve Śiva had become so consuming by this time that, along with gainful employment, he gave up marriage. In Jaffna, he explained, the bride provided the bridegroom with everything—house, lands, garden, jewels—and took in return, presumably, his independence.[11] But to give up career and marriage without having formally renounced both to become an ascetic appeared to others as self-indulgent and irresponsible. The married and prosperous householder was believed to be the social and ritual basis of Dharma.

Consequently, when Nāvalar left Percival's employ to run his school, few supported him. With meager resources he set the school up in a house opposite the Vaidīśvaran Temple where he preached. Six months later he moved it into the temple's monastery. Its teachers were his own students who received no salary except from donations. In addition to the usual curriculum of the Tamil school they taught sectarian Śaiva texts, for Āṟumuga Nāvalar wanted to produce Śaivas able to refute the doctrines of others. He named the fledgling institution The School of Śaiva Splendor (*Śaivaprakāśa Vidyāśāla*).

Āṟumuga Nāvalar's concept of a sectarian Śaiva school was something new, an adaptation of the Protestant schools he knew intimately. Operating within the boundaries of Dharma, the traditional Tamil school was nonsectarian. It served the immediate and practical educational needs of the higher castes of all sects by imparting the values of Dharma they all shared.[12] Writing, reading, arithmetic, literature, and ethics were taught according to a fixed syllabus to a group of boys, perhaps fifteen to twenty-five in number, but taught individually, each pupil moving according to his ability to imitate, memorize, and comprehend. The texts were in poetry accompanied by difficult prose commentaries. And the teacher explained them in vernacular Tamil to each pupil as he progressed at his own rate. Compared to the British and American methods of classroom instruction, where all the students were instructed simultaneously in the same subject and progressed at the same rate, the Tamil system, one British scholar observed, "turns out every pupil a fair scholar, though at a great waste of labour. The class system ensures a much higher average, but permits confirmed dullards."[13]

Once an unusually motivated and talented student completed this education, he might want to pursue higher studies in Śaivism, but it was left to him to find a teacher. The degree of sophistication in Śaiva thought that anyone attained, therefore, depended entirely upon individual talent, motivation, and personal circumstances. Most of the literati absorbed their Śaivism through stories, songs, and temple festivals, or through family instruction or through whatever expositions of the Epics and Purāṇas (ancient lore) they cared to attend in the temples. A few among them received scriptural initiations and instruction in the esoteric meanings of the rites to which they committed themselves. Fewer still systematically studied literature and theology at the monasteries.[14]

From the Śaiva point of view, individuals seek out instruction in Śaiva Orthodoxy according to their own responses to Śiva as he dances out their lives in history. Śiva as teacher is known as Dakṣiṇāmūrti, the village teacher, so to speak, whose classroom is the cosmos and whose pupils are the world's embodied souls. Having all the time in the world he teaches each pupil individually until he or she masters the revealed curriculum, assimilates its transcendent knowledge, and "graduates" into Eternal Freedom (*Mukti*).

Āṟumuga Nāvalar had decided, however, that this system was no longer adequate. Śiva was calling for new developments. As he had indicated already in 1842, Śiva was chastising the Tamils through the missionaries in order to elevate them. Using modern methods to educate Śaivas was Nāvalar's devout response. Śaiva education now had to be efficient and use the classroom and the subject matter of the West, replacing its Christian doctrine with Śaiva doctrine. That meant, of course, a complete change in teaching methods. Instead of relying on palmleaf books that students would copy out by hand and memorize at their own rate, the new system needed printed books that everyone in the same class could read, memorize, and understand simultaneously. Difficult poems and commentaries had to be put into comprehensible prose, but the prose itself had to be sufficiently elegant to convey the contents of the poems and to elevate the thinking of the students.

By founding the School of Śaiva Splendor in 1848, Āṟumuga Nāvalar had taken on three enormous tasks: the construction of a Śaiva curriculum designed for sequential classes, the creation of an appropriate style of Tamil prose in which to write it, and the establishment of a press in Jaffna on which to print it. Those tasks shaped the rest of his career.

Within a year he had gained enough financial backing to purchase a printing press. Leaving the school in charge of its teachers, he and a colleague set out for Madras to buy one. Crossing the Palk Strait, they visited a prestigious monastary whose leaders had heard of Āṟumuga Nāvalar's unusual learning in Śaiva Orthodoxy and his efforts to rejuvenate it. The monks and scholars examined his knowledge, heard him preach, and conferred the coveted title Nāvalar, The Learned. This honorary degree from the scholastic heart of Śaiva Orthodoxy stamped his efforts as authentically Śaiva and based on a sound knowledge of scripture and tradition.

While he waited in Madras for his press, Āṟumuga Nāvalar commenced his career of editing and publishing unusually reliable editions of Tamil texts from various palmleaf copies. To nurture Śaiva education and devotion, he published a Tamil dictionary and a poem to the Goddess.[15] In Jaffna he set up his press in a donated building near the school and hired workmen trained at the

American mission press to run it. He named it The Preservation of Knowledge Press (*Vidyānubālana Yantraśāla*). In order to supervise both it and the school, he slept at the adjacent monastery.

The Preservation of Knowledge Press started publishing early in 1850, producing a list of pamphlets and books that Āṟumuga Nāvalar had been working on for some time. His first two volumes of graded readers, *Lessons for Children*, appeared that year and the next. A third volume of thirty-nine advanced essays appeared in 1860. In clear and dignified prose they discussed subjects such as "God," "The Soul," "The Worship of God," "Crimes Against the Lord," "Grace," "Killing," "Eating Meat," "Drinking Liquor," "Stealing," "Adultery," "Lying," "Envy," "Anger," and "Gambling." Contrary to one missionary's judgment, *Lessons for Children* was not the "blending in conflict and compromise of Hinduism and Christianity,"[16] but was simply the presentation in a modern textbook manner of the values taught in the traditional Tamil school and in the Veḷḷāla culture of Śaiva Orthodoxy. Many of those values happen to be shared by Christians.

Publications from this period reveal how important the practice of piety was to Āṟumuga Nāvalar and how far from satisfactory he found it among Jaffna Śaivas. In one he observes that although many people do not like sins and the negative fruits they produce, they nevertheless do not perform deeds that will generate benefits for their own future well-being:

> Human birth is rare to obtain, even more so birth in this virtuous land of Bhārata [South Asia] where Veda and Āgama, the true books, are esteemed. Birth among those who perform asceticism is even rarer. And most rare of all is birth in a lineage of Śaivas. Nevertheless, many Śaivas do not value these things in the slightest. They have studied and heard about the greatness of Lord Śiva, the treasure of compassion, and about meritorious deeds and sins and their fruits, but they do not comprehend them. They detest sins but they do not perform meritorious deeds. They thus spend their lives in vain, turning themselves into food for burning hell. A few, however, do try to perform a few meritorious deeds one way or another, but they have no idea at all how to perform them correctly...and so they only go on gathering more sins for themselves.[17]

Āṟumuga Nāvalar's first major literary publication appeared in 1852. It was the prose retelling of the twelfth-century hagiography of the Śaiva saints, *Periya Purāṇam*. The models of piety provided by these saints would inspire Śaivas to remove their ignorance, he believed, and this belief fueled the enormous labor required to turn the medieval poetry into two hundred and seventy-two pages of faithful but modern prose.[18] Noteworthy is the fanatical devotion of those whose love for Śiva pushed them beyond the normal order of Dharma.[19] This volume set a new standard for prose in Tamil, a standard that earned Āṟumuga Nāvalar recognition as the "father" of modern Tamil prose.

Nāvalar's attitude toward prose retellings of sacred poetic works revealed his sense that tradition had degenerated. The *Periya Purāṇam* is written in finely wrought poetry, he wrote in his introduction to his prose rendering, but nowadays only scholars who are not sick or confused understood it. In contrast, this prose version was for everyone, for learned scholars, failing scholars, literate laypeople, and the illiterates who listened as it was read aloud. It was a Purāṇa about Śiva and thus even though it was in prose it would confer spiritual benefits on those who read and listened to it in the proper ritual context and with the appropriate attitude.

The ritual qualifications he prescribed for hearing the *Periya Purāṇam*, even in its prose rendering, revealed Nāvalar's firm position within tradition. Readers and listeners, he said, must first have been initiated and must live in purity. This meant they did not eat meat or drink liquor, they applied sacred ash daily to their bodies, they used consecrated *rudrākṣa* beads for reciting the five-syllable mantra, and they worshiped regularly in a temple. The ritual he prescribed for reading the scripture further illustrated his conservatism:

> Those who want to read aloud any books that speak of Lord Śiva's majesty should first purify their bodies and perform the required rites, and then place a throne in a pure place, set the sacred scripture on it, worship both it and the teaching priest [*ācārya*] who will explain it, sit down, and with love that softens and melts the mind begin reading. Anyone who wants to listen while it is being read should listen in the same manner. The Śiva Āgamas and Śiva Purāṇas declare that anyone who does not recite it or listen to it in this manner will not receive the fruits that such acts produce. Since this [prose version of] *Periya Purāṇam* is one of those books, this is the way it should be read and heard too.[20]

His prescription, of course, can also apply to the evangelical Protestant ritual of reading the Word of God to a congregation. In fact his motivation for rendering sacred texts into a modern prose that he had to create and then to print reminds one of Martin Luther. Indeed his work is analogous to the Bible translation he had assisted Peter Percival with for eight years. To his mind prose did not alter the sacred nature of the poetic text but did enhance its ritual use, just as Percival's translation was meant to enhance the reading of the Bible in Tamil Protestant worship. Both efforts sought to generate pious understanding and pious feeling through the communal act of hearing sacred words about God.

Nāvalar's most controversial use of the press was the publication of anti-Christian tracts, adding to the Tamil polemical literature that had begun to circulate early in the century. Three examples will convey the flavor of these polemics. Christians in 1853 had begun to aim their verbal weapons in public at Śiva's son, Murugan. According to popular stories that Śaivas celebrated annually in temple festivals, Murugan married one woman properly and subsequently seduced another into marrying him too.[21] The Protestants said that Murugan was hardly a decent moral example for people to follow. How could he thus be God?

Not willing to abide this sneering slander of the Lord he believed to be Śiva himself, Nāvalar explained in a tract entitled *Radiant Wisdom* that there are different levels of meaning in the Murugan stories.[22] At the same time he compiled examples of indecent language from the Christian scriptures he knew so well and published them as "Disgusting Things in the Bible."[23]

His most effective literary weapon appeared in 1854. It was a seventy-two page training manual addressed to Śaivas for use in disputations with Protestants. Entitled *The Abolition of the Abuse of Śaivism*, the booklet circulated widely among Tamils in Sri Lanka and Madras, was reprinted at least twice in the nineteenth century and eight times by 1956.[24]

The *Abolition of the Abuse of Śaivism* expressed the "evangelical" nature of Ā<u>r</u>umuga Nāvalar's Śaivism. In his introduction he urged his readers to study the booklet for their own salvation. Do not leave off piety for the next birth, he said, for birth as a Śaiva is the boundary of the end of all births. He also urged them to use his analysis of the Bible against Christians whenever they abused Śaivism. The booklet presented his full comparison of the rituals of Śiva's temple with those of the temple in Jerusalem.[25] It also argued against the Protestant belief that the rituals of the "Old Dispensation" no longer serve a valid function in the "New Dispensation."

In his introduction Nāvalar also described a Śaiva "methodism" that had decisive consequences for the interaction of Śaivas and Protestants in the latter half of the nineteenth century. His methods drew upon those of the Wesleyan mission and are another example of his modernization of Śaivism from within. The *Periya Purāṇam*, for example, contains vivid stories portraying the vigorous opposition Śaiva saints are believed to have given to the "abusers" of Śiva a thousand years earlier and he alluded to those stories here.

Nāvalar first described the problem Jaffna Śaivas faced. Missionaries, he said, do not bother to study Śaivism on its own terms but nevertheless describe it and then attack their own false understanding in printed pamphlets which they circulate widely.[26] The Śaiva scriptures tell us that we must oppose this enormous abuse. To avoid opposing it out of fear, or out of friendship, or out of desire for wealth is a great sin. Moreover, the British government will not punish Śaivas if they openly oppose the missionaries, he said reassuringly, for even though the government is Christian, it protects all religions equally. It has even threatened to throw missionaries out of Sri Lanka if they continue to harass Hindu temples.

Nāvalar then provided a theological perspective. Even if Śaivas who aggressively oppose such abuse suffer because of it, it is Śiva's will. Śiva is the one in charge of events, Śiva knows all of our deeds, and Śiva determines what we shall experience at a given time. The purpose of this birth after all, he said, is to serve Śiva and to attain Eternal Freedom (*Mukti*), not to gain the pleasures of the body. And, Nāvalar declared, martyrs for Śiva are guaranteed salvation: "Have not the Śiva scriptures themselves confirmed that those who give up their bodies in order to get rid of such great sins as the abuse of Śiva are certain to attain release?"[27] Fear no one but Śiva, contemplate him alone, rely only on his grace, and oppose the missionaries who abuse him. Refute their "vile" Christian doctrine and work to establish Śaivism, the true religion (*satsamaya*).[28]

Nāvalar then prescribed seven methods for developing individual piety and social action. First, pray every day to Śiva with deep devotion, asking him to remove the obstacles to this meritorious work. Second, give generously for the support of it. Third, use the collected money to purchase books printed by the press and read them carefully, over and over. Fourth, explain these books clearly to others so they will not fall into the "Christian pit." Fifth, whenever missionaries and their catechists abuse Śiva and preach Christian doctrine, "do not at all try to please them, but stand up against them, refute the abuse they heap on Śaivism, oppose their doctrine, and shut their mouths."[29]

Sixth, do not let your children mix with those of other doctrines and at the right age have them initiated and properly instructed in Śaivism. And seventh, appoint men outstanding in their knowledge and devotion to be preachers who will preach each week about Śiva to everyone in the temples, monasteries, and other pure places of the villages. Through these methods, he says, the splendor of Śaivism will spread throughout the Tamil lands and will destroy the darkness of other doctrines and will bring many to Eternal Freedom.

By this time Āṟumuga Nāvalar's fame had spread and marriage offers were pressed upon him. To ward them off once and for all, in 1854 he and a friend underwent the final Śaiva initiation, the *nirvāṇa dīkṣa*. Its daily liturgical requirements prohibited the initiate from generating the pollutions normal to the householder's life. Marriage with its requisite sexuality was now closed to him. At thirty-two, Nāvalar was a recognized celibate, a *naiṣṭika brahmācāri*, free to devote the rest of his life to his work. But unlike a formal renunciant, an ascetic *sādhu*, he was free to move among ordinary people to achieve his ends.

Āṟumuga Nāvalar lived for twenty-five more years, a stalwart, vigorous example of the Śaiva piety he taught, respected as a person by Hindus and Christians alike. These years were his most active and productive, but in them he did not open new fields; rather he tended and harvested the ones already sown, expanding his efforts to both sides of the Palk Strait. To the printing press in Vaṇṇārpaṇṇai he added one in Madras; to the School of Śaiva Splendor in Vaṇṇārpaṇṇai he added one in Chidambaram; to the battles against Brāhmans in Jaffna who infringed the scriptures, he added battles with the Dīkṣitar priests in Chidambaram; to struggles against "false" Śaivism in Jaffna he added struggles against "false" Śaivism in Madras. And everywhere he disputed the claims and refuted the abuses of the Protestants. Wealthy benefactors to whom he frequently made ardent appeals for support came to his aid in both Sri Lanka and India, and in both places he led efforts to restore Śiva's temples that were in decay.

Āṟumuga Nāvalar's literary production was astonishing. Among his approximately ninety-seven Tamil publications, twenty-three are his own creations in a prose largely of his own making, eleven are his commentaries, and forty are his editions of those works of grammar, literature, liturgy, and theology he thought important for nurturing Tamil culture. His own recovery, editing, and publishing of ancient works, in fact, dug the foundations for the renaissance in Tamil literature later in the century.[30]

Nāvalar's School of Śaiva Splendor was the first Hindu school in Sri Lanka to succeed and flourish. The school he established in India, in Chidambaram, survives to this day, but it spawned only two others in nearby towns. In Sri Lanka, however, the School of Śaiva Splendor soon became the center of eleven, all but one in the Jaffna region, and eventually spawned more than one hundred and fifty schools.[31] Graduates from those schools carried Āṟumuga Nāvalar's work into the twentieth century, nurturing and spreading the belief that to be Tamil, and especially to be a high-caste Tamil, means to live in the realm of Dharma at whose center stands the temple of Śiva.[32]

Responses of Krishna Piḷḷai and Muttaiya Piḷḷai in Tinnevelly District

Veḷḷāla Hindus across the Palk Strait in Tinnevelly District shared the same religious culture as the Veḷḷālas in Jaffna. But there were three important differences. The Veḷḷālas in Tinnevelly composed about 20 percent of the population and were numerically inferior to the larger population of lower-status castes. The Veḷḷālas in Tinnevelly, unlike those in Jaffna, were not exclusively Śaivas, for there was a large minority of Śrī Vaiṣṇavas devoted to Viṣṇu. And finally, the District was involved in the social and political dynamics of India rather than of Sri Lanka, even in such distant events far to the north in Delhi as the revolutionary efforts of 1857 to remove British rule.

About a decade after Āṟumuga Nāvalar had launched his "evangelical" Śaivism with its preaching, its school, and its press, a small group of Protestants emerged among the Veḷḷālas of Tinnevelly. They illustrate exactly the kind of response to the Protestants that Nāvalar sought to prevent. Between 1857 and 1860 fourteen men ages sixteen to twenty-nine formally left their Vaiṣṇava and Śaiva traditions in favor of the Protestantism of the Church of England. They formed the nucleus of a Christian "caste" that over the years expressed itself persistently as Protestant, Veḷḷāla, and Tamil.[33]

From the time of their formal conversions, the converts lived in Palamcottah, the mission center of the Church Missionary Society (CMS), and in the neighbouring Veḷḷāla hamlet of Murugankuṟicci. Before converting, most them had been teachers and students in Palamcottah's four CMS educational institutions. In the mid-1860s some of them launched other careers as merchants, doctors, lawyers, government officials, and landowners. Veḷḷāla conversions between 1876 and 1886 further enlarged the community to about two hundred people comprising twenty-seven to thirty households.

The cultic center of this Protestant "caste" was Trinity Church near Murugankuṟicci. Its members worshiped there with Christians of all other castes, having renounced in principle the purity and pollution basis of caste differentiation at baptism. Nevertheless, they consciously sustained their Veḷḷāla identity, a matter of increasing importance to them over the years as the rapidly growing Protestant population in the District drew heavily from the lower castes.

Two brothers belonging to the early nucleus of this Murugankuṟicci community provide insights into these conversions. They were the only two surviving children of a well-educated, pious, and prosperous Śrī Vaiṣṇava couple. The father managed other people's lands and the family lived in various parts of the District, far from schools where the sons could learn English. The father died when his older son, Krishna Piḷḷai (1827-1900), was fifteen and his younger son, Muttaiya Piḷḷai (1835-1895), was eight. ("Piḷḷai" is a Veḷḷala caste title.)

Being seven years apart in age, the brothers grew up in different circumstances. Krishna Piḷḷai was treated by his parents in the traditional manner of the older son. As a child he studied Tamil and, since English was not available, Sanskrit. He was married at the age of thirteen to a girl who was nine. When his father died he assumed his position as the manager of lands, assisted by his mother and two uncles. And he received initiation as a *prapanna* of Viṣṇu.

In the Śrī Vaiṣṇava sect to which Krishna Piḷḷai's family belonged, the prapanna is one who formally relies on Viṣṇu's grace for attaining the goal of Eternal Freedom (*Mukti*). This goal of life and the means to it are the same, namely Viṣṇu. One's own efforts, except for that of taking refuge in Viṣṇu, are inconsequential. Śrī Vaiṣṇavas appeal to many models in Hindu literature and tradition for this doctrine, but the most significant is the life of their their greatest theologian, the teaching priest (*ācārya*), Rāmānuja. The grace that

Viṣṇu bestowed on Rāmānuja when he took refuge is so immense, they believe, that it passes on to all of Rāmānuja's disciples in all generations. Initiation as a prapanna constitutes initiation as Rāmānuja's disciple and qualifies one for the promised grace. By virtue of this initiation, Viṣṇu guarantees the prapanna Eternal Freedom at death. For such a prapanna, there is no rebirth.[34]

This Śrī Vaiṣṇava doctrine, in which God is both the goal of life and the means to it, is shared by Śaivas but formulated differently. Śaivas link ritual action and yogic discipline to divine grace in the attainment of Eternal Freedom. Śrī Vaiṣṇavas stress the predominant role of divine grace in reaching that goal, with little place given either to ritual action or to yoga. The Śrī Vaiṣṇava position closely approximates that of the nineteenth-century evangelical Protestants. The crucial difference between the two beliefs, of course, is that for the Protestant the refugee falls not at the feet of the ācārya Rāmānuja, but at the feet of the crucified Jesus. And the formula for salvation differs. Śrī Vaiṣṇavas use an ingestive metaphor: divine grace absorbs human sin to release the innate purity of the soul. Protestants use a judicial metaphor: the righteousness generated by Jesus' atoning sacrifice clothes the impure soul when it faces absolute justice.[35]

As befits a prapanna, Krishna Piḷḷai learned Śrī Vaiṣṇava doctrine and ritual and, until the crisis of his conversion, took his prapanna status seriously. Muttaiya Piḷḷai, in contrast, was never initiated and did not share the same formal commitment to the tradition. From his eighth year his elder brother was his paternal authority. In his twenties he studied English, but never Sanskrit. He married only at the age of thirty. Less saddled with responsibilities, he was more adventuresome than Krishna Piḷḷai. Not surprisingly it was he who was the first to become a Christian.

The brothers grew up with almost no understanding of Christianity, encountering it only in low-caste field workers their father managed. At the age of ten, however, Krishna Piḷḷai had read a Tamil pamphlet written by Peter Percival, the missionary scholar with whom Āṟumuga Nāvalar would translate the Bible. The pamphlet was *The Avatār of Grace*.[36] Krishna Piḷḷai paid no attention to Percival's long discussion of Jesus, he later recalled, but he did take note of Percival's attack on the supposed immorality of Viṣṇu's ten avatārs.

Due to growing opposition to the spread of Christianity among the lower castes, in 1845 the situation of the brothers radically changed. Krishna Piḷḷai, now eighteen, had participated with his two uncles in Hindu attacks on low-caste Christians during October and November. They had not opposed Christianity, he recalled, but those nominal Christians who had "harassed" non-Christians. The violence provoked government action. Fearing arrest, Krishna Piḷḷai fled secretly to Palamcottah where the family owned a house. His uncles were jailed. His mother, brother, and wife joined him and they resided in Palamcottah permanently, living on family wealth.

Krishna Piḷḷai and Muttaiya Piḷḷai spent the next seven years studying Tamil literature to qualify as Tamil teachers. They made close friends with other Veḷḷāla young men who shared similar aims. The best jobs in the District for these young men turned out to be with Protestant missions. In 1853 Krishna Piḷḷai took a job in a mission school outside of Palamcottah teaching low-caste Christians. Muttaiya Piḷḷai, who started with a missionary elsewhere in the District, landed a position in 1855 at a mission school in Palamcottah.

By 1857 Muttaiya Piḷḷai and Krishna Piḷḷai, each in his own way, had become familiar with Christian doctrine, had been persuaded by it, and after much internal anguish had decided to testify to their faith by public conversion. We can identify five factors in their conversion. First, they discovered that the missionaries to whom they taught Tamil each day exemplified many of their own Hindu ideals of the true devotee. They could not deny their distant admiration for them. Second, they encountered the intellectual, moral, and religious issues posed by these missionaries in their own mother tongue, through Tamil pamphlets and books passed to them by a few Veḷḷāla Christians at the schools and through periodicals like the *Morning Star* published in Jaffna. The same journal that offended Āṟumuga Nāvalar's sensibility as a Hindu nurtured their intellectual inquiry. Third, in this literature, Christian theology was presented as a rational system that harmonized with the history, geography, and science of a five-thousand-year-old world. This knowledge, outdated to us but modern to them, was moreover the knowledge of the class in power, the ruling British elite. Fourth, they discussed these ideas with trusted Hindu friends, a close community of like-minded Veḷḷālas involved in some way with the Palamcottah mission schools.

Now unlike Āṟumuga Nāvalar, who read the Bible alone and no doubt secretly, Krishna Piḷḷai and Muttaiya Piḷḷai had a mutual friend whose interpretation of the Bible they found persuasive. His hermeneutical role may have been decisive. The friend was a young aristocratic Veḷḷāla of Śrī Vaiṣṇava background who, as a student at the Native English School, had become persuaded to the Christian view. He first helped Muttaiya Piḷḷai to understand the Bible in the Protestant fashion. Then, implicitly drawing upon the Śrī Vaiṣṇava theology of the prapanna, he helped Krishna Piḷḷai to understand how the doctrine of Jesus' atoning sacrifice applied to him personally. Krishna Piḷḷai thus came to believe that the crucified Christ was, as he put it, the "manifestation of Dharma" (*Dharmamūrti*).

The belief that Jesus on the cross manifests Dharma introduces the fifth and final factor in the conversions. It was evident to Krishna Piḷḷai and Muttaiya Piḷḷai, and to any other thoughtful person of the time, that Dharma in Tinnevelly of the 1850s was changing. Āṟumuga Nāvalar had already realized it in Jaffna and was responding accordingly. Fifty years of British rule had made an impact. Schools throughout the District now taught the worldview of the British ruling class, while its judiciary enforced notions of justice that flowed from it. Thousands from the Tamil lower castes were converting and asserting new rights. The Christian government had disestablished Hindu temples, and local customs governing agriculture and temple rituals were slowly weakening.

Compared, moreover, to the rational vigor and political power of British institutions, Hindu institutions appeared stagnant. Since their disestablishment, temples were increasingly involved in misappropriation and embezzlement of funds. Except for polemical tracts, Hindu scholars, monks, and priests had little other than the apologia of other eras to use in meeting Christian ideological attacks. No Āṟumuga Nāvalar had emerged in Tinnevelly District. Copies of his booklet of 1854, *The Abolition of the Abuse of Śaivism*, may have been available in the region but there was no circuit of Śaiva preachers to exploit it. The brothers and their friends did turn to Hindu books for guidance, but other than their trusted friends they did not dare turn to Hindu people. The social threat posed to their families by any serious consideration of conversion on their part was so great that they feared the hostile reactions of their own kin.

Hindu opposition to Christian converts in these years was impassioned and frequently violent. When Muttaiya Piḷḷai and his aristocratic friend and another Veḷḷāla went to the missionaries in Palamcottah to seek baptism, the police had to protect the other two from their own families. When Krishna Piḷḷai sought baptism, he made the long trip to Madras to avoid estranging his wife, in vain it turned out. In 1858 high-caste Hindus in Tinnevelly Town led mass protests to the procession of low-caste Christian corpses along public streets running through high-caste areas. In one incident, Indian soldiers were stoned and ten demonstrators were killed and nineteen wounded.

Eventually, as the British asserted their control, Hindu and Christian conflicts subsided. In the early 1860s the converts settled down in Murugankuṟicci, gradually persuaded their wives to join them, and developed their lives as high-status Christians, a witness, the missionaries hoped, to the Veḷḷālas and Brāhmans of Palamcottah and Tinnevelly Town that conversion did not mean loss of identity or culture. Missionary attitudes toward these Veḷḷālas, however, were ambivalent. They would have liked the Christians of all castes, high and low, to create a single Christian "caste" by interdining and intermarrying freely, but they would not. Not just the Veḷḷālas wanted to retain their caste identities.

And few of the Veḷḷāla converts wanted to "Europeanize" their lives. Prior to baptism, for example, Muttaiya Piḷḷai and Krishna Piḷḷai and others had refused to cut off the sign of their "Aryan" status, the long uncut hair known as *kuṭumi* that offended the missionaries. The missionaries reached a compromise with them and rapidly the kutumi became a hairstyle for Tinnevelly

Christian men. Like other Veḷḷālas, Muttaiya Piḷḷai and Krishna Piḷḷai kept vegetarian kitchens and continued those daily ritual and social customs of their Hindu past that they believed did not conflict with their new faith. On these matters they often opposed the missionaries.

Partly to seek freedom from missionary control, in fact, Muttaiya Piḷḷai left his mission employ in 1864 to start an import and retail business with a friend. Two others later did the same. In 1865 Krishna Piḷḷai left Murugankuṟicci to resume the teaching position he had held before his conversion. He remained there a decade before returning to Palamcottah. Unlike his younger brother, Krishna Piḷḷai remained a teacher, scholar, and poet in mission employ most of his adult life.

These Veḷḷāla Protestants nurtured their intellectual life through the Tamil and English literature produced by the various Protestant missions. Their most common reading material was the *Friendly Instructor*, published in Palamcottah from 1848.[37] This Tamil periodical regularly provided them a Protestant framework of thought and information about events in the British Empire in India and elsewhere. It was also a channel for publishing their own thoughts. Tracts and pamphlets circulated widely, providing them a Protestant perspective on the Hindus, Muslims, and Catholics of their environs.

Significantly, to understand the religions of their relatives and neighbors, and of their own past, they turned to European rather than to Indian sources, especially to Robert Bren's *The Test of Religions, or Hinduism and Christianity Contrasted and Examined*. It had been translated into Tamil and published in Jaffna in 1858.[38] Bren's book probably served them less well as a source of genuine understanding of the religions around them—and indeed of their own past—than as a means for sustaining the plausibility of their new ideological stance. As we shall see, toward the end of his life, Krishna Piḷḷai attempted to provide a genuinely Indian alternative.

Muttaiya Piḷḷai and Krishna Piḷḷai wrote a great deal of literature as Christians, all of it in Tamil. Muttaiya Piḷḷai found doctrinal controversy, apologetics, and social issues engaging. In 1863 he wrote a booklet responding to questions about Christianity raised by a follower of Advaita Vedānta in Jaffna, a metaphysics of absolute nondualism in which God as person dissolves finally as illusion. In 1878 he wrote a booklet attacking the Catholic veneration of Mary. In 1887 he wrote a pamphlet responding to another follower of Advaita Vedānta in Madras. And in 1894–95 he published articles in the *Friendly Instructor* to explain the essence of this nondualist metaphysics. He did so, he explained, because many learned Hindus acknowledged its authority and European scholars increasingly found it of interest.

In 1894 Muttaiya Piḷḷai wrote and published *The Manners and Customs of Native Christians, and the Rules and Regulations of the European Missionaries*.

He argued in it against missionary efforts to eradicate caste observances among Tamil Christians.[39] The local context for the pamphlet was caste rivalry within Trinity Church. The Veḷḷālas were a decided minority in the congregation, but he wrote against the missionaries on behalf of all the other castes involved. The pamphlet had a larger context as well. Muttaiya Piḷḷai's thinking reflected a developing non-Brāhman political self-consciousness among Tamils, formulated largely by Veḷḷālas, which contained decidedly anti-Brāhman elements.[40] The non-Brāhman movement, interestingly, had found inspiration in the earlier Śaiva educational efforts of Āṟumuga Nāvalar. And the non-Brāhman movement was, of course, an aspect of nationalism developing throughout India.

In *The Manners and Customs of Native Christians*, Muttaiya Piḷḷai insisted that in "sinless" matters or in those that are not divine commands, missionaries should leave Tamil Christians alone to organize their lives according to indigenous rather than British social categories. Castes were natural groupings of people according to cultures and functions, he asserted, and had not derived from the notion of purity and pollution. Purity and pollution was a Brāhman idea imposed by Brāhmans on indigenous Tamil practice. Christianity in India must be indigenous, he said, and to be indigenous it must follow those local customs that did not conflict with the gospel. Caste observances change in history naturally, he observed. But changes among Tamil Christians must come from the Tamil Christians themselves, according to their own judgment. They must not be imposed by foreign missionaries. Caste hierarchy was acceptable to him rather in the way it was to the Buddhists of Sri Lanka, as an inevitable cultural fact based in the nature of humans but malleable to "natural" processes of social change. It did not, however, reflect the relative purity and pollution of peoples.

Now, while Muttaiya Piḷḷai's creative thinking moved outwards toward society, Krishna Piḷḷai's creativity turned inwards to poetry and theology. Unlike his younger brother, he never addressed his writings to social issues. In the early 1860s, Krishna Piḷḷai composed a work on Tamil grammar to use in his teaching. And he began a compilation of nearly twenty-five hundred stanzas from the best Hindu poets to replace the "immoral" Tamil works prescribed for University of Madras examinations. In 1868 he wrote a long poem for his five-year-old son, and another poem of one hundred verses in which he ruthlessly rejected his own Hindu past. But in the 1870s he wrote a number of devotional poems which he patterned after poems by Hindu saints. These he set to music for Christians to use in their morning and evening worship. He hoped they would cultivate the same devotion as found among Hindus, an intense love for God in which "feeling and thought unite, dissolve and melt, a great sigh arises, tears flow, the tongue stammers, the Spirit's fire kindles in the heart, and the love of the supremely merciful Śrī Christu fills the heart."[41] Such a description of devotional feeling, with suitable modification, might have been written by Āṟumuga Nāvalar.

Krishna Piḷḷai's fame as a Tamil poet, however, derives from his epic retelling of John Bunyan's *Pilgrim's Progess*. He had read Bunyan in translation before his conversion. He had planned to retell the story in one thousand Tamil verses, and in 1878 they began to appear serially in the *Friendly Instructor*. But after a malaria attack in 1879, and in response to the urging of friends, he decided to expand the telling into a courtly epic that followed Tamil literary models, for example the Tamil *Rāmāyaṇa* which he had studied as a Śrī Vaiṣṇava youth. He gave his finished work of three thousand eight hundred verses the title *The Journey of Salvation*, and it appeared in print in 1894.[42] Sixteen years in the making, some judged it the most significant Tamil poetry of the nineteenth century.

Significantly, the mythic structure Krishna Piḷḷai gave to the story followed the map of the maṇḍala we earlier saw was important to Āṟumuga Nāvalar's thought. Following Tamil tradition, he applied this maṇḍala with its center of light and its periphery of darkness to the cosmos.[43] At the center of the cosmos he placed the Kingdom of God and he placed its capital city, Eternal Freedom (*Mukti*), on the three-peaked central mountain of Meru. The Ganges of Life descends from Meru and provides abundance for the king's subjects who are all souls who have attained salvation and now live forever in the kingdom of Eternal Freedom. This divine kingdom is unmanifest. It is made of being, of knowledge, and of bliss, the *sat-cit-ānanda* of the Brahman which Veda says is the essence of all reality.

Outside of the kingdom of Eternal Freedom, on the other side of the River of Death, Krishna Piḷḷai placed the dark wilderness. It is the realm of manifest time and space (*prapañca*). God had originally created this realm through an act of speech. It was to be unmanifest and pure. But the Demon (*Pēy*) entered and instantly it became defiled and manifest. The Demon now rules this degenerate realm from its capital, the City of Delusion (*Māyāpuri*), and he keeps his subjects trapped in the sin and the sorrow of sensual life.

The Kingdom of God and the Kingdom of the Devil are part of one single whole. Like the border on the maṇḍala map that separates the dharmic realm from the wilderness, the walls surrounding the two realms—the unmanifest realm of being, knowledge, and bliss and the manifest and defiled realm of sensual sorrow and death—touch one another. And, like space and time in Hindu thought, the manifest and defiled realm exists as a verbal emanation from the unmanifest and pure realm and depends on it for its continuation. In these and other details, Krishna Piḷḷai echoed a common Hindu cosmography.[44]

For all his adaptation of Hindu myths and symbols, however, Krishna Piḷḷai scathingly identified his own Śrī Vaiṣṇava past with the demonic realm of darkness. The City of Delusion, he said, is Śrī Raṅgam. One of the more ancient Śrī Vaiṣṇava temples, Śrī Raṅgam contains seven encircling walls and serves Śrī Vaiṣṇavas as the cultic heart of the tradition in the way the temple of Śiva at Chidambaram serves Śaivas. Krishna Piḷḷai had made a pilgrimage there with his wife in his early twenties to seek the birth of a child. The Demon who rules the defiled manifest realm of sin and death, thus, is Raṅganātha, the reclining iconic form of Viṣṇu at Śrī Raṅgam. Krishna Piḷḷai had once taken refuge in Raṅganātha as a prapanna. The poet's renunciation of his Śrī Vaiṣṇava past was unambiguous.

Like Bunyan's Vanity Fair, the City of Delusion comprises all the countries of the world, but Krishna Piḷḷai added to them the "false" doctrines and the caste distinctions of India. India, he said, is the oldest area of the world, and is wealthy and lusts for harlots. India is where the Vedas, the Purāṇas, and the Hindu sects entice men. On Judgment Day, he said, atheists, advocates of nondualist Vedānta, those who believe in rebirth, and those who believe there are many paths to Eternal Freedom will not escape the wrath of God. Some of his statements were so harsh, in fact, that editors at the Christian Literature Society in Madras omitted them from later editions of the work.

In Krishna Piḷḷai's version of the maṇḍala, he explicitly placed the Hindu concept of Dharma and certain Hindu sects in the demonic wilderness. And he explicitly placed Christian doctrine in the center. Significantly, though, his wilderness list did not include theistic Hindu theologies like the Śrī Vaiṣṇavism of his own past and the Śaiva Siddhānta of Āṟumuga Nāvalar. They similarly reject nondualistic Vedānta. The question thus arises, insofar as they approximate Christian theism, did Krishna Piḷḷai implicitly view Hindu theistic traditions as standing nearer the center of the maṇḍala than Advaita Vedānta?

There is some evidence that Krishna Piḷḷai did hold that view. As he was preparing *The Journey of Salvation* for publication, he was also writing his only prose work, a more reasoned discussion of comparative religion. It appeared serially in the *Friendly Instructor* between 1894 and 1896 and was published separately in 1898 as *The Determination of the Religion of Salvation*.[45] To improve upon the studies and refutations of Hindu thought used by the missionaries, such as Bren's *The Test of Religions*, he read widely in Hindu treatises and followed traditional Indian methods of disputation. He presented the theological position of each tradition on a given topic in its own terms and then attempted to refute each position logically to prove Christianity superior.

In his summary of the doctrines held in common by all the theistic traditions of the Tamils, Christianity included, Krishna Piḷḷai suggested that in contrast to the nondualist Vedānta in the wilderness, the theistic traditions share some common ground on the maṇḍala map. They all agree, he said, that there is only one God and that he alone is the cause of the world. Possessing faultless qualities, he creates, sustains, and destroys the universe. They all agree that from the very beginning he has revealed himself to mankind through a line of great souls. They all agree that Eternal Freedom and Hell exist and that those who adhere to God's divine commands and prohibitions with purity of mind, body, and speech will attain Eternal Freedom while others will attain Hell. And they all agree that God's punishment of those who commit sins is matched by his friendliness toward those who perform meritorious deeds.

Beyond these doctrinal agreements the traditions diverge widely. Krishna Piḷḷai's task was to show that Protestant doctrine stands at the center, shedding light on them all. Whatever the success of his effort, by following the indigenous maṇḍala mapping, he had in principle moved beyond mere polemic to understanding. His approach provided the possibility that a Christian like him and a Hindu like Āṟumuga Nāvalar might one day find themselves consciously sharing common religious ground.

Krishna Piḷḷai and Muttaiya Piḷḷai never met Nāvalar Āṟumuga Piḷḷai. They did, however, connect with him indirectly. By the time Krishna Piḷḷai had gone to Madras in 1857 for baptism, Peter Percival had moved there from Jaffna and was registrar of the Presidency High School. Krishna Piḷḷai worked for him for about five months. Like Āṟumuga Nāvalar before him, he served as a Tamil teacher in Percival's school and as his private Tamil tutor. Similarly, in the 1860s Muttaiya Piḷḷai served as the Christian Missionary Society's Tamil referee for the Bible translation that Percival and Nāvalar had spent years working on. The British Methodist missionary Peter Percival, it turned out, had been a significant common element in two very different responses to the Protestantism he represented.

Conclusions

The mixture of change and continuity in these differing responses is noteworthy. Āṟumuga Nāvalar changed Śaiva Orthodoxy by creating a new Śaiva school system that fused modern knowledge with sectarian ideas and by revitalizing Śaiva culture through temple reform, preaching, and the printing press. He created an "evangelical" Śaivism by stressing scripture over custom and by seeking an individually motivated spiritual regeneration of culture. Krishna Piḷḷai and Muttaiya Piḷḷai changed their own lives by renouncing their Śrī Vaiṣṇava heritage, by gathering their lives around a new and foreign cultic center, and by working out creatively the intellectual and social implications of their Tamil Christian devotion. In the process they changed Protestantism in

Tinnevelly District, indigenizing it socially, devotionally, literarily, and intellectually. All three opened doors in Tamil culture to a new level of discourse between religions, using inherited models of comparative religion in ways that in the midst of argumentation suggested more genuine critical understanding.

In their changes they shared strong continuities with their past and with the culture around them. They all believed in a "God of history" and agreed that he used the missionaries to elicit responses from the Tamils, but disagreed, of course, over who God is and what he intends those reponses to be. They believed in common that true devotion is expressed individually at times of prayer in the emotional experience of thought and feeling fusing and melting at the feet of God. They all chose to express their own devotion to the Tamil-speaking people around them, using printed forms of their mother tongue rather than the increasingly prestigious and more cosmopolitan English.

All three men accepted the validity of a just order of society, of Dharma, but conceived of it differently. Āṟumuga Nāvalar appealed to Śaiva scripture both to change local custom and to perpetuate the purity and pollution distinctions between castes. Muttaiya Piḷḷai appealed to Christian scripture to eliminate purity and pollution as a basis for social differentiation, invoking instead a secular notion of caste as an indigenous form of social organization expressing the "natural" processes of society. Krishna Piḷḷai, who thought of the crucified Christ as the manifestation of Dharma, regarded caste a sign of the corrupted world of delusion, but he nevertheless respected its social distinctions in his own life. All three men affirmed their heritage as Veḷḷālas; and Āṟumuga Nāvalar and Muttaiya Piḷḷai actively opposed missionary efforts to create "one caste." All three, finally, shared the idea of the maṇḍala with its center of light moving out to the demonic darkness. They disagreed profoundly, of course, about whose splendor stands at the center and who it is that dwells in the dark wilderness outside.

Notes

1. This study derives from research supported by the Fulbright Program in Madras, India, 1968–69 and 1983–84, and by Smith College. For a recent account of Christianity in India, see Stephen Neill, *A History of Christianity in India*, 2 vols. (Cambridge: Cambridge Universtiy Press, 1984, 1985). For a recent analysis of Jaffna culture and the place of Veḷḷālas in it, see Bryan Pfaffenberger, *Caste and Tamil Culture: The Religious Foundations of Sudra Domination in Tamil Sri Lanka* (Syracuse University: Maxwell School of Citizenship and Public Affairs, 1982).

2. For easy recognition I have transliterated Tamil words according to Sanskrit conventions where appropriate. The following biographical information about Āṟumuga Nāvalar comes from "Nāvalar vāḻkkaiyil mukkiya campavaṅkaḷ [Important events in Nāvalar's life]", in *Nāvalar ñuṟṟāṇṭu malar 1979* [Nāvalar Centenary Souvenir 1979]), ed. K. Kailāsapati (Colombo and Kottāvil, 1979), 299-304; and from three biographies: Ve. Kaṉakarattiṉa, *Āṟumukanāvalar carittiram* [The biography of Āṟumuga Nāvalar] (Jaffna, 1882, reprinted 1968); T. Kailāsa Piḷḷai, *Āṟumukanāvalar carittiram* [The biography of Āṟumuga Nāvalar] (Madras, 1918, with an expanded edition in 1955); and V. Muttukumaraswamy, *Sri La Sri Āṟumuga Nāvalar, The Champion Reformer of the Hindus (1822-1879): A Biographical Study*, new rev. ed. (Colombo [?], 1965). For the larger context of Tamil intellectual responses to the West in which Nāvalar played a crucial role, see D. Dennis Hudson, "The Responses of Tamils to Their Study by Westerners 1600-1908," in *As Others See Us: Mutual Perceptions, East and West*, ed. Bernard Lewis, Edmund Leites, and Margaret Case (New York: International Society for the Comparative Study of Civilizations, 1985), 180-200 [*Comparative Civilizations Review* 13 (Fall 1985) and 14 (Spring 1986)]. (But note one correction in the study: S. Radhakrishnan was a Telugu Brahman, not a Tamil.) For a fuller discussion of Nāvalar's early career, see Hudson, "Āṟumuga Nāvalar and Hindu Renaissance among the Tamils," *Religious Controversy in British India: Dialogues in South Asian Languages*, ed. Kenneth W. Jones (Albany, New York: State University of New York Press, 1992), 27-51 and 246-255. For his later career see Hudson, "Winning souls for Śiva: Āṟumuga Nāvalar's Transmission of the Śaiva Religion," in *A Sacred Thread: Transmission of Hindu Traditions in Times of Rapid Change*, eds. Raymond B. Williams and John B. Carman (Chambersburg, Pennsylvania: Anima Press, 1992), 23-51.
3. The map of the maṇḍala as applied to Hindu sects is derived from Sabhāpati Nāvalar, scholar (*vidvān*) of the Tiruvāvaṭuturai Ātīṉam, in "Varālaṟu", *Śivasamavātavuraimaṟuppu* by Śivajñāna Yogi (Cidambaram: Siddhānta Vidyānubalāna Yantraśāla, 1893), 1-6.
4. *Utaya Tārakai—Morning Star* II (1842): 287.
5. The meeting was reported in a letter printed in *Supplement to the Utayatāraki—Morning Star* II, 20 (Thursday, October 20, 1842): 249. The author was Ādinārāyana Cēṭṭiyār Śivapprakāśan, a pseudonym I think of Nāvalar Āṟumuga Piḷḷai. A very different version of the meeting is given by S. Tannayerperagasan (in volume II: 284-287) who tells us that Āṟumuga Piḷḷai was the recording secretary.
6. Published four months later in *Supplement to the Utayatārakai—Morning Star*, III (Thursday, January 26, 1843): 21-23. The editors' lengthy reply is spread over numbers 3-6 of volume III (1843). For a detailed discussion of this letter, see D. Dennis Hudson, "A Śaiva Response to the Protestants: Āṟumuga Nāvalar of Jaffna (1822-1879)," paper prepared for the Annual Meeting of the American Academy of Religion, November 1986.

7. In 1875, for example, Nāvalar published three pamphlets addressed to the officials of the temple, reprinted in *Śrī La Śrī Āṟumukanāvalar Perumāṉiṉ Pirapantattiraṭṭu* [The Collected Essays of the Great and Venerable Āṟumuga Nāvalar], 2 vols, ed. T. Kailāsa Piḷḷai (Madras: Āṟumuka Nāvalar Vidyānubālaṉa Accakam, 1954), II: 1-97.
8. E. J. Robinson lists the topics of twenty-nine sermons given between February 18 and November 17, 1848, in *Hindu Pastors: A Memorial* (London: Wesleyan Conference Office, 1867), 124-25. Kaṉakarattiṉa also gives examples in *Āṟumukanāvalar carittiram*, 20, repeated by Muttukumaraswamy in *Śrī La Śrī*, 20.
9. Sabapathy Kulandran discusses Āṟumuga Nāvalar's work with Percival on the Bible translation in "The Tentative Version of the Bible or 'The Nāvalar Version,'" *Tamil Culture* VII (1958): 229-250, and in *Kiṟistava Tamiḻ Vétākamattiṉ Varalāṟu (A History of the Tamil Bible)* (Bangalore: The Bible Society of India, 1967), 117-49.
10. His statement is reprinted by Kailāsa Piḷḷai, *Āṟumukanāvalar carittiram*, 19-21.
11. This was probably a form of the "shifting matri-uxorilocal pattern" shared by Tamils on the east coast of Sri Lanka. See Dennis B. McGilvray, "Mukkuvar Vannimai: Tamil Caste and Matriclan Ideology in Batticaloa, Sri Lanka," in his *Caste Ideology and Interaction* (Cambridge: Cambridge University Press, 1982), 34-97, esp. 43-46.
12. Charles E. Gover describes this system in "Pyal Schools in Madras," *Indian Antiquary* II (February 1873): 52-56.
13. Gover, "Pyal Schools in Madras," 55.
14. On the monastery or *maṭha* in south India as an educational institution, see S. Gurumurthy, *Education in South India: Ancient and Medieval Periods* (Madras: New Era Publications, 1979), 13-25. Contemporary *maṭhas* are described briefly in "Maths in South India," *Vedanta Kesari* 44.4 (August 1957): 148-81. For an example of a nineteenth-century householder teacher at a *maṭha*, see the English versions of U. V. Swāminātha Aiyar's autobiography, *The Story of My Life by Dr. U.V. Swaminathaiyer* trans. S.K. Guruswamy, ed. A. Rama Iyer (Madras: Mahamahopadhyaya Dr. U.V. Swaminathaiyar Library, 1980); and his biography of his own teacher, *A Poet's Poet: Life of Maha Vidwan Sri Meenakshisundaram Piḷḷai: Based on the Biography in Tamil by Mahamahopadhyaya Dr. U.V. Swaminathaiyer* (Madras: Mahamahopadhyaya Dr. U.V. Swaminatha Iyer Library, 1976).
15. The dictionary was the *Cūṭāmaṇi nikaṇṭu*. The first ten parts contain about eleven thousand words and this is the section Nāvalar appears to have published. It was republished five times before the last two parts were added. See S. Vaiyapuri Piḷḷai, "History of Tamil Lexicography," *Tamil Lexicon* I (Madras: University of Madras, 1982 [1936]), xxv-xliv, esp. xxi-xxviii; and *Cūṭāmaṇi nikaṇṭu: mūlamum uraiyum*, vols. 1-10 ed. by Ārumuka Nāvalar; vols. 11 and 12, ed. Ko. C. Ponnambala Piḷḷai (Madras: Ārumuka Nāvalar Vi. Accakam, 1966). The poem was the Tamil version of the Sanskrit poem, *Saundaryalaharī* by Vīrai Kavirājapaṇḍitar with the explication by Śaiva Ellappa Nāvalar.
16. Robinson, *Hindu Pastors*, 125.

17. Āṟumuga Nāvalar, *Civālayataricaṉaviti* [Śivālaya-darśana-vidhi [The Rule for Worship in a Śiva Temple], 5th ed. (Madras: Vidyānubālaṉa Yantraśāla, 1882), 40.
18. Āṟumuga Nāvalar, *Tiruttontar periyapurāṇam...kattiya rūpamākacceytu* [The Great Purāna of the Holy Saints...Rendered into Prose] (Jaffna, 1852).
19. For a discussion of this, see D. Dennis Hudson, "Violent and Fanatical Devotion among the Nāyaṉars: A Study in the *Periya Purāṇam* of Cēkkilār," *Criminal Gods and Demon Devotees*, ed. Alf Hiltebeitel (Syracuse: State University of New York Press, 1989), 373-404.
20. Āṟumuga Nāvalar, *Tiruttoṇtar Periyapurāṇam...kattiya rūpamākacceytu*, 5.
21. For a sympathetic discussion of the story, see David Dean Shulman, *Tamil Temple Myths: Sacrifice and Divine Marriage in the South Indian Śaiva Tradition* (Princeton: Princeton University Press, 1980), 275-85. For a discussion of the festivals in Sri Lanka that celebrate the story, see Gananath Obeyesekere, *The Cult of the Goddess Pattini* (Chicago and London: University of Chicago Press, 1984), 470-74, and Obeyesekere, *Medusa's Hair: An Essay on Personal Symbols and Religious Experience* (Chicago and London: University of Chicago Press, 1981).
22. *Cuppirapōtam* [Śubhra-bodha], (1853), reprinted in *Āṟumukanāvalar Pirapantat-tiraṭṭu* I, 3rd ed., 3-16.
23. Cited by Kailasa Piḷḷai, *Āṟumukanāvalar carittiram*, 55.
24. Āṟumuga Nāvalar, *Caivatūṣaṇaparikāram* [Śaiva-dūṣaṇa-parihāra] (Madras: Vidyānubālaṉa Accakam, 1956). The India Office Library lists a 1868 edition and the British Library lists a 1890 edition.
25. For a discussion of this aspect of *The Abolition of the Abuse of Śaivism*, see D. Dennis Hudson, "A Hindu Response to Torah," *Between Jerusalem and Benares: Studies in Comparative Jewish and Hindu Religion*, ed. Hananya Goodman (Albany, N.Y.: SUNY Press, forthcoming).
26. He names " Blind Way" (*Kuruṭṭuvaḻi*), "Attributes of the Hindu Triad" (*Mūmūrtti Lakṣaṇam*), and "News of Depravity" (*Tūrācāraviruttāntam*).
27. Nāvalar, *Caivatūṣaṇaparikāram*, 9.
28. Ibid., 10.
29. Ibid., 11.
30. Damōdharam Piḷḷai of Jaffna in particular continued this work, himself once a Christian who became a Śaiva because of Nāvalar. Tiru. Vi. Kalyāṇasundaram used an architectural metaphor to describe Āṟumuga Nāvalar's role: Āṟumuga Nāvalar dug the foundations for the recovery of Tamil classics, Damōdharam Piḷḷai built its walls, and Swāmināṭha Aiyar of Tanjore put on the roof and made it into a temple. The temple was Tamil literature which each man believed housed Śiva. See *Tiru. Vi. Kā. Valkkaik Kurippukkaḷ* [Autobiographical Notes of Tiru. Vi. Ka.] (Madras: South Indian Śaiva Siddhanta Works Publishing Society, 1969 [reprint of 1944]), I, 160. For a description of the way Swāmināṭha Aiyar became involved in this Tamil literary renaissance, see D. Dennis Hudson, "Renaissance in the Life of Sāmināta Aiyar, a Tamil Scholar," *Comparative Civilizations Review* 7 (Fall 1981): 54-71.
31. *Sri Lanka: A Survey*, ed. K. M. De Silva (Honolulu: The University Press of Hawaii, 1977), 389.

32. Nāvalar's student's student, N. Katirvēl Piḷḷai of Jaffna (d. 1907), was influential on Tiru. Vi. Kā. in Madras. In his youth, Maṟaimāl Aḍigaḷ (formerly Swāmi Vedāchalam) participated in the Śaiva Siddhānta Sabhā in Nāgapaṭṭiṇam led by a friend of Nāvalar. See Tiru Pulavar Aracu, *Tiru. Vi. Kaliyāṇacuntaraṇār* (Madras, 1982), 21-22; and Tavattiru Āḻakaraṭikaḷ, *Maṟaimalaiyaṭikaḷar varalāṟṟu māṭci* (Madras, 1977), 185-91.
33. The following discussion is based on my unpublished Ph.D. thesis, *The Life and Times of H. A. Krishna Piḷḷai (1827-1900): A Study in the Encounter of Tamil Sri Vaishnava Hinduism and Evangelical Protestant Christianity in Nineteenth Century Tirunelveli District* (Claremont Graduate School, Claremont, California, 1970).
34. Patricia Y. Mumme explained this theology in "From Mediator to Savior—The Development of the *Ācārya* Figure in Tenkalai Śrīvaiṣṇavism," a paper prepared for the Association of Asian Studies Annual Meeting, 1985. H. Daniel Smith explored the topic earlier in "Prapatti—The Sacrament of Surrender—Its Liturgical Dimensions," a paper prepared for the American Academy of Religion Annual Meeting, 1969. He also produced an eight-minute film on the topic, "The Hindu Sacrament of Surrender (*prapatti*)," distributed by the Syracuse University Film Rental Library, Syracuse, New York.
35. For further discussion, see D. Dennis Hudson, "Hindu and Christian Theological Parallels in the Conversion of H. A. Kṛṣṇa Piḷḷai, 1857-1859," *Journal of the American Academy of Religion* 11, no. 2 (June 1972):191-206.
36. *Āruḷavatāram* [Incarnate Grace], 4th ed. (Jaffna: American Mission Press, 1849).
37. *Naṟpōtakam* [Friendly Instructor] (Palamcottah: C.M.S. Press, 1848—[monthly]).
38. Robert Bren, *Samayapar̄ṭcai: The Test of Religions or Hinduism and Christianity Contrasted and Examined. The Former, on its own Evidence, Proved to be Erroneous, and the Latter, by Many External and Internal Proofs, Shown to be from God*, 2nd ed. (Palamcottah: C.M.S. Press, 1867).
39. For a further discussion of this pamphlet and the events that led up to it, see D. Dennis Hudson, "Christians and the Question of Caste: The Veḷḷāla Protestants of Paḷaiyankōṭṭai," *Images of Man: Religion and Historical Process in South Asia*, ed. by Fred W. Clothey (Madras: New Era Publications, 1982), 244-58.
40. See Eugene F. Irschick, "The Intellectual Background of Tamil Separatism," in his *Politics and Social Conflict in South India: The Non-Brahman Movement and Tamil Separatism, 1916-1919* (Berkeley and Los Angeles: University of California Press, 1969); 275-310.
41. H. A. Krishna Piḷḷai, *Irakṣaṇiya maṉōkaram* (Rakshanya Manoharam: The Joy of Salvation, Prayer and Praise in Verse), 3rd ed.(Madras: Sir David Devadoss, 1951), 14.
42. H. A. Krishna Piḷḷai, *Irakṣaṇiya yāttirikam [The Rakshanya Yathrikum]: A Tamil Poetical Work Based on the Story of the Pilgrim's Progress of John Bunyan* (Madras: The Christian Literature Society, 1894).
43. Krishna Piḷḷai's use of the maṇḍala is revealed by analyzing his mythic structure as described in part three and elsewhere in *Irakṣaṇiya yāttirikam*. For a general discussion, see Hudson, *The Life and Times of H. A. Krishna Piḷḷai*, 485-89.

44. See for example, *Kauṣītakī Upaniṣad* 1.
45. H. A. Krishna Piḷḷai, *Irakṣaṇiya samaya nirṇayam* [The Determination of the Religion of Salvation], 2nd ed. (Tuticorin: K. Ci. A. Vētarattiṉam, 1956).

CHAPTER 6

Indigenous Protestant Churches in China, 1900–1937: A Pentecostal Case Study

DANIEL H. BAYS

Introduction

Between 1900 and 1937, Protestant Christianity in China became much more diverse than it had been before 1900. In the mission sector, a great variety of new Christian mission groups established themselves, some of them rather sectarian in theology or practice, such as Pentecostals or Adventists. Many more independent or "faith" missionaries came to China, not tied in with the traditional mission societies. Meanwhile those established mission societies, with not only churches but a plethora of institutions such as schools and hospitals, also grew substantially, especially between 1900 and the mid-1920s.

Yet the really important phenomenon during this period was the growth of independent or indigenous churches. These were of two categories:

Within Mission Churches

One category of independence was that pursued within the general structure of the foreign mission churches in China. This had a slogan: the "three-self" aim of Chinese Christians being responsible for "self-management, self-support and self-propagation" in the churches. Many foreign missionaries, and Chinese Christian leaders working within the mission-related structures of the day, promoted this goal. From the early 1910s and the formation of the China Continuation Committee, this goal was pursued gradually, reaching a watershed in the National Christian Conference (NCC) of 1922, out of which came the ecumenical Church of Christ in China, a Sino-foreign body with a significant degree of Chinese leadership and responsibility. The National Christian Council, a national Protestant coordinating and liaison body, was also a product of this period.

Not all denominations or mission groups joined the Church of Christ in China and/or the NCC. Some of them, like the Anglicans and Lutherans, pursued their own forms of Sino-foreign unity and nurturing of Chinese leadership. Others, like the China Inland Mission (CIM), continued basically a foreign-dominated operation at the top but tried to promote sensitivity to and encouragement of Chinese Christians' aspirations to responsibility and autonomy at the local level.

These phenomena were all important ones, and deserve more detailed and understanding treatment than they have so far received at the hands of scholars.[1] However, a broad judgment on these events and trends is that within the mission-related structures there was not a great deal of movement toward an authentically autonomous or indigenous Chinese church before 1937—or before 1949 for that matter. Attitudes of paternalism remained frequent among foreign missionaries, and the power of foreign financial subsidy remained a potent, if usually an implicit, factor in most Christian organizations. Even capable Chinese Christian leaders within these structures sometimes did not seem to push as hard as they might have for full independence and authority. I will say no more about this whole topic, important though it is.

The Extra-Mission Indigenous Sector

There was, however, an altogether different sector of Chinese Christianity which came into being in the 1900–1937 period, one which was to a high degree independent of foreign missions, autonomous in operations, and truly indigenous in ideas and leadership. This sector of Chinese Christianity has been sorely neglected by scholars of Chinese history and of the history of Christianity as well. It is a diverse sector, made up of a combination of organized church groups (some nationwide with hundreds of congregations) and of individual congregations or even individual Christian workers who made their mark in a more local setting. Some of these coexisted with and interacted with the mission churches; others were quite separatist and had almost no contacts with other Christians, Chinese or foreign.

Having worked on the subject of twentieth-century Chinese Christianity for several years now, collecting considerable amounts of scattered data, I believe that this sector was far more interesting and significant than might previously have been thought. An example of completely overlooking most of this sector is a 1936 publication on Chinese Protestant Christianity put out by the National Christian Council, which theoretically was designed to serve the whole Chinese church (*1936 Handbook*). This volume includes vast statistics on each of the mission societies and related Chinese church bodies, but does not even mention the names of the True Jesus Church, the Assembly Hall, the Jesus Family, or the China Christian Independent Church federation, all of which were well established by that time and had at least several tens of thousands of adherents between them. In the preface of this handbook an estimate of five thousand is made for communicants in the generic category of "independent churches" (*1936 Handbook*, xi).

I also believe that this sector was much larger than most have surmised. In the 1940s, the various independent Chinese Protestants may have accounted for 20–25 percent of all Protestants, or as many as 200,000 persons. Moreover, judging from what we know of the churches in China today, it seems that a great many of the older Christians whose experience dates to before Liberation (1949) came out of these indigenous churches (they do not for the most part openly retain those identifications today, but some still do).[2]

A comprehensive survey of this subject would properly include the following:

1. Church federations made up of independent congregations most of which had previously been mission churches but had become self-supporting and self-governing. There were at least two of these federations, one in North China centered in Shandong and organized as early as 1912, called the China Christian Church (Zhonghua Jidu jiaohui), the other begun before 1910 with headquarters in Shanghai, called the China Christian Independent Church (Zhongguo Yesujiao zilihui). The latter at one point in the 1920s had well over one hundred congregations affiliated with it. These churches usually remained on fairly good terms with mission groups, participated in some ecumenical activities, and retained their original denominational creeds and practices, often a variety of Presbyterianism.
2. The True Jesus Church (Zhen Yesu Jiaohui), a Pentecostal church established before 1920, to be treated in some detail below.
3. The Assembly Hall (Juhuichu or Juhuisuo) or "Little Flock" (Xiaoqun), organized in the mid-1920s and led before 1937 by Ni Duosheng ("Watchman Nee"). This was a strongly proselytizing church influenced by Brethren ideas of church polity, rather exclusivist and often in conflict with denominational and mission churches.

4. The Jesus Family (Yesu Jiating), a unique Pentecostal communitarian church first established in rural Shandong province in the late 1920s.
5. The Spiritual Gifts Church (Lingenhui), the least organized of those mentioned thus far. This was centered in Shandong province in the late 1920s and 1930s, and is perhaps best seen as a Pentecostal movement, not an ecclesiastically organized body. The movement encompassed Chinese churches and pastors who broke away from denominations which refused to accept their Pentecostal doctrines and practices, and also touched foreign mission communities as well, making the famous Shandong Revival of the early 1930s a joint Sino-foreign experience.
6. A host of individual Chinese Christian pastors, traveling evangelists, writers, and teachers. Some of the best known were Wang Mingdao, Song Shangjie ("John Sung"), Wang Zai ("Leland Wang"), Jia Yuming, Ji Zhiwen ("Andrew Gih"), and Chen Chonggui ("Marcus Cheng"). Many of these worked with conservative evangelical mission churches or groups in revivals, seminary teaching, publications, and so forth, but all had essentially autonomous status, and most were careful to retain their independence from foreign control or subsidy.

The great majority of individuals and groups in the above list of six categories were quite conservative, even fundamentalist, in theology or doctrines.[3] A partial exception was some of the churches in the federations of category one, which were more liberal or moderate Presbyterian in belief (though a "liberal Presbyterian" would still be considered "conservative" by some).

A Case Study: The True Jesus Church

The remainder of this chapter will be devoted to drawing a profile of one of the most interesting of the examples of indigenous Chinese Christianity, the True Jesus Church, before 1937. The True Jesus Church was the first Chinese Christian group since the mid-nineteenth-century Taipings to generate a creative and self-defined set of doctrines, and it was also the largest of the indigenous churches by the 1930s, spread over several provinces. Another comparable group was the Jesus Family, a local rural communal Christian church, even more doctrinally creative, which spread but remained confined to North China, especially Shandong, before 1937. Both were distinctly Pentecostal in belief and practice, and both were influenced by foreign Pentecostal missionaries or their literature at key stages of development. As will become apparent, I believe that Christian Pentecostalism, new to the Chinese scene after 1900, provided a particularly effective bridge between some essentials of Christianity and those of traditional Chinese popular sectarian "heterodox" religion. This correspondence centers on millenarianism, self-interpreting direct divine revelation, and healing.

Before proceeding to a detailed description of the True Jesus Church, I will establish a baseline for analysis by introducing and describing the essential features of some of the "new" Christian doctrines in the form of Pentecostalism which entered China after 1900. It is important to stress that these doctrines were not very visible in nineteenth-century missionary Christianity in China.

Pentecostalism Comes to China: Missionary Progenitors

Pentecostalism, and the missionaries who were an integral part of it, were products of the convergence of several forces in Christianity at the turn of the century (Anderson 1979; Synan 1971; Wacker 1984) Some of these forces were a reaction against the advancing secularization and institutionalization of largely middle-class Protestant denominational churches. Not all of these forces or elements were unique to the United States, but they came together there in a dramatic way, so that early Pentecostalism can be seen as a product of U.S. society.

These forces included: (1) The energies of the post–Civil War Holiness movement, which by the 1890s had split into many groups, all looking for the power to achieve personal holiness; some had begun fixing on the idea of the baptism of the Holy Spirit as the secret. (2) An ardent and expectant millenarianism, based theologically on a position of premillennialism. (3) An urge for pristinization. This was manifested in a belief that in the present, which was a special new age leading up to the second coming of Christ, it was necessary to replicate the Apostolic age of the early Church.[4] (4) A search for a *sign* to signify one's appropriation of the power of holiness, received through the baptism of the Spirit; eventually this sign came to be considered speaking in tongues.

All these elements coalesced in the particular conditions of the United States. Soon after 1900, the Apostolic Faith movement emerged, and then came the great watershed of the formation of the modern Pentecostal movement, the Azusa Street revival in Los Angeles, 1906–8.[5] From Azusa Street came the people and forces to form the U.S. Assemblies of God in 1914, and smaller American Pentecostal groups. But right from the beginning in 1906, there was a remarkable missionary thrust coming out from the Azusa Street phenomenon. Within weeks, Christians transformed by the power of the Holy Spirit were heading off to foreign lands, not a part of any mission society, but as "faith missionaries," certain that God would meet their needs.[6] The destination of many of them was Asia.

What were the characteristics of these early Pentecostal missionaries and the message they brought? One was millenarianism, bringing the excitement of the conviction that one was living in the last stage of history, where Christ could return literally at any moment. A second theme was the tremendous power of the Holy Spirit, gained through the baptism of the Holy Spirit, manifested in healings and miracles of all kinds, some quite spectacular. Another characteristic was going through ecstatic personal experiences such as prophecy, possession of one's faculties, or being transported to another realm or dimension. The final theme was speaking in tongues as a sign of confirmation for the individual that he or she had received Holy Spirit baptism.[7]

As far as I can tell, the first avowedly Pentecostal missionaries arrived in China in 1907.[8] Almost immediately they put down roots in at least three places which later strongly influenced the development of Chinese Pentecostalism. These were Hong Kong, Hebei province, and Shanghai.

Alfred G. Garr, who was pastoring a Los Angeles church when the Azusa Street revival began in 1906, was one of the first pastors to receive the baptism of the Spirit and the gift of tongues. Within days he felt a call to go as a missionary to India and points East, and almost immediately set off. He spent some time in India in 1907, then arrived with his wife in Hong Kong in October 1907, where he joined a handful of Pentecostal single women who had come to Hong Kong from Seattle in the late summer or early fall of 1907 (Ward n.d.; Downey 1984). Garr had considerable impact in Hong Kong. A Congregational church of the American Board of Commissioners for Foreign Missions (ABCFM) permitted him to hold meetings there, where he began to present Pentecostal doctrines. One Mok Lai Chi (Mo Lizhi), a forty-year-old school proprietor who was the Sunday School superintendent and a deacon in that ABCFM church, was Garr's interpreter. Soon Mok received the baptism and the gift of tongues. Within two months the ABCFM church committee banned the Pentecostals from the premises, and they had to move elsewhere. But Mok let them use his school, and in January 1908, Mok as editor put out the first issue of a Chinese monthly paper, *Pentecostal Truths* (*Wuxunjie zhenlibao*); Mok remained editor for many years. By 1909 six thousand copies were being printed and mailed nationwide.[9] This group and newspaper are important because the paper directly influenced the North China founders of the first major Chinese Pentecostal church, the True Jesus Church. The extant issues of the paper which I have seen, beginning with 1909, are in the headquarters of the True Jesus Church in Taichung, Taiwan. Moreover, a brief history put out by the True Jesus Church mentions Mok and this paper as an early forerunner.[10]

There was also a very early Pentecostal base in North China, in Zhengding xian, near Shijiazhuang, Hebei province (called Chihli province before 1912). Like the Hong Kong base, it was a direct product of Azusa Street in Los Angeles. In about 1904, a certain Mr. Berntsen went to a south Hebei mission, probably a station of the South Chihli Mission.[11] Late in 1906 he got his hands on one of the first issues of the "official" Azusa Street publication, the *Apostolic Faith*, and was so excited by its description of events there that he immediately left China and sailed back to the United States, headed for Los Angeles. The rapid transmission of this early sectarian publication all the way from Southern California to the hinterland of Hebei is itself remarkable. At any rate, in the words of a 1907 issue of the *Apostolic Faith*, "Berntsen went to the altar at Azusa Mission, and soon fell under the power, and arose drunk on the new wine of the kingdom, magnifying God in a new tongue. As soon as he could speak English, he said, 'This means much for China.'"[12]

Berntsen stayed around Los Angeles for a time, then helped form a group of about twelve Pentecostal missionaries who headed for China. They decided to open a new independent mission station in an area where famine had been raging, and chose Zhengding, on the rail line just north of Shijiazhuang, Hebei, not far from Berntsen's earlier station. Berntsen kept in touch with the Azusa Street people, and letters from him are included in issues of the *Apostolic Faith* until the last issue in May 1908. The Zhengding mission had some permanence. Berntsen and his wife were still listed as being there, along with a few others, in 1915.[13]

The group at Zhengding began to put out a newspaper in 1912. This was called the *Tongchuan fuyin zhenlibao* (*Popular Gospel Truth*), and gives us some important information. First, it identifies the church name under which this Pentecostal group operated, the Xinxinhui (Faith Union). This name appears in none of the mission directories or other sources of the time.[14] It is important to know because later, both of the two major Chinese founders of the True Jesus Church were profoundly influenced in Beijing by members of the Xinxinhui. Like the early Hong Kong Pentecostal paper, the two 1912 issues of this paper which I have seen are in the Taichung, Taiwan True Jesus headquarters, and the church's own history identifies the Zhengding paper as a forerunner.[15] The Zhengding paper is also interesting because it highlights so plainly, among other themes, the millenarianism that drove Pentecostal beliefs. On the paper's masthead, above the title, is the phrase *Yesu jisu huilai* (Jesus will return soon).

Besides Hong Kong and Hebei, a third early Pentecostal group settled in at Shanghai. This group also was a product of the Azusa Street revival, although a slightly indirect one. As early as in the summer of 1906, Pastor M. L. Ryan of Salem, Oregon, heard in detail of the inspiring events in Los Angeles, and was profoundly affected.[16] Soon he moved to Spokane, where he gathered a Pentecostal congregation which in the summer of 1907 sent a whole band of missionaries to Asia, led by Ryan himself.[17] Interestingly, as they were leaving Seattle in late summer 1907, they met and overlapped a few days with Brother Berntsen from Hebei, who was landing there on his way to Los Angeles (Berntsen in *Apostolic Faith*, Jan. 1908, 2). The Ryan group encountered some confusion and scattering in East Asia, but by the fall of 1907 at least two of its single women members had gone on to Hong Kong, where they soon joined up with A. G. Garr arriving from India, and were in on the founding of the Pentecostal movement there which I have already described. Others of Ryan's group went on to Shanghai, where they were settled and operating before 1910, along with some other missionaries in the Shanghai area who had abandoned their denominations and come over to join one or another Pentecostal band, or just operated independently.

I have taken some pains to pinpoint the above three places—Hong Kong, Zhengding in Hebei, and Shanghai—as sites of very early Pentecostal activities in China, because of the linkage of all three to the formative stages of the True Jesus Church. But after 1910, there was a rapid growth of Pentecostal missions all across China. These missionaries were not very visible among the general run of foreign missionaries.[18] They preached where they could, held healing services, and expected miracles. Many if not most had no regular financial support, and they seem to have been more peripatetic than most missionaries, perhaps because they generally did not build institutions like clinics and schools (although some did have orphanages).

The Pentecostals were not accorded much respect by the "missionary establishment." One British Baptist source referred disparagingly to "certain sects from America" which entered Shandong after 1912 (Williamson 1957, 344). The China Inland Mission, by now the largest Protestant mission body in China with over one thousand members, found increasing tension within its ranks on the issue of Pentecostalism or the "tongues movement" after 1910. Some of its missionaries were attracted to the phenomenon, a number were repelled by it, and the all-powerful CIM China Council at Shanghai spent much time debating the proper relationship with the movement during 1914–15. The more they saw, the less they liked it. After consultation with the home councils in Britain and North America, in April 1915 the China Council adopted a long statement condemning the Pentecostal movement, whose meetings were allegedly "characterized by disorder and by manifestations which in some cases have led to mental derangement and maniacal ravings" (China Inland Mission 1915). And a Chinese-language church newspaper published by the American Presbyterians in Shanghai specifically warned in 1915 that in quest of the "gift" of speaking in tongues, people had been known to go insane and kill themselves

(*Tongwenbao* 1915, 2). The Pentecostals obviously had an uphill task in public relations, at least in the missionary community.

Despite their pariah status among fellow missionaries, these Pentecostal pioneers persevered. Buoyed by the immediacy of their spiritual experiences and by millenarian expectations, they lived on the precipice of history, having direct communication with Jesus and being filled with the awesome power of the Holy Spirit, all this confirmed for them by the tongues phenomenon. Their message, quixotic or heretical as it seemed to many other missionaries, did in fact find a Chinese audience.

One feature of the earliest Chinese participants in the Pentecostal movement was that they were nearly all already Christians, but searching for a deeper and more immediate religious experience that they did not find in their particular denominations. Early adherents came variously from Methodist, Presbyterian, China Inland Mission, Congregational, Seventh Day Adventist, and other backgrounds. In Hong Kong the second, third, and fourth Pentecostal converts were all members of the ABCFM church where A. G. Garr first preached.[19] Later, the two most important founders of the True Jesus Church came from Presbyterian and London Mission Society churches, respectively, and the founder of the Jesus Family had a Methodist background.

Early Chinese Pentecostals: A Profile of the True Jesus Church

The True Jesus Church in effect had two co-founders. One was Mr. Zhang Bin of Weixian district in northeast Shandong province (Zhen Yesu jiaohui 1979). Zhang, who had been an elder in the Weixian Presbyterian church for several years, in 1909 was told by his son about an Apostolic Faith Mission (Shitu xinxinhui) in Shanghai where one could "receive the Holy Spirit." The elder Zhang set off on a quest that would take him far and wide. He went to Shanghai, where the Pentecostal missionaries (very likely Mr. and Mrs. Lawler, Azusa Street products) laid hands on him, but he did not receive his Spirit baptism. He continued earnestly to seek it at home, and finally in December 1909 he received the Holy Spirit and the sign of tongues. In 1910 he went to Suzhou and was rebaptized (by immersion in water, apparently), and sometime after that he went to the north, including Beijing, where he received instruction from two members of the Xinxinhui or Faith Union, one of them probably Brother Berntsen from Zhengding (who may have been visiting in Beijing or perhaps came there regularly to tend to Faith Union activities; the two Faith Union members were surnamed Pen and Kui, and Berntsen's Chinese surname was Pen).[20] Sometime before 1916 Zhang, who by now had renamed himself Zhang Lingsheng ("spiritual life"; later he would add Bide, "Peter"), received a "revelation" (*qishi*) from God that only Sabbath day worship was acceptable. Zhang then formed a church or group based on this Seventh-Day Pentecostalism which had the name Jesus's True Church (Yesu zhen jiaohui). The missionary Pen Dexin (Berntsen?) agreed to the seventh-day worship in 1916, according to True Jesus sources. Zhang spent at least some of his time between about 1912 and 1918, perhaps most of it, back home in Shandong. His relationship with his old Presbyterian church during these years is unknown to me.

Many aspects of Zhang Lingsheng's story, which comes entirely from True Jesus Church sources, cry out for elaboration or clarification. Where did his Sabbatarian beliefs come from? From U.S. Seventh Day Adventists? Was the group he formed (Jesus's True Church) a congregation, or more like a study group of believers within other churches? The sources indicating this very early activity of Zhang Lingsheng may have the ultimate purpose of showing that a later rival of the church leadership and excommunicant, Barnabas Zhang, was *not* a founder of the church (Zhen Yesu jiaohui 1947); does this make the alleged early activities of Zhang Lingsheng too suspect? What contacts did Zhang retain, if any, with his original Presbyterian church in Weixian, where he had been an elder? Nevertheless, despite these questions we seem to have here in Zhang an eclectic and peripatetic Christian seeker, constituting one of the two strands eventually forming the True Jesus Church.

The other strand was provided by Mr. Wei Enbo, a native of Hebei province who was from a poor family background and had very little education. Sometime after 1912 Wei, a Beijing silk dealer and a member of a London Missionary Society congregation, was plagued with a lingering illness. Wei encountered an elder of the same Faith Union with which Zhang Lingsheng had interacted, Xin Shengmin (I am uncertain whether Chinese or foreign, but Xin is an unlikely true surname), who laid hands on him. Wei was miraculously healed, and joined the Faith Union. Later, at a meeting he received the Holy Spirit and tongues. All this must have taken place between about 1912 and 1916. A good guess is the fall of 1916 (Zhen Yesu jiaohui 1947, M6).

Wei Enbo then had the key experience which launched his career as prophet and church founder. By his own detailed account, in March 1917 he heard the voice of God speaking clearly to him, directing him to receive the same kind of baptism Jesus had received, which was a "face-down" baptism by immersion (Zhen Yesu jiaohui 1947, M4). Then he received further direct revelations, along with direct visual sightings of Moses, Elijah, and others, calling him to be a warrior for the True God, to defeat Satan and his forces, and to "correct" (*geng-zheng*) the mistaken path of all the world's churches. Militant terms of warfare run through Wei's description of his commission. He received the power to undertake these tasks after a thirty-nine-day fast, which he was also told to carry out. He took the name Paul (Baoluo), as well. There is no claim in his own later account, written in early 1919, of his receiving at this point (1917) a revelation on Sabbath worship.[21]

By May 1917 Paul Wei was preaching his new doctrines in and around Beijing, with stress on the power of the Holy Spirit, miracles, the imminent return of Christ, and the need for the correct (i.e., face-down) water baptism. His target was the Christian churches. He went directly to the churches at worship times, challenged the pastors by calling them false teachers of false churches, and called on the parishioners to join him. Some did, but at the same time Wei was variously vilified, chased away, beaten, cursed, and twice even jailed. When undergoing abuse, he would publicly pray for his critics—although when in jail he had the wits to claim his rights under the freedom of worship clause of the new constitution. He did not yet use the name True Jesus Church, but the Universal Correction Church (Wanguo gengzheng jiao). Thus we see here a dramatic call by a prophet-like Wei, himself directly commissioned by God, to purify and restore to pristine truth all of China's Christian churches. My rough estimate of the number of Paul Wei's followers before 1918 is fewer than two hundred.

During 1918 the movement took more precise doctrinal shape. The key place was Tianjin, where Paul Wei first met Zhang Lingsheng of Weixian, Shandong, who as we have seen was already a Pentecostal of many years' standing. They seem to have hit it off well together. Wei laid hands on Zhang in an act of ordination or legitimation, and the two of them (though other names also appear by now in the accounts) apparently put together the doctrinal foundations of a new church. The name of the church became the two former church names combined, the Wanguo gengzheng jiao zhen Yesu jiaohui (Universal Correction True Jesus Church), soon shortened to the latter, or True Jesus Church (Zhen Yesu jiaohui 1947). They had agreed on a long set of doctrines and practices by the time they put out their first newspaper in February 1919—the *Universal Correction Church Times* (*Wanguo gengzhengjiao bao*).

Some of the most important doctrines and practices adopted at this time were as follows (*Wanguo gengzhengjiao bao* 1919, 1:1). Believers must:

1. receive full immersion face-down baptism;
2. seek the baptism of the Holy Spirit, with speaking in tongues as evidence;
3. keep Saturday as the Sabbath for worship;
4. seek the power of healing and of exorcising demons;
5. in communion break the bread, not cut it;
6. implement the sacrament of footwashing among church members;
7. have ordination by laying on of hands;
8. have no time limit for Sabbath worship;
9. all have the right to speak during services;

10. all be permitted to pray aloud during services;
11. seek revelation of the Holy Spirit in choosing overseers (*jiandu*, "bishops"), elders (*zhanglao*), and deacons (*zhishi*);
12. if evangelists, not receive a set salary;
13. devote their heart, spirit, and livelihood to the Lord, and give at least 10 percent of their income.

Interestingly, a brief comment after this list says that *only* those who abide by these provisions are true Christians.

Another set of clauses defined a series of corrective measures which must be taken by other Christian churches in order to become proper or pure. Other churches must:

1. stop using the term *Shangdi* for god and use *Zhenshen* ("True God");
2. eliminate the appellation and the office of "pastor" (*mushi*) and ordain only overseers, elders, and deacons;
3. stop teaching the doctrine of the Trinity (*sanwei iti*) and teach the unitary and undivided (*shu'i wu'er*) true God;
4. baptize only in the name of Jesus, not that of the Father, Son, and Holy Spirit;
5. stop using denominational names and call themselves the True Jesus Church;
6. stop depending on finances or influence of foreigners;
7. stop baptizing by sprinkling, and only use immersion;
8. honor the Sabbath as the only proper worship day;
9. not restrict the right of prayer to only one person in the assembly; all must have it;
10. not give set salaries to evangelistic workers;
11. not put time limits on worship services.

The above sets of church regulations and demands upon other churches appeared in the first issue of the church paper in February 1919. They show a highly developed set of orthodox doctrines, as well as a striking exclusiveness in their presumption to dictate drastic changes to other churches. Remarkably, these doctrines basically have not changed in the over seventy years since their promulgation in 1919, at least not for the mainstream of the True Jesus Church with its headquarters in Taiwan. The doctrines were (and still are today) presented in a context of urgent millenarianism, and also one of distinct antiforeignism. I have mentioned Paul Wei's evangelism strategy of challenging the mission churches. Several articles in the first few issues of the *Wanguo gengzhengjiao bao* directly attacked foreign-run churches, and foreign pastors, as "big sinners" or "big deceivers," headed for Hell if they did not repent and recognize the truth. One article, entitled "The Cry of the Angel of the East" (implying that Paul Wei, or the True Jesus Church as a whole, was this angel), specifically said that the bloodletting of World War I in Europe showed conclusively that Western Christianity was on the wrong track (reprinted in Zhen Yesu jiaohui 1947, F3).

Thus by early 1919 the True Jesus Church had established itself in the Beijing-Tianjin corridor as a militant, millenarian sectarian church. There was no assurance that it would survive, however. The first place to which the church expanded beyond the Beijing-Tianjin area was Shandong. After becoming Paul Wei's partner in this new religious venture, Zhang Lingsheng returned to Weixian. There a relative Zhang Dianju, an antique dealer who had become a Pentecostal convert of Zhang Lingsheng years before, and other locals as well, became followers of the new church. The Weixian group implored Paul Wei to come to Shandong, which he did in mid-1919, making Weixian his base but influencing many in east-central Shandong. Wei laid hands on Zhang Dianju and ordained him as an elder. He now took the name Barnabas (Zhang Banaba). Barnabas Zhang was to become an outstanding and powerful missionary of the True Jesus Church during the next several years, spearheading the rapid expansion of the church into central and south China. But in the meantime the movement's top leaders remained in Weixian for a time in the summer of 1919. The second issue of the church paper was edited in Weixian in July 1919 (Zhen Yesu jiaohui 1947). There were also some dramatic incidents of confrontation and violent clashes between the new sect and the established Presbyterian church in Weixian, as some converts came out of the older churches to join the new group.[22]

After 1919, the True Jesus Church grew at an impressive rate. Ironically, it did so without the two founders. Paul Wei died in the fall of 1919, and Zhang Lingsheng soon confined his activities to his home area of Shandong. But Isaac Wei (Wei Wenxiang), son of Paul Wei, and Barnabas Zhang of Weixian, as well as several other gifted missionaries and evangelists, spread the movement to other areas in the early 1920s. Henan province, and in particular Hunan province, became hotbeds of growth of the church, and by the mid-1920s Hunan was becoming its center of gravity. The early 1920s saw a number of internal crises and challenges, especially a diverse set of heresies, defections, and splitoffs. Heresies, or doctrinal/leadership challenges, seem to occur especially easily in a church where much store is put on direct revelation and self-interpreting glossolalia. For example, for a time about 1920 everyone in the church took the surname Ye (for Yesu, Jesus), on the strength of a revelation to one influential elder. Other heresies were more serious, with self-styled prophets setting up their own separate churches; most of these died out. Yet the basic doctrinal core of 1918–19 seems to have remained quite firm. A serious blow to the church came in the late 1920s, when Barnabas Zhang, the powerful apostle to central-south China, claimed overall leadership, and the church split for a few years into northern and southern factions. A crucial national conference of 1931 excommunicated Barnabas Zhang and reunited the church under the leadership of Isaac Wei, the founder's son. By 1936, in an anniversary yearbook, the True Jesus Church claimed 480 churches and meeting points, almost a quarter of them in Hunan, and several tens of thousands of members.[23]

The church remained quite exclusivist. Interestingly, it did send representatives to the huge ecumenical National Christian Conference in Shanghai in 1922; Isaac Wei represented Hebei, and Barnabas Zhang Shandong (National Christian Conference 1922, 3, 6). But the True Jesus Church showed no interest in joining any of the interchurch bodies coming out of that conference, and I know of no other cases of direct positive contact or cooperation with foreign Christian elements, or even other native Chinese churches, after this. The church continued in fact to have a great deal of conflict with mission churches, since it drew many of its members from established Christian congregations.

Conclusion

What conclusions can be drawn from this brief narrative and profile of the True Jesus Church?

First of all, this story of the early True Jesus Church constitutes a fascinating case of "transnational relations" (Nye and Keohane 1972). There was a crucial input by maverick individual foreign missionaries, which occurred outside the established channels of intellectual/religious transmission (Christian colleges and publications, denominational mission churches). Yet the resulting Chinese church paid scant acknowledgment, let alone deference, to its foreign progenitors.[24] Nevertheless, the Chinese Pentecostal Christian community, the numerical majority of which was represented by the True Jesus Church for much of the twentieth century, must be reckoned as a legitimate part of the twentieth-century Pentecostal/Charismatic movement, an international transnational phenomenon of the first magnitude.

One cannot help but be struck by the remarkable eclecticism of the church's founders in creating a Chinese Seventh-Day Unitarian Pentecostal church. This is seen in stark terms in the basic tenets of the church adopted in 1919, which I have already recounted. Several of these—Holy Spirit baptism, tongues, and healing—are classic Pentecostal doctrines. Even the "Jesus only" anti-Trinitarian position probably came from Pentecostal sources; the "Jesus only" impulse was quite strong among early Pentecostal missionaries in the mid-1910s, especially in China (McGee 1986, 89). The Saturday worship conviction likely came from early American Seventh-Day Adventist missionaries and their publications; they were increasingly active in China after 1902 (Luke 1983). Yet some of the other doctrines—for example the "sacrament" of footwashing, the face-down baptism—are not so obvious in origin. Many of the church's early regulations plainly reflect a profound congregational egalitarianism or anti-ecclesiasticism-—for example, denial of the term "pastor," leaders to be chosen by revelation, the right of all to speak, pray, and participate in worship services. Perhaps related to this was the suspicion and outright denunciation of foreign control or financial support.

Yet it should be remembered that this whole synthesis of ideas and practices was largely held together, at the beginning at least, by Paul Wei's startling visions and direct communication with God, as well as by an underlying current of intense millenarianism, in this case a variety of Christian millennialism—the eschatological conviction that Jesus would soon return. It is here where the correspondence between foreign-derived Pentecostal ideas and Chinese sectarian religious ideas seems potentially significant.

Some of the most insightful research into late imperial Chinese society over the past decade has been in the area of Chinese religious sectarianism and its place in Chinese popular culture.[25] Plainly, certain of the themes and characteristics manifested by many Chinese sectarian groups seem echoed in Pentecostal Christianity. For example, Pentecostalism implicitly legitimized, and sometimes openly encouraged, direct Holy Spirit revelation of God's will, even explicit divine instructions. This kind of practice in the form of shamanism or spirit possession was familiar in Chinese sectarian religion, and of course it strongly characterized the Taipings, earlier creative adaptors of Christianity who were also political rebels in the mid-nineteenth century. Likewise, Pentecostalism highlighted and was even predicated upon millenarianism, another standard feature of heterodox Chinese religion. Again, the Taipings earlier had a strong dose of millenarian underpinning, although theirs evolved from a spiritual to a dynastic political manifestation. And note that another twentieth-century foreign millenarian church, the U.S. Seventh-Day Adventists, grew very rapidly in China after its relatively late beginning in 1902; it, of course, had adventism foremost in its doctrines. Finally, the Pentecostal emphasis upon miracles, especially divine healing, perhaps corresponded well with the healing practices of some traditional Chinese sects.

I submit that none of these key themes was significantly present in nineteenth-century mission Christianity in China. The millenarianism was there in theoretical but usually muted form; the direct revelation and dramatic physical healings hardly at all. It was only in the early twentieth century that this set of new but authentically "Christian" themes appeared in China, originally brought by Pentecostal and other sectarian missionaries. When these currents did appear in China, plainly they were able to tap into corresponding themes of the long-existing Chinese popular heterodox religious syndrome. In addition to the basic resonances of millenarianism, direct revelation, and healing, it may be that the traditional sectarian reverence for the White Lotus-derived Wusheng laomu ("The Eternal Mother") in late imperial times predisposed some early Chinese Pentecostal Christians to find congenial the "Jesus only" Unitarianism that became orthodoxy in the True Jesus Church—this despite the vague gender change from (more or less female) Eternal Mother to (more or less male) True Jesus. Moreover, the intense lay congregationalism and anticlericalism of the True Jesus Church seem closer to the egalitarian "congregational style" of White Lotus sectarians than to that of at least some denominational Christians.[26] It may even be possible that the still fairly recent Boxer cataclysm of 1900 in North China, with its destructive denouement, encouraged some Chinese who were interested in millenarian sectarianism to shy away from a traditional White Lotus variety and try a Christian variety instead.[27]

All this is to say that some Chinese certainly did join the True Jesus Church to become Christians, as other Chinese joined other churches to become Christians. But at the same time that they were adopting Christianity, True Jesus converts and other Pentecostals did so in a manner that satisfied some assumptions or inclinations that derived directly from the Chinese sectarian tradition, which remained strong in the early twentieth century. In that sense, the new elements of the Christian Pentecostal message may have been more effective bridges to certain parts of traditional Chinese society than had been the nineteenth-century Christian message.

Notes

1. It is remarkable that even after a half-century, one of the major sources on the Chinese church in this period is Latourette (1929). The late M. Searle Bates died before he could finish his monumental work on the Chinese church in the twentieth century, but an outline of his drafts and excerpts are in Bates (1984). An institutional history of the Church of Christ in China by a former leader is Merwin (1974). A capsule summary of movements toward independence is in Brown (1983, 40-43).

   The best work in Chinese on indigenous developments in this period is the series of articles by Cha (1981, 1982, 1984). For some issues of the 1920s in particular, see the dissertations by Chao (1986), and Lam (1978).

   What is needed are some balanced, in-depth studies of some major denominations or church groups, as well as of important individuals in the Chinese church, researched on a bilingual basis.

2. Impressions from reading the twenty-odd issues of *Bridge*, a bilingual magazine published since 1983 by the Tao Fong Shan Ecumenical Centre, Hong Kong. Each issue contains detailed descriptions of local churches in China, often including substantial data on the believers' personal histories and present diversities.
3. The term "fundamentalist" was just coming into broad use in the 1920s, and sharp divisions among missionaries in China was one aggravating factor in the "fundamentalist-modernist controversy"; fundamentalists held to the literal truth of traditional Christian dogma, the inerrancy of scriptures, and the need for individual repentance and a personal faith for salvation, with social reform efforts secondary.
4. The code term for this was the "latter rain." I am especially indebted to Grant Wacker for insights on this "pristinization."
5. All the standard sources on Pentecostalism deal with this event. I have used a reprint of the newspaper published at Azusa Street, the *Apostolic Faith*.
6. Faith missionaries were not a new phenomenon, but there were very few in China before 1900. A major 1907 survey, based on statistics of about 1905, notes over one hundred missionaries categorized as "unconnected" or "independent" (MacGillivray 1907, 551-2). But only two or three dozen of these were real "faith" missionaries, with neither a mission society nor a home base of financial support.
7. In attempting to understand the key characteristics of Pentecostalism, it should not be thought that doctrine was necessarily the main dividing line between them and other Christians. Many Christians sought holiness, and were in theology premillennialist. The essential differences were perhaps in social behavior. For a stimulating essay on this theme, see Marty (1976).
8. Some missionaries who had been in China since well before 1907 later became Pentecostals.
9. *Wuxunjie zhenlibao* (April 1909, 1). A brief biography of Mok is in an anonymous article, "Good News from the Land of Sinim" (1909). After Garr left Hong Kong (about 1911–12), Mok became leader of the Hong Kong Pentecostal group.
10. Zhen Yesu jiaohui (1979, 2).
11. For a brief description of the South Chihli Mission, see MacGillivray (1907, 535-37).
12. *Apostolic Faith* (Sept. 1907, 1).
13. *The China Mission Year Book, 1915* (1916, Directory 78).
14. The 1915 mission yearbook, which places Berntsen and others at Zhengding, does not include their church name in English or Chinese.
15. Zhen Yesu jiaohui (1979, 2), where the group putting out the paper is mistakenly identified as the Shitu xinxinhui, Apostolic Faith Church, a name which many early Pentecostal missionaries adopted. But the newspaper itself clearly identifies the mission under the name Xinxinhui.
16. He has a letter in the very first issue of the *Apostolic Faith* (Sept. 1906, 2).
17. See *Yearbook of Apostolic Assembly of Spokane, Washington* (1907). In addition to fourteen missionaries listed for China and Japan, over twenty others are variously listed for Africa, South America, India, and Europe.

18. For example, the 1915 mission yearbook usually does not have Chinese names for these organizations and individuals, as it does for the more established missions, and many are not listed at all.
19. Mok Lai Chi, already mentioned, and Mr. and Mrs. T. M. Sung; Sung's father-in-law was a pastor. Sung succeeded Mok as leader of this Hong Kong church after the latter died in 1926 (Sung 1938, 14-16).
20. In Suzhou he may have been baptized by Antoinette Moomau, a former Shanghai Presbyterian missionary who, like Berntsen, went back to Azusa Street and then on to Suzhou as an independent worker after her return to China. The True Jesus history identifies the Faith Union representative as Pen Dexin, which I originally thought was Peterson, because another True Jesus source refers to a Mr. Peterson. But Berntsen's surname was Pen, according to *The China Mission Year Book, 1915* (1916, Directory 78). Unfortunately, only his surname is given in that source. I cannot tell if "elder Kui" (Kui zhanglao) was Western or Chinese.
21. But Zhang Lingsheng later claimed that Wei did receive a revelation on Sabbath worship in 1917, at the same time as his other revelations (Zhen Yesu jiaohui 1947, M6).
22. There is interesting documentation on this in U.S Presbyterian records, as well as in the issue of *Wanguo gengzhengjiao bao* (no. 2) published in Weixian in the summer of 1919.
23. This paragraph is based on Zhen Yesu jiaohui (1936) and Zhen Yesu jiaohui (1947). In future I will be doing much more detailed work on these events, which are outside the main purview of this essay.
24. Among the other major indigenous churches I have mentioned, the Assembly Hall or Little Flock also tended toward open friction with the foreign sector of Christianity in China.
25. The literature on this research area is becoming quite extensive. The initial opening of the field began with Overmyer (1976) and Naquin (1976). Some of many later important contributions have been Overmyer (1981); Harrell and Perry (1982); several essays in Johnson et al. (1985); Shek (1986); Jordan and Overmyer (1986).
26. See references in note 25.
27. This is not to say that the Boxers themselves were of the exact socio-religious types which later became Pentecostal Christians. Joseph Esherick (1987) has shown that the Spirit Boxers, who became the "Boxers" of history, were not even White Lotus sectarians, and came from a variety of cultural origins, not just sectarian religious origins. Nevertheless, the particular spirit possession practice of the Spirit Boxers does seem similar to one of the key Pentecostal religious experiences, the "infilling" of the Holy Spirit which comes with Holy Spirit baptism and often brings supernatural powers.

References

Anderson, Robert M. 1979. *Vision of the Disinherited: The Making of American Pentecostalism*. New York: Oxford Univ. Press.

Apostolic Faith. 1906–8. Los Angeles (reprinted 1981).

Bates, M. Searle. 1984. *Gleanings from the Manuscripts of M. Searle Bates: The Protestant Endeavor in Chinese Society, 1890-1950*. New York: National Council of Churches.

Bridge 1983—. Hong Kong.

Brown, G. Thompson. 1983. *Christianity in the People's Republic of China*. Atlanta: John Knox Press.

Cha Shijie. 1981. "Minguo Jidujiaohui shi 1 (1911-1917)" (History of Christian churches in the Republic period, part 1, 1911-1917), *Guoli Taiwan daxue lishixuexi xuebao* (Journal of the History Department, National Taiwan University) 8:109-45.

———. 1982. "Minguo Jidujiaohui shi 2 (1917-1922)," ibid., 9:257-94.

———. 1984. "Minguo Jidujiaohui shi 3 (1922-1927)," ibid., 10-11:375-435.

Chao, Jonathan T'ien-en. 1986. "The Chinese Indigenous Church Movement, 1919-1927." Ph.D. dissertation, Univ. of Pennsylvania.

China Inland Mission. 1915. Council minutes, 100th session, April 13-14, 1915.

China Mission Yearbook, 1915. 1916. Shanghai.

Downey, Rose P. 1984. Tape of interview, in Assembly of God archives.

Esherick, Joseph W. 1987. *The Origins of the Boxer Uprising*. Berkeley: Univ. of California Press.

"Good News from the Land of Sinim." 1909. From *Latter Rain Evangel* (Dec. 1909).

Harrell, Stevan, and Elizabeth J. Perry. 1982. "Syncretic Sects in Chinese Society: An Introduction." *Modern China* 8, no. 3:283-303.

Johnson, David, A. Nathan, and E. Rawski, eds. 1985. *Popular Culture in Late Imperial China*. Berkeley: Univ. of California Press.

Jordan, David K., and D. Overmyer. 1986. *The Flying Phoenix: Aspects of Chinese Sectarianism in Taiwan*. Princeton, N.J.: Princeton Univ. Press.

Lam Wing Hung. 1978. "The Emergence of a Protestant Christian Apologetics in the Chinese Church during the Anti-Christian Movement in the 1920's." Ph.D. dissertation, Princeton Theological Seminary.

Latourette, Kenneth S. 1929. *A History of Christian Missions in China*. London: SPCK.

Luke, Handel H. T. 1983. "A History of Seventh-Day Adventist Higher Education in the China Mission, 1888-1980." Ph.D. dissertation, Andrews Univ.

McGee, Gary B. 1986. *This Gospel Shall Be Preached: A History and Theology of Assemblies of God Foreign Missions to 1959*. Springfield, Mo.: Gospel Publishing House.

MacGillivray, D. 1907. *A Century of Protestant Missions in China (1807-1907)*. Shanghai: American Presbyterian Mission Press.

Marty, Martin E. 1976. *A Nation of Behavers*. Chicago: Univ. of Chicago Press.

Merwin, W. C. 1974. *Adventure in Unity: The Church of Christ in China*. Grand Rapids: Eerdmans.

Naquin, Susan. 1976. *Millenarian Rebellion in China*. New Haven: Yale U. Press.
National Christian Conference. 1922. *The Chinese Church as Revealed in the National Christian Conference*. Shanghai: National Christian Conference.
1936 Handbook of the Christian Movement in China under Protestant Auspices. 1936. Ed. C. L. Boynton and C. D. Boynton. Shanghai: Kwang Hsueh Publishing House.
Nye, J., and R. Keohane. 1972. *Transnational Relations and World Politics*. Cambridge: Harvard Univ. Press.
Overmyer, Daniel L. 1976. *Folk Buddhist Religion: Dissenting Sects in Late Traditional China*. Cambridge: Harvard Univ. Press.
———. 1981. "Alternatives: Popular Religious Sects in Chinese Society." *Modern China* 7, no. 2:153-90.
Shek, Richard. 1986. "Religion in Chinese Society: Orthodoxy versus Heterodoxy." Unpublished manuscript.
Sung, T. M. 1938. "The Story of My Conversion: History of the Hong Kong Pentecostal Mission." *Latter Rain Evangel* (June 1938):14-16.
Synan, Vinson. 1971. *The Holiness-Pentecostal Movement in the United States*. Grand Rapids: Eerdmans.
Tongchuan fuyin zhenlibao (*Popular Gospel Truth*). 1912– .
Tongwenbao (*The Chinese Christian Intelligencer*). 1915. No. 34:2.
Wacker, Grant. 1984. "The Functions of Faith in Primitive Pentecostalism." *Harvard Theological Review*, 77, nos. 3-4:353-75.
Wanguo gengzhengjiao bao (*Universal Correction Church Times*). 1919– .
Ward, W. A. n.d. "The Trailblazer." n.p. In Assembly of God archives.
Williamson, H. R. 1957. *British Baptists in China 1845-1952*. London: Carey Kingsgate Press.
Wuxunjie zhenlibao (*Pentecostal truths*). 1909– .
Yearbook of Apostolic Assembly of Spokane, Washington. 1907. In Assembly of God archives.
Zhen Yesu jiaohui (The True Jesus Church). 1936. *Zhen Yesu jiaohui zongbu shizhounian jinian zhuankan* (*Commemorative Volume on the Tenth Anniversary of the General Headquarters of the True Jesus Church*). Shanghai.
———. 1947. *Zhen Yesu jiaohui chuangli sanshizhounian jinian zhuankan* (*Commemorative Volume on the Thirtieth Anniversary of the Founding of the True Jesus Church*). Shanghai.
Zhen Yesu jiaohui Taiwan shenxueyuan (Taiwan seminary of the True Jesus Church). 1979. *Zhen Yesu jiaohuishi* (*History of the True Jesus Church*). Taizhong, Taiwan.

CHAPTER 7

The Messiah and the Masked Man: Popular Ideology in Mexico, 1810–1821

ERIC VAN YOUNG

> There does not exist, nor ever will exist, any community or group of communities whose mythology and ethnography... can be known in their entirety...since we are dealing with a shifting reality, perpetually exposed to the attacks of a past that destroys it and of a future that changes it. For every instance recorded in written form, there are obviously many others unknown to us; and we are only too pleased with the samples and scraps at our disposal.
>
> —Claude Lévi-Strauss, *The Raw and the Cooked*

Chelm in New Spain

The mythical Jewish town of Chelm has been the subject of innumerable jokes, anecdotes, and homilies for many generations, and one of these stories will be my starting point in this chapter. It seems the good citizens of Chelm had heard many rumors about the coming of the Messiah. Naturally they did not want to miss such an event, so they hired a poor but honest man of the town—we shall call him Chaim—to keep watch. He was to sit in a wooden tower they had built just beyond the edge of the town and run in to inform the people when he should spy the Messiah approaching. Weeks passed, then months and years, during which Chaim kept his vigil faithfully, but with no sign of the Messiah's approach. The town's elders even lost hope, but out of habit Chaim stayed at this post with food and pay. Finally one of the town's scoffers (for even Chelm had such people) came to the tower and expressed incredulity that the man should still be keeping watch. "Chaim," he shouted, "don't you know the Messiah is never going to arrive?" To which Chaim answered, with a philosophical shrug of the shoulders, "Yes, but after all it's a living."[1]

The story about Chelm illustrates that messianic expectation was for some not only a way of making a living, but also a way of life and a habit of mind. In the years around 1810 country people all over central Mexico seem, like the citizens of Chelm, to have been awaiting some sort of a messiah to lead them to a more perfect time and place, ill-defined or unconscious as these hopes were. Popular messianic longings had not arisen, of course, just with the eruption of Miguel Hidalgo's revolt, and in the very first years of the new century rumors of conspiracy, foreign invasion, Indian saviors and kings, and massive rural uprising ricocheted about the countryside of New Spain. The year 1801 was possibly even to have marked the advent of an Indian millennium in Mexico. At least two Indian pseudo-messiahs were reported to have appeared, one in the area of Durango and another near Tepic, evoking near-hysterical responses from the central authorities in Mexico City and weary embarrassment on the part of these same authorities when no massive insurrections had materialized.[2]

By far the most serious of these incidents was the appearance of an Indian pretender named Mariano in the isolated, rugged country of the western *sierra madre*, near the important coastal town of Tepic, in the waning days of December 1800. Mariano claimed to be the son and heir of the deceased Indian governor of Tlaxcala, an independent pre-Columbian city-state and colonial province in eastern central Mexico, and further claimed to have journeyed to Spain where King Charles IV confirmed his shadowy rights to sovereignty. His coronation was to take place on 6 January 1801 (Epiphany in the Christian calendar, the twelfth day after Christmas—significantly, "Día de los Reyes" in Spanish ["Day of the Kings," or Magi]) at Tepic, preceded by a full-scale royal entry into the town to the accompaniment of mounted horsemen, flags bearing the image of the Virgin of Guadalupe, and the attendance of Indian and royal officials. His program consisted of only two elements: the restoration to local Indian communities of land in the possession of non-Indians, and the abatement or elimination of tribute payments. In an openly chiliastic gesture, he specified that he was to be crowned not with gold or silver, but with the crown of Jesús Nazareno (Jesús the Nazarene, belonging to a local religious effigy), "since he came to suffer in order to free his sons." In the event the conspiracy to crown King Mariano was discovered, several hundred Indian conspirators were arrested and shipped off to Guadalajara, and military units in much of western Mexico were put on alert through the end of 1801 to face a major insurrection which never came to pass.[3] The Mariano episode, occurring in the twilight years of Spanish colonial rule in Mexico, had a number of predecessors in the form of messianic/millenarian movements among the rural Indians of the country. One may thus legitimately speak of a long tradition of such collective manifestations beginning immediately after the conquest (or even before it, if one wishes to take that view) and stretching through the eighteenth century, with something of a hiatus after about the early 1760s.[4]

With particularly sharp irony, in many instances around 1810 these messianic hopes were focused on the ferociously reactionary figure of the Spanish king Ferdinand VII ("El Deseado"—"The Longed-for One"), who would have found himself perfectly in sympathy with the ruthless military repression carried out in his name by some royalist commanders in New Spain. And yet while much of the Mexican countryside was awash with this amalgam of rumor, hope, and messianic expectation centering on the king of Spain or surrogate figures, Indian peasants were brutally assassinating European-born Spaniards in village jacqueries (violent, short-lived uprisings) and on backcountry roads. The almost preternatural violence of this Spaniard-bashing—mobbings, torture, and gratuitous *coups de grâce* were not unusual—often took on a compulsive, sacrificial tone clearly beyond political assassination.[5] Thus we are faced with an apparent sharp contradiction between two elements of collective belief and their associated forms of social action: the monarch, the archetypal figure of intrusive and oppressive colonial authority, was being venerated with messianic fervor, while European-born colonists were being slaughtered with an almost ritualistic enthusiasm.

In accordance with the broad topic of this volume, the central theme of this chapter is the process whereby elements of Christian religious doctrine intermeshed with an indigenous cultural tradition to underwrite an ideology of collective action within the context of political upheaval and widespread popular violence. In tracing this process I will examine two questions. First, how did Indian messianism function as an element of popular ideology in the Mexican struggles for independence from Spain? In answer to this question I will develop the following hypothesis: that messianic belief within the context of large-scale political upheaval functioned to focus popular—that is to say, largely Indian and peasant—energies on the struggle for a political break with Spain, but for reasons very different from those of the elite creole ideologues of the movement, and even in substantial degree opposed to them. It is my contention, in fact, that Indian messianic hopes represented a primitive political irredentism: a basically conservative, even reactionary ideology combining elements of naive monarchical legitimism with those of a rigidly localocentric worldview, a kind of spontaneous peasant Fourierism. But messianism took different forms in different regions of colonial Mexico, and some passing attention to these variations can tell us a good deal about the spatially and temporally uneven process of acculturation which took place during the colonial period. Furthermore, the fact that one sees messianism linked to mystical kingship in popular ideology, and in *no instance* to a full-blown millenarian formulation, but only to the vaguest of programs, provides some hints as to the overall shape of colonial popular culture and the worldview of major segments of the Mexican population.

This formulation leads us to the second question: in what respects did popular and elite rebel ideologies differ from each other, and at what points, if any, did they converge? It was largely the concept of mystical kingship and its role in linking ideas about social structure, political constitution and legitimacy, and religion that provided the interface between elite and popular rebel ideologies, and allowed apparently concerted action against the Spanish colonial state at points. But behind this convergence lay very different goals and ideas about the structure of political and social relationships. At its heart, it seems to me, this ideological and social rift in the ranks of the rebels amounted to a fundamental contradiction of purpose in which the elite creole directorate of the rebellion was launched in an effort at a sort of proto-liberal state- and nation-building, while Indian rebels and rioters were bent on preserving the autonomy of communities which survived outside the state or nation. The exploration of this contrast—a kind of binary opposition almost fortuitously Lévi-Straussian in its symmetry (hence the epigraph of the chapter)—explains much about the nature of Mexican colonial society and the upheaval which sundered it from Spain.[6] Other themes demonstrate a similar contradiction—attitudes toward the Church and its priests, toward political independence itself, toward the social constitution of New Spain and the distribution of its wealth, especially land—but none of these encapsulates so clearly the global vision of popular rebels, in particular. In developing my argument I will place considerably more emphasis on the issue of popular messianic expectation than upon elite thinking because the former has hardly been studied at all and is of considerable interest, while many shelves in libraries sag under the weight of books devoted to the latter and attract the social historian rather less.

Creole Nationalism

The concept of nationhood occupied in the thinking of elite creole ideologues the central place that mystical kingship, tinged or conflated as it was with messianism, occupied in that of the popular masses of the country. Certainly monarchism within the ranks of the early autonomist thinkers, before the actual outbreak of the insurgency of 1810, was the rule. Father Miguel Hidalgo, the parish priest who initiated the armed independence struggle in the fall of 1810, himself espoused the candidacy of Ferdinand VII to be monarch of New Spain provided his legitimacy could be proved uncompromised, and monarchical projects were frequently proposed by other creole thinkers, though because of the situation in Spain the issue was murky until the restoration of Ferdinand in 1814.[7] In this light, the continuing discussion of the possibility of inviting King Ferdinand to rule the colony, as the Brazilians had done with the Portuguese King Joao VI, appears natural. Furthermore, a constitutional monarchy of some sort, linked indissolubly to religious sanction, seemed to many Mexican autonomists the logical solution to the problem of state-building, so that the short-lived Mexican Empire (1821–22) of Agustín de Iturbide seems less cynical and idiosyncratic when it comes along.[8] On the whole, however, it seems fair to say that more than the monarchy, or republicanism, or the instrumentalities of state-building, what engaged the attention of creole thinkers most centrally was the concrete issue of political autonomy and behind it the larger question of Mexican nationhood.

Although there occurred a certain amount of *Sturm und Drang* about constitutional forms, the rebel Act of Independence of 1813, the constitution which took shape in the following year, and the loose program associated with them were anything but Jacobin.[9] There is a good deal of controversy among modern scholars as to the liberal content of these documents, some claiming they were essentially quite conservative and others that they followed closely the lines of the French revolutionary constitution of 1793.[10] What one sees in the Constitution of Apatzingán is an insistence on political autonomy from Spain, popular sovereignty, representative forms, separation of powers, an established and exclusive Catholic church, and so forth.[11] Although the issue of state-building was of considerable importance to the directorate of the independence movement, there is little if any evidence to indicate that it mattered a fig to their followers.

More interesting from the perspective of comparing elite creole with popular worldviews is the question of emerging Mexican nationhood and its place in the respective thinking of the two groups. As with constitutional forms, there is little if any evidence to indicate that creole ideas about nationhood resonated in the least with popular concepts of personal and community identity (we shall have more to say on this below). While it is true that popular and elite rebels were often able to draw together under the banner of the Virgin of Guadalupe and a fairly virulent anti-*gachupín* sentiment (European-born Spaniards were often called by the pejorative epithet *gachupín*), it is also true that these symbols and their associated behaviors represented different things to the two groups.

In the case of the Virgin of Guadalupe, creole patriots tended to see in her advent and cult evidence of the providentialism associated with the historical formation of the Mexican nation, while popular groups probably saw in her especially a protectress and in Marianism in general an echo of ancient mother-gods.[12] The victimization of European-born Spaniards, on the other hand, had for the creoles the flavor of a fraternal struggle over concrete political prizes and for the Indian masses of the colony a function of displacement from a frontal assault on dominant white society in general.

The creole patriotism whose origins David Brading has traced so interestingly, and which began developing into a genuine nationalism in the decades after independence, was a very different ideology from the localocentric Indian peasant worldview often linked to messianic expectation.[13] In fact, creole patriotism was undergirded by certain racist ideas regarding the Indians of New Spain and their "degraded" condition at the close of the colonial period, ideas which originated in the attempt of creole ideologues to distance themselves from the stain of *mestizaje* (race mixture) and the prevailing negative scientistic concepts about the nature of man in the New World popularized by such European writers as Buffon, Raynal, de Pauw, and Robertson. In any case, creole thinking of the independence era was shot through with an attempt to create a Mexican nation, even if not yet with coherent nationalist imagery. The locus of community for most creole autonomist thinkers was in the nation, and their struggle throughout the next century and a half was to realize a coherent ideology and a state structure congruent with their community of sentiment.

Permutations of Popular Messianism

While ideologues among the elite creole directorate of the rebels were struggling with the knotty problems of nationhood, political legitimacy, and the constitution of the Mexican state, some resolving it in favor of an essentially conservative republicanism and others in favor of a constitutional monarchy with representative institutions, popular insurgent ideology was taking a rather different tack. Fragmentary but persuasive evidence points in the direction of a widespread, subterranean messianic or crypto-messianic expectation focusing, in large part, on the figure of King Ferdinand VII. Although the documented cases of this are comparatively few, it seems not unreasonable to assume that the recorded pronouncements represented a more generalized belief among the Indian rebels of the colony, and probably even among many thousands and tens of thousands of Indian villagers who did not actively take up arms. Of the group of young Indian insurgents of both sexes from Celaya captured in November of 1810, for example, all but two clearly believed they were following the orders of the king of Spain, who was physically present in Mexico, riding about the countryside in a mysterious black coach, and who had himself commanded Father Hidalgo to take up arms against the Spanish colonial authorities. Furthermore, the king had enjoined them, through the headman (*gobernador*) of their village, to kill the Viceroy and all other European-born Spaniards and divide their property amongst the poor.[14] Another captured rebel was reported to have said that "a person is coming in a veiled coach, and when people come to see him, they kneel down and go away very happy."[15] About the same time a woman from a village near Cuautla told her neighbors that the king was traveling in the company of Father Hidalgo and wearing a silver mask.[16] In the late winter of 1810–11 and spring of 1811 King Ferdinand VII was variously reported to be approaching Cuauhtitlán, or with Ignacio Allende's insurgent forces at Querétaro.[17] Yet another captured rebel stated emphatically that King Ferdinand had appeared in New Spain by a particular and miraculous intercession of the Virgin of Guadalupe.[18]

The king was masked; he was invisible; he was traveling alone in a closed coach; he was with Father Hidalgo or Ignacio Allende (a creole militia officer and the priest's co-conspirator); he was working in concert with the Virgin of Guadalupe to destroy the Spanish armies. One of the most interesting of these "sightings" of the king in Mexico was that by two Indians in the area of Cuernavaca in early 1811, who sought to defraud a number of local village officials of a small quantity of cash by concocting a letter supposedly authored by the Indian governor of Tlaxcala (a significant echo of the Mariano and mad messiah episodes I have treated elsewhere).[19] The letter stated that the king was about to enter the village of Cuauhtitlán, to the north of Mexico City, and that he commanded complete secrecy from the *gachupines* as well as financial support from Indian village officials, on pain of death. What is interesting about this incident, of course, is not the fraud itself, but the fact that its perpetrators thought it credible.[20] Some rebel leaders even feared that news of King Ferdinand's restoration to the throne in 1814 might undermine the loyalty of their Indian followers. This thinking apparently lay behind the effort of Father Marcos Castellanos, the insurgent commander of the besieged island of Mezcala in Lake Chapala, to suppress the information from his entirely Indian forces as late as 1815.[21] Leaders on both sides of the rebellion were aware of beliefs concerning messianic, mystical kingship among the Indian masses and considered the matter a delicate one which might compromise their political positions. In the summer of 1808, for example, the creole lawyer Francisco Primo de Verdad, in addressing the assembled viceregal and municipal authorities in Mexico City, made an eloquent case for (colonial) popular sovereignty, employing the concepts of an "original people" and despoiled monarch. But neither Primo de Verdad nor his European-born political opponents elaborated on these ideas much in debate, presumably because the governors of the quasi-autonomous Indian districts of the city (Tenochtitlán and Tlatelolco) were attending the meeting and with them the shades of several despoiled and assassinated Aztec monarchs.[22]

Occasionally Indian villagers or other country-dwellers made emphatic pronouncements against the *gachupines* in general, while exempting the king as the object of special veneration.[23] An example of such behavior occurred in the village of Epazoyuca, just a few miles to the northeast of Mexico City, during a public procession in the fall of 1808. The Indian official Pablo Hilario, bearing a standard with the image of the Virgin of Guadalupe, was standing next to the Indian governor of the village, bearing upon another standard the likeness of King Ferdinand VII. When the large, ethnically mixed crowd began yelling "Viva Fernando Séptimo!" Pablo Hilario chimed in with "Viva Fernando Séptimo y mueran todos los gachupines!" ("Long live King Ferdinand VII and death to all Spaniards!"). One Spanish witness to the incident observed that Hilario's statements were "very like those indecorously repeated even in the public plazas."[24] Translated into action, such naive monarchism very often took the form of Indians being recruited to the insurgent cause by rebel leaders astute enough to invoke the name of the king in calling for adherence to the cause of Hidalgo and Allende. The statements of captured Indian rebels show no trace of any cognitive dissonance in this regard: apparently the yawning contradiction in terms was for them no contradiction at all.[25]

There were, interestingly enough, candidates alternative to "El Deseado" to whom messianic expectation was attached. It is often stated and widely believed that the objects of messianic veneration by the Indian masses of the country were the priests who led the rebellion in its early phases, most especially Miguel Hidalgo and José María Morelos.[26] While this is not an unreasonable assumption, it is probably due more to the retrospective mythification of the progenitors of Mexican national identity than to any marked popular sentiment at the time of the independence struggle itself. Apart from a very few scattered references to the imminent return of Hidalgo and Morelos at the head of avenging armies after their widely publicized deaths, there is very little evidence of the kind of apotheosis ("spontaneous canonization" in Jacques Lafaye's expression) of these popular leaders undergone in more recent times by such men as Emiliano Zapata, Pancho Villa, or Che Guevara.

A more widely venerated, or at least more widely spoken of, figure in the messianic mold, oddly enough, was Ignacio Allende, a wealthy creole militia officer from the Bajío town of San Miguel el Grande, a co-conspirator of Hidalgo's who became the priest's second-in-command during the short-lived 1810-11 rebellion. A less likely candidate for popular veneration would be hard to imagine, but Allende was apparently nonetheless more closely associated with messianic expectation himself, and also with the figure of King Ferdinand, than the priests. In a number of documents Allende was linked closely with "El Deseado," or even conflated with him and the Virgin of Guadalupe, as very notably in the case of an Indian uprising and rebel invasion in the Cuernavaca area in late 1810.[27] Allende was quite widely perceived among Indian villagers and many other insurgents as the paramount leader of the rebel forces even during the apogee of Hidalgo's power, until he engineered a kind of coup against the older man in early 1811. A seditious Indian magistrate from a small pueblo in the Chalco district said in the early summer of 1811 that "would to God Allende would come, and he would go with him though it cost him his home." In the Texcoco district, near the viceregal capital, many Indian officials sympathetic to the rebellion were awaiting an emissary from Allende (not Hidalgo) in November of 1810, and the insurgent army was on more than one occasion referred to as Allende's army (not Hidalgo's).[28] His name appeared in seditious verses espousing national liberation (in one case substituted for that of Archduke John of Austria, and America replacing Italy) and his image in an allegorical sketch purchased by an Indian peasant from the country in one of the capital's major plazas; he was mentioned in people's prayers and seen by some to have been sent by God as scourge for the *gachupines*; and one ingenuous captured rebel even referred to him as "His Serene Highness."[29] Among the ranks of the creole insurgent leadership Ignacio Allende was more socially conservative than most, yet he was seen by many Indians as a great avenger and killer of *gachupines*, social equalizer, abolisher of tributes and fixer of prices, and even as an agrarian reformer.[30] In at least one instance—significantly, in the rough and isolated further reaches of the sierra of Metztitlán—while his capture was being denied as a lie (at almost exactly the same time that he was being executed in the north of the colony, in Chihuahua), Allende was being proposed as a popular candidate for king: "and now he is going to obtain the crown of Mexico and in a few days we will fall at his feet, and kiss his feet and hands, because he is going to be our Catholic King [*nuestro católico*]."[31]

The Etiology of Popular Messianism

This apparently bizarre spate of messianic, crypto-messianic, and quasi-messianic popular expressions did not, however, spring out of a political or cultural vacuum, but had its own cultural antecedents—preconditions necessary but not sufficient for the rapid development and activation of such ideas at the end of the colonial period. At this point, then, let us take a step back from the rebellion itself to take a look at those antecedents.[32]

The connection in Western religious/eschatological thought of the millennium with a cyclical closure or recurrence in time is too well known to require extended comment here. Indeed, the idea of the Second Coming itself partakes of such a circularity, even though the outcome of this central event of Christian eschatology, in which messiah and millennium are inextricably associated, is traditionally thought to be an end of history, a kind of perfect stasis, and not the initiation of a new cycle.[33] This is a particularly notable characteristic of the nativistic or revitalization movements which have frequently sprung up in the ex-colonial world, and which often assume the form of messianic/millenarian cults or uprisings. In such collective fantasies the perfect age to come may appear as a regeneration, the recovery by oppressed social groups of what has previously been lost—political autonomy, economic resources, cultural integrity, cosmological coherence, and so forth—so that, in Sylvia Thrupp's words, "time [is] bent back...to recapture some state of harmony in which the world began."[34] How much more powerful must the appeal of such doctrines be, therefore, if they resonate strongly with an indigenous intellectual and religious tradition of cyclical cosmology, even if the latter has been systematically suppressed in the name of a hegemonic evangelical Christianity?

Such a resonance was, in fact, one of the major antecedents of popular messianic belief in late colonial Mexico, and played an important role in the link between messianic expectation and collective violence. As with the cyclical aspect of millennial belief, the cyclical (or perhaps helical, Aztec thought allowing for some evolution) nature of Mesoamerican cosmological thought is familiar enough to require only brief comment here.[35] The mythicohistorical memory of the Aztecs told of a succession of ages, or "suns," of exactly the same length, at the end of which mankind had in each case been destroyed cataclysmically; and predicted that the same fate awaited the people of the Fifth Sun, the Aztecs themselves. Within this overall scheme elaborate astronomical calculations and the intermeshing of two calendars divided mundane time into shorter cycles (of fifty-two years), at the end of which the universe held its breath awaiting its contingent renewal. Intertwined with this cyclical view of time there existed a strong mythicohistorical tradition of man-gods and messianic prophecy, stretching back through the Mesoamerican classic era and embodied most strikingly in the figure of Quetzalcoatl, a pan-Mesoamerican deity who was also regarded as having been a real historical figure. It was, in fact, the prophesied return of Quetzalcoatl after centuries of exile, coinciding as it did with the arrival of Fernando Cortés early in 1519, that lent the advent of the Spanish such an enormous psychosocial impact on the Aztecs, facilitating the conquest of a far-flung Indian empire numbering tens of millions of inhabitants by a ragged army of a few hundred European adventurers.[36] Exactly how explicitly or widely preserved by the eighteenth century were the

Aztec traditions of cyclical cosmology and messianic expectation is impossible to determine, given the conditions prevailing in the colony and the surviving documentation, but it seems likely that they existed side by side with other beliefs (shamanism, for example) as part of the substrate of Indian popular culture.[37] At the very least such beliefs would have predisposed large segments of the colony's rural masses, in times of stress, to form the highly cathected relationship with a single charismatic figure typical of messianism.[38]

The enduring matrix of popular messianic expectation, however, was only one of the ingredients in the singular alchemy of collective action. Another was the existence and wide recognition among the colonial rural masses of a protective, patriarchal tradition of monarchical government at whose center stood the quasi-thaumaturgical figure of the Spanish king himself. The great rambling edifice of royal Indian protectionism constructed piecemeal during the three centuries of colonial rule leaked like a sieve, to be sure, and laws for the protection of the Indian populations were frequently honored more in the breach than in the observance. Nor was a large measure of cynical *raison d'état* absent from Crown Indian policy, since from the very first the monarchy sought to counteract the centrifugal, feudal tendencies of the colonial enterprise in the New World by interposing itself and its agents, insofar as possible, between the colonists and their indigenous labor supply.[39] Nonetheless, the Indians of New Spain (and elsewhere) enjoyed a set of legal privileges, exemptions, and protections which significantly interfered with their complete integration into colonial society, and kept them in a legal bubble of tutelage ruptured only with the advent of independent Mexican nationhood in the third decade of the nineteenth century.[40]

On the negative side this protected status meant demeaning tribute payments, a serious abridgment of civil rights, and perennial interference in Indian affairs from secular and ecclesiastical authorities. But on the positive side it meant exemption from certain kinds of taxes, generally more lenient criminal penalties than meted out to non-Indians, a high degree of municipal autonomy, access to a special court system, and so forth.[41] On the whole, given the Indians' subordinate and disadvantaged position in colonial society, they adapted remarkably well to the colonial judicial system and enjoyed considerable success in the courts, both local and viceregal, in defending, for example, their rights to private and communal lands. To cite but one instance among many thousands extant in the colonial documentation, in the early 1780s a number of Indian officials and villagers from several pueblos in the Cuauhtitlán area, to the north of Mexico City, were complaining bitterly about the alienation of Indian farming lands through rentals and sales, both to wealthier Indians and to non-Indian farmers of the region. Elements of coercion, fraud, and collusion on the part of local royal officials in such land transfers were uncovered after a lengthy investigation ordered by the viceroy, and hundreds of agreements were abrogated and the lands in question returned to the control of poor Indian villagers. Furthermore, a viceregal decree was issued reinforcing previous prohibitions of 1778 and 1780 against many such arrangements.[42] The point here is that where these and other legal and administrative remedies were applied in favor of the Indians of colonial New Spain, they were applied in the king's name. Furthermore, religious and civic ritual of all kinds constantly stressed the centrality of the Spanish king to the colonial commonweal, and his benevolence and fatherly concern with the welfare of his weakest subjects.[43] Such associations surely contributed powerfully to popular veneration of the Spanish king, especially among the Indians who often sheltered under his protective, patriarchal mantle, and made of his figure a preeminent candidate for messianic expectation.

In addition to considerations of politics, culture, and cosmology, we must take into account the particular social and intellectual conditions under which the mass of rural Indians lived in Mexico at the close of the colonial period. While it is true that messianic and millenarian movements have been common enough in the West and in Western-dominated areas of the world since the medieval period, it is also true that in terms of mainstream religious belief these cults and movements must be regarded as heterodox, even (or most especially) if they adapt, distort, or invert ideological elements from orthodox religious thought. Many observers of such collective phenomena have noted that they tend to flourish in culturally "backward" or isolated areas or among marginal or transitional populations, where heterodox beliefs or older cultural elements are likely to persist.[44] Heterodox belief, a longstanding tradition of religious syncretism, lack of education, and geographical and cultural isolation were certainly typical of large parts of New Spain even at the end of the colonial period. The characterization of the rural Indians constantly repeated by many parish priests and local officials at the end of the colonial period—that they were ignorant, lazy, drunken, vicious sodomites, naturally prone to violence, barbarism, and rebellion—must certainly be taken with a large grain of salt.[45] Nonetheless, there is plentiful evidence that heterodoxy and an often exceedingly imperfect understanding of approved religious teaching, combined with the resilience of ancient indigenous belief systems, were widespread, and it seems reasonable to assume that these conditions provided an environment nourishing to messianic beliefs.

Institutions of secular education—village schools—for Indians and other country-dwellers were common enough in New Spain at the close of the colonial period, but they seem to have achieved indifferent results at best. A survey of villages completed in 1773 in the large province of Sayula in western central Mexico, for example, indicated that most Indian schools, though they existed on paper, were nearly moribund in fact. Communities lacked the wherewithal to pay the schoolmasters from village funds, and most families were so poor that paying on an individual subscription basis was impossible for them. Aside from this financial constraint, Indian attitudes about non-Indians (schoolmasters were often drawn from this group) living in their villages, resistance to acculturation, and the oft-mentioned need to have children working in the fields and other productive activities rather than attending schools, made school attendance very low and progress in educating Indian children slow or nonexistent.[46]

Even more important than the lack of secular education among the Indian population in nourishing a tradition of messianic expectation, however, was religious heterodoxy of various sorts. Now, while it is true that one man's heterodoxy may be another's intense piety, it is also true that notions of cultural relativism and individual piety were not widespread in the period of which we are speaking. Furthermore, both the active practice of heterodox religious rites and the more passive resistance to traditional religious indoctrination at the parish level were explicitly acknowledged by colonial authorities as often being linked to an overall rejection of the Spanish colonizers and their culture. To cite but one example, the Franciscan curate of the Indian town of Poncitlán, on the northern shore of Lake Chapala, reported in 1731 concerning the hostility of the local Indian villagers, particularly in the nearby pueblo of Mezcala. The problem of inducing the local villagers to attend mass and observe the other Christian sacraments had for decades past been a difficult puzzle (*quebradero de cabeza*) for all the priests who had dwelt there. The Franciscan stressed, however, as did other local Spanish witnesses, that the Indians also held an "enmity...to the Spaniards" and a "repugnance" to having any non-Indian living in their villages (as we have noted with schoolmasters). Riots against their curates and the occasional attack upon local secular authorities (on one occasion resulting in the murder of a royal deputy magistrate) were fairly regular occurrences. In one pueblo of the district in the 1720s the Indians had attacked the priest in his church. One man among the rioters broke into the sacristy, ate all the sacramental wafers, and to the horror of several onlookers, while running through the cemetery to his home he burst and died on the spot.[47] Occasionally such conflicts with village priests were related not only (one suspects not even principally) to matters of religious observance, but also to the payment of ecclesiastical subventions and demands for labor and other services on the part of parish clergy.

The complaints of parish clergy regarding the irreligion and ignorance of their Indian flocks were so generalized over New Spain right up to the end of the colonial era (and beyond) as to indicate that evangelization had indeed been shallow, at least insofar as formal religious observance was concerned. The priest of Calimaya, for instance, just a few miles west of Mexico City, asserted in 1792 that of his five thousand backsliding parishioners, mostly Indians, not a hundred knew the simplest prayers. In an 1809 letter the priest of Apaxtla, near Taxco to the southwest of the capital, lamented the "deplorable" moral state of his parish and the "tears of blood which should be shed for the loss of their souls, since they have completely abandoned religion." In nearby Zacualpan about the same time, the curate complained that although he had attempted to teach some elements of Christian doctrine to his Indian parishioners after the mass on Sundays, they refused to stay in the church, physically pushing and abusing the ushers who tried to make them stay seated for lessons. A similar situation prevailed among the Indians resident in the sizable town of Celaya, in the Bajío (a major grain-producing, mining, and industrial region) to the north of Mexico City, where neither kindness nor punishment sufficed to discipline them into learning elements of the faith.[48] Indian parishioners in many villages regularly went for years without hearing mass, taking communion, or confessing, and they lived together out of wedlock, refused to baptize their newborn, and buried their dead outside church cemeteries.

If ignorance of formal religious elements, resistance to indoctrination, and conflict with ecclesiastical authorities were endemic in the late colony, more active forms of heterodox behavior seem to have been common enough, although by their very nature less well documented. The most extreme form of this, of course, was the advent of Indian messiahs. One such figure was Antonio Pérez, active in the area of Yautepec, in the Morelos sugar zone, about 1760. He preached nothing less than a total inversion of the social order then prevailing in the colony, clothing his prophetic visions in a language compounded of traditional apocalyptic and pre-Columbian imagery (the soul of Christ was composed of kernels of maize, etc.). Some years later memories of Pérez, his cult, and his followers were still fresh in the area, and by the late 1770s there was even some suggestion that traces of the cult survived in and around Tepoztlán.[49] Similar though less well-known cases of Indian messianism were those of Mariano, in the Tepic area in 1800–1801, and the mad messiah of Durango, about the same time, both cited above.

But these spectacular manifestations of Indian heterodoxy were certainly outnumbered by the day-to-day practices of shamanism, witchcraft, fertility cults, and so forth. In 1817, for instance, the vicar of the village of San Lorenzo Huichichilapan, near Toluca, just a few miles west of Mexico City, reported the arrest of a number of men of the pueblo for participating in what were apparently propitiatory rites dedicated to a traditional Indian god of the hills. The celebration of the cult included icons of Christ and the Virgin, but also certain "dolls" (*muñecos*) presumably representing pagan deities; dancing and singing by both sexes; offerings of food (tamales, most prominently); and other ritual elements.[50] Roughly similar "idolatrous" practices were uncovered by a local priest as close to the viceregal capital as the district of Xochimilco in 1813, where local shamans oversaw a syncretic cult, with overtones of fertility rites, in a secret chapel in a cave.[51] In the pueblo of Tecualoya, to the west of Cuernavaca, a local Indian woman was prosecuted for witchcraft in 1818, with ample supporting testimony from a number of villagers.[52]

Parallel with resistance to religious indoctrination, messianism, and active heterodoxy ran a strong tradition of what can most appropriately be called popular piety—religious celebrations, processions of various kinds associated with liturgical events or the veneration of local icons, spontaneous cults and chapels, and so forth. Before about the last third of the eighteenth century, manifestations of such popular piety had been tolerated or even encouraged in keeping with the exuberance of the baroque Church and the doctrines of Tridentine Catholicism. After that turning point, however, the Mexican church shifted its position with the advent of the Bourbon reforms sponsored by the enlightened Spanish monarchy. Popular forms of piety were thenceforth sanitized, restricted, or suppressed outright, provoking considerable resistance, even violent resistance, on the part of Indian villagers in particular.[53] Indeed, it even seems possible that several of the village jacqueries that erupted in connection with the Hidalgo rebellion in late 1810 may have been linked to frustrations with clerical attempts to suppress popular religious celebrations, especially those of All Saints.[54] The point to be made here is that certain forms of popular religious piety identified as noxious by the enlightened Mexican church entered, *ipso facto*, the substratum of Indian ideology which nourished heterodoxy and an oppositional political stance readily associated with it.[55]

Awaiting the Messiah: A Reprise

In the heated political atmosphere of the years around 1810 it should come as no surprise that political imagery and religious imagery were widely blended in both rhetoric and action. The communal identity of villages under attack by internal and external pressures—a long-term process with significant political dimensions—had traditionally been linked to religious expression, a relationship most economically described by the concept of "campanilismo"—the tendency of villagers to see the social (and political) horizon as extending only as far as the view from their church tower. Indian villagers were forever ringing their church bells as a symbol of community identity, even over the strong objections of parish clergy. In one case, in the pueblo of Atlautla in the Chalco district near Mexico City, for example, villagers in an argument with the local curate, when enjoined by another local priest to stop ringing the church bells to gather people in the plaza, replied to him "that they would ring them as much as they wanted, since they had paid for the bells and not I."[56] About the same time (1799), in the village of Zapotlán el Grande in the Lake Chapala area in western Mexico, Indian villagers complained bitterly against the policy of the local curate in burying only non-Indian householders (*gente de razón*) in the churchyard, that the bells were "not rung for any Indian," and that the customary peels on the occasion of Indian religious fiestas had been eliminated. An Indian delegation from the village stated:

> It is a hardship, a hardship we repeat, that it being our pueblo we are treated with such disdain, and that the church serves only the non-Indians, since they are the only ones buried in it. And the Indians, being on their own land, and in their own village, are disdained and treated with inhumanity as we are seeing in the present case, since for the non-Indians, who are only newcomers to the town, there are church burials, peels of bells, and everything they want, and for the unhappy Indians, whose village it is, there is the treatment we are seeing.[57]

Indian villages identified so strongly with their religious processions that the least innovation in their procedures or variation in their routes could provoke a major disturbance, as many a parish priest found to his regret.[58] Perhaps the most heinous form of attack upon a pueblo was the removal of its holy images from the village church.[59]

Campanilismo, however, had an important secular aspect, as well, which underscores the difference between popular and elite political worldviews, the raw version and the cooked. There seem to have prevailed, as I have tried to suggest, very different ideas between village-dwelling Indians, on the one hand, and the superordinate, largely urban white groups, on the other, regarding the appropriate level of reference in political and social action. The distinction here would correspond roughly to a popular "Gemeinschaft" model of society and an elite "Gesellschaft" model, respectively. While the case for a stark polarity between the two worldviews would be impossible to make (a continuum with one ideal type at either end would certainly be the more accurate representation), it is nonetheless true that village rebels most often acted as though their horizon of reference stretched only to the boundaries of their communities, while the creole directorate of the independence movements acted as though they had a broader vision of Mexican society as a whole, one which I have referred to as proto-liberal. It would not be unreasonable, therefore, to suggest a kind of von Thünen's ring-like structure in the moral space of small communities, in which as one approached the outer rings the social reference group and the definition of community became ever more attenuated and the likelihood of outward-directed hostility greater. Crime outside the community, for example, is likely to have been defined much more narrowly than crime within it; that is, certain acts would be considered less deviant outside the furthermost ring than within the innermost. This is not to suggest that once beyond the boundary markers of their communities Mexican country-dwellers suddenly developed gaping super-ego lacunae, but simply that definitions of deviance, wrong-doing, and legitimacy became progressively more blurred along the outward trajectory.

In the context of late colonial Mexico, however, there is a striking anomaly in the actual behaviors one sees in such situations—a disturbance, as it were, in the neat pattern of outward rippling hostility and aggression which found their center in the rural village. This anomaly is found precisely in the relationship of the local community in rebellion to the Spanish king, and in the conversion of the latter in many instances into a figure of messianic veneration. The anomaly is more apparent than real, however, and can be explained by an analysis of the ideological substrate beneath rebellion, as I have attempted in this essay. For the present it is important to note that the apparently anomalous behavior was not evenly distributed in New Spain, but tended to occur in the central parts of the colony as opposed to the more peripheral areas. New Spain, of course, was not socially isotropic, but was characterized by uneven patterns of economic activity, settlement, and zones of acculturation. For many of the villagers of central Mexico, therefore, rebellion against the Spanish king was no crime because it was no rebellion, since the royal persona was thought to support it, urge it, and even join in it.

Once the rebellion itself had broken out, formal and informal rhetoric and collective action were suffused with religious imagery on both sides of the conflict, though this was perhaps most notable among the insurgents because of the popular nature of the revolt. On the royalist side, military necessities sometimes joined with those of propaganda, as in the "cruzada" regiment personally outfitted and led by Bishop Cabañas of Guadalajara in late 1810 before the capture of the city by Hidalgo's forces. An admittedly unsympathetic eyewitness called the bishop's regiment a "pious farce," and described it marching out from the Cathedral every morning in late 1810 led by the bishop himself, blessing the company as he went. Following the prelate came several ranks of mounted priests, swords in hand, bearing a white banner with a red cross on it, and last a crowd of boys, each wearing a red cross on his chest and yelling in concert "Long live the Holy Catholic Faith!"[60] Loyalist priests, sent out to "missionize" pacified areas of the realm, were prone to suggest that the rebels were in league with the Anti-Christ.[61] On their side the rebels marched behind banners displaying the Virgin of Guadalupe, of course, but employed religious practice and imagery in other ways, too. They celebrated masses regularly to honor the birthday of the insurrection and other occasions, and prohibited priests in rebel-held areas from administering the sacraments to *gachupines*, on one occasion refusing baptism to a newborn baby.[62] Villages and towns which resisted the rebels militarily risked having their religious icons kidnapped or burned to ashes, as happened in Calpulalpan and Tamazunchale, respectively, in 1812.[63] Saints of the Church had political labels affixed to them, some being referred to as "insurgentes" and others as "acallejados" (adherents of the royalist general and viceroy [1813–16] Félix María Calleja).[64] And on one notable occasion the Indian villagers of a remote pueblo, sympathetic to the rebel cause, crucified their governor and all the members of his family.[65]

It is in such a context, then, that one sees the invocation of the Spanish king Ferdinand VII up and down a continuum ranging from revilement to veneration. The act of rebellion itself, of course, was recognized by the colonial authorities and many amongst the rebels as *lèse-majesté*, but short of this it should hardly be surprising that the king's figure was frequently enough the object of openly seditious statements. References to regicide (especially worrying to the authorities because of the Paris events of 1791) were reported, as well as punishments less terminal but more earthy, such as sodomizing the king and defecating upon him.[66] One particularly imaginative and thorough seditionary and blasphemer jailed in Oaxaca was said by several witnesses to have stated that "he said screw the King, and he wished Morelos would come and finish them all off, that God was as much a cunt as the Virgin and all the saints." On other occasions he said he "shit on God and on the King and his crown," and that the king should not be called "Fernando Séptimo" but "Fernando Suéltame" instead.[67] Interestingly enough, the only seditious statement of this sort from Indians that I have been able to document comes from mid-1809, before the outbreak of the insurrection, and was made in a tavern in the heat of a drunken argument by an Indian pulque-seller from one of the Indian districts of Mexico City, apparently in response to what he construed as a racial insult from a non-Indian. This was a veiled reference to regicide, cast in the quite sophisticated form that the French (regicides) had had the right idea, "and that the time will come when the Indians will do the same."[68] In the rural setting, denials of the king's authority or even of his person occasionally are recorded, as when the Indian insurgent *cabecilla* (chieftain) Luis Vite, in the remote mountainous area of Molango, in the sierra of Metztitlán to the north of the capital, insisted that his followers "not believe [or] obey the King."[69]

A more normal or expectable range of expression from Indians regarding the figure of the Spanish king fell in the category of what we may call naive legitimism. This was ideologically associated, certainly, with the patriarchal stance of the monarchy toward the Indians and their veneration of the king, but was a pre-messianic form of it which found its own spontaneous modes of expression. The Indian commune of Juchipila, for example, in western central Mexico (in an area which, like parts of the Huasteca and the eastern *sierra madre* on the other side of the country, was to be an endemic focus of rebellion for several years after 1810), annually celebrated a fiesta dedicated to the king of Spain, even when the local curate tried to discourage it.[70] Within the context of the insurrection, it is in this naive legitimism that one begins to see the "splitting" of Spaniards into "good king" and "bad *gachupines*" mentioned above.[71] In its most sophisticated and secularized aspect this might appear as a discussion of the French "usurpation" of the Spanish throne, a form of sedition apparently more likely to appear amongst Indian villagers in the center of the country, near the capital or other large cities. One particularly droll manifestation of this was the story circulating in 1808 among the Indians of the market town of Zempoala, to the northeast of the capital, that the Spanish royal family had been sent back to Spain by Napoleon, but all embalmed, in wooden boxes (a metaphor of legitimacy without authority?).[72] And extending the continuum of veneration for the Spanish monarch and messianic veneration a bit further would bring us to sightings of the king and the mysterious redeemer we have already examined in some detail above.

Conclusion

In concluding, let us now take up some of the evidence from an interpretive point of view. Our rather tortuous route has led us from creole autonomist ideology to popular messianic expectation and the cultural matrix which nourished it, through a final detour into crime and communal identity. I would suggest that the paths of popular and elite ideology in fact converged hardly at all. And where they did apparently converge—in the person of a monarch (and I say "a" monarch rather than "the" monarch pointedly)—the raw and cooked versions touched different emotional chords and expressed different social aspirations. To mix the metaphor even more hopelessly, popular and elite rebel groups were engaged in a dialogue of the deaf in which there was considerable noise but little exchange of information. Furthermore, as I have tried to point out in my discussion of crime and rebellion, the Indians particularly among popular rebel groups, at least in the heartland of New Spain, tended to blur or chop out of their political cosmology the very middle-level structures represented in creole thinking by the concept of a nation, while popular ideas of the "state" seem largely to have been limited to monarchical legitimacy.

To take up another aspect of the evidence, how are we to account for the central importance of Ignacio Allende, himself an improbable candidate for messiah-hood, in popular ideology in this period? A possible explanation—a working hypothesis—lies in the nature of the mediating role played by the lower clergy in village cosmology. Rural priests like Hidalgo and Morelos, along with hundreds of other country clerics who fought under the banner of the Virgin and many more who did not, were mediators between their parishioners and the supernatural powers represented by God, Jesus, the Virgin, and the Saints.[73] As such, their brokerage function may have been held such an inherent aspect of their personae, and their personalities so familiar, that they were able to attract little if any of the powerful emotional cathexis whose formation was necessary to the development of a popular messianic figure. Perhaps priests, therefore, were simply not expendable in the moral economy of the peasant village universe. Then, too, Allende ostensibly shared a number of characteristics with the king against whom he rebelled: relative youth, whiteness, social distance, a politicomilitary vocation, and so forth.

The question is not easily answered, of course, why Allende should have been elected as an alternative messiah at all. One strong possibility consists of regional (or even personal) variations among the Indian and other popular insurgents. What does seem clear is that Allende and not the Spanish king was the preferred object of messianic hope in remoter areas of the colony, such as in the Metztitlán case cited above, while their roles may have been interchangeable in the center of the country, in the Mexican *oikoumene*. In the same general area of the country, the authority and legitimacy of King Ferdinand were being denied at the same time that he was being exalted further to the south. Here we may also recall the episodes of Indian messiahs at the beginning of the century—those of Mariano and the mad messiah of Durango—alluded to at the beginning of this chapter. Although little is recorded of messianic pronouncements by insurgents in the near north and northwestern reaches of the colony, the areas in which the turn-of-the-century episodes occurred, it seems reasonable to assume that messianic expectation and social unrest there did not burn themselves out in 1801. If there *had been* such manifestations in the 1810–21 period, they would probably have focused not on King Ferdinand, or even on Ignacio Allende, but on Indian figures, possibly associated (as were the earlier two and related incidents across the colony) with the mythified history of Tlaxcala, a powerful symbol and metaphor for a countercolonial Indian shadow-state. We may posit, therefore, an important continuum in the objects of messianic expectation, ranging from the more northerly, remote, and less acculturated areas of the colony (in which roughness of terrain and/or difficulty of access may serve as a surrogate for distance), where Indian king/messiahs predominated, to the central, densely populated, highly acculturated areas closer to the Valley of Mexico, where such hopes were attached to the figure of the Spanish king himself.

The sociospatial continuum proposed here has two suggestive branching implications, regarding the messianic object-choice of Indians and the elaboration or lack of elaboration of millenarian or quasi-millenarian programs.

If it is true, as Gruzinski has suggested, that the priestly and political functions earlier fused in the Mesoamerican tradition were split apart in the post-classic period, before the advent of the Europeans, then it would appear that by the late colonial era, despite the tendency of the Spanish state to conflate divine and secular authority, the split had become a permanent one.[74] This would explain why the specialized priestly class of the colony—parish curates such as led the insurgency in many areas—failed to emerge as political/religious messiahs. From this point of view, Father Hidalgo may have been just another Nahua priest reciting auguries. Following this same interpretation, the hints of fusion—expressed as chiliastic grandiosity—one sees in Mariano and the mad messiah of Durango would be characteristic of the colonial periphery because of the less thorough process of acculturation (or deculturation) there. Furthermore, the lack of specific programmatic elements, for the most part, in the ideology of Indian rebels in the more central regions of the country would correspond precisely to the same considerations, since one does see such programmatic elements in the earlier, more peripheral movements, as also in earlier messianic episodes in central New Spain.[75] Even if the peripheral Indian prophet-kings elaborated only primitive millenarian programs, this was still more than one saw a decade later in the center of the country. Here Indians of a messianic persuasion seem to have been operating with an amputated cosmology in which, if a New Jerusalem existed, it was co-terminous with the edge of each embattled peasant village which looked to the king or his surrogate as messianic saviors.

Finally, messianic expectation among the Indian villagers of New Spain may have served them as a kind of ideological lever against the local political structure—against local officials, merchants, landowners, and sometimes against their own priests. It represented in a time of social crisis the invocation of a reciprocal relationship in which the distant royal government (and by extension its viceregal surrogates) had done much the same thing in reverse—built the large, rambling, leaky edifice of royal Indian protectionism as a counterweight to the centrifugal tendencies present in the New World in general and New Spain in particular. The political symbiosis, of course, had its limits, and there were strains within it which neither party, on its side, openly admitted. The village-dwelling Indians almost certainly looked no further than the boundaries of their communes, and admitted as legitimate only certain claims on the part of the monarch, while the monarchy (or Spanish state) on its side saw the Indians not as potentially free and equal citizens, but as perennial minors living under royal tutelage, paying taxes and supplying labor.[76] The system represented, therefore, a kind of disingenuous alliance. There was about this situation a certain structural symmetry if one places the creole elite with its allied social groups in the middle, its aims radically opposed to both Indian villagers and the monarchy since it sought to seize and, to a degree, spread political power on the one hand and pulverize Indian communitarian values on the other. The focus of Indian messianic expectation on the Spanish king (or on surrogate figures such as Ignacio Allende) embodies the kind of contradiction between popular and elite ideology often found in mass insurrectionary movements, therefore, and undermines the traditional wisdom that all the rebels in New Spain had the same thing in mind when they took up arms against the colonial regime.

Notes

1. I have been unable to reference this anecdote, though anthologies of Jewish humor and folklore typically include large numbers of stories about Chelm. See, for example, Nathan Ausubel, ed., *A Treasury of Jewish Folklore: Stories, Traditions, Legends, Humor, Wisdom, and Folk Songs of the Jewish People* (New York, 1948), and Harry D. Spalding, ed., *Encyclopedia of Jewish Humor, from Biblical Times to the Modern Age* (New York, 1969).
2. For a detailed discussion of an Indian messiah in Durango in the years 1800-1801, see Eric Van Young, "Millennium on the Northern Marches: The Mad Messiah of Durango and Popular Rebellion in Mexico, 1800-1815," *Comparative Studies in Society and History* 28 (1986), pp. 385-413. Conspiracies and village riots in the Tepic area at about the same time, centering on the mysterious Indian messiah named Mariano, are dealt with by Christon I. Archer, *El ejército en el México borbónico, 1760-1810* (Mexico City, 1983), pp. 132-35.
3. Important documentation on the Tepic episode is to be found in Biblioteca Pública del Estado, Fondos Especiales, Guadalajara (hereafter BPE), Criminal, paquete 34, exp. 9, ser. 763, 1801-1806. Other documentary references include Archivo General de la Nación, México, Mexico City (hereafter AGN), Historia, vol. 428, fols. 37r-76r, 1801; AGN, Historia, vol. 413, exp. 5, fols. 248r-339r, 1801; AGN, Infidencias, vol. 13, exp. 6, fols. 125r-155r, 1816-17; and AGN, Indiferente de Guerra, vol. 46A, no pagination, 1801. I am grateful to Christon Archer for bringing some of these sources to my attention.
4. For an interesting and exceedinly suggestive treatment of four such figures and their followers, see Serge Gruzinski, *Les Hommes-dieux de Mexique. Pouvoir indien et société, xvie-xviiie siécles* (Paris, 1985); and for a discussion of messianic/millenarian elements in the Tzeltal revolt in early eighteenth-century Chiapas, Robert Wasserstrom, *Class and Society in Central Chiapas* (Berkeley, 1983), pp. 76-86 and passim.
5. Numerous instances of what I have elsewhere described as almost ritualistic assassinations occurred; some examples are discussed and analyzed in Eric Van Young, "Who Was That Masked Man, Anyway?: Popular Symbols and Ideology in the Mexican Wars of Independence," Rocky Mountain Council on Latin American

Studies, Annual Meeting, *Proceedings* (Las Cruces, N. Mex., 1984), vol. 1, pp. 18-35; and Van Young, "Millennium on the Northern Marches."

6. The epigraph of this paper is drawn from Claude Lévi-Strauss, *The Raw and the Cooked* (New York, 1979), p. 5. I have not meant to draw any invidious comparisons between popular and elite creole ideological formulations by referring to them herein, respectively, as raw and cooked. Nonetheless, when one pieces together testimony, description of collective action, and the odd bits and pieces of (especially Indian) programmatic pronouncements on the part of the popular rebels, and compares them with the basically rationalist, Western thinking in formal manifestos, pamphlets, newspapers, and so forth, produced by creole insurgent thinkers, one is forced to recognize a striking contrast, analogous to the primary process thinking of individuals as opposed to their ego-censored everyday thought processes.
7. On Hidalgo's political ideas, see Alfonso García Ruiz, *Ideario de Hidalgo* (Mexico City, 1955).
8. Royalist thinkers and propagandists also stressed the religious underpinning of the Bourbon monarchy and the king's authority, of course, and attempted to hammer this home to the "humble portion of the people." On this point, see Hugh M. Hamill, Jr., "The Rector to the Rescue: Royalist Pamphleteers in the Defense of Mexico, 1808–1821," VI Conference of Mexican and United States Historians, Chicago, 1981; and also Hamill's "Royalist Propaganda and 'La porción humilde del pueblo' during Mexican Independence," *Americas* 36 (1980), pp. 423-44.
9. For a brilliant analysis of these questions, see David A. Brading, *The Origins of Mexican Nationalism* (Cambridge, 1985), esp. pp. 51-52.
10. The former position would be occupied by Brading, the latter by José Miranda, whose book *Las ideas y las constituciones políticas mexicanas* is glossed by Luis González, *Once ensayos de tema insurgente* (Zamora, 1985), p. 122. One reason for the difficulty in characterizing creole political thought, of course, is that after the initial crisis of 1808 the intellectual community of New Spain was severely divided, and many creole intellectuals switched sides back and forth; Hamill, "The Rector to the Rescue," p. 2. Furthermore, María del Reafugio González points out that distinct differences between Mexican conservatives and liberals were late in coalescing; "Ilustrados, regalistas y liberales," Symposium on the Independence of Mexico and the Creation of the Federal Republic, University of California, Irvine, February 1987.
11. For a pithy discussion of the constitution of 1814, see González, *Once ensayos*, pp. 109-28. See also Ernesto de la Torre Villar, *La Constitución de Apatzingán y los creadores del estado mexicano* (Mexico City, 1978), and *La independencia mexicana*, 3 vols. (Mexico City, 1982).
12. On the role of the Virgin of Guadalupe in the formation of Mexican creole patriotism, see Jacques Lafaye, *Quetzalcóatl and Guadalupe: The Formation of Mexican National Consciousness, 1531-1813*, trans. Benjamin Keen (Chicago, 1976).
13. Brading, *The Origins of Mexican Nationalism.*
14. AGN, Criminal, vol. 134, exp. 3, fols. 36r-50r, 1810.

15. AGN, Criminal, vol. 454, no exp. no., no pagination, 1811.
16. AGN, Criminal, vol. 175, no exp. no., fols. 369r-392v, 1811. The figure of the messianic, disguised king ("el encubierto") is familiar from Spanish history, as well, as Angus MacKay points out in his interesting paper, "Ritual, Violence, and Authority in Castile," Bronowski Renaissance Symposium: The Art of Empire—Culture and Authority in the Spanish Empire, 1500-1650, University of California, San Diego, April 1986.
17. AGN, Criminal, vol. 204, exp. 10, fols. 191r-205v, 1811; vol. 194, exp. 1, fols. 1r-13r, 1811.
18. AGN, Infidencias, vol. 22, exp. 10, fols. 179r-183v, 1810. The miraculous intercession of the Virgin, by the way, goes some way toward meeting the criterion of supernatural intervention seen to be essential in the definition of messianic/millenial expectation developed by Norman Cohn, "Medieval Millenarism: Its Bearing on the Comparative Study of Millenarian Movements," in Sylvia L. Thrupp, ed., *Millennial Dreams in Action: Studies in Revolutionary Religious Movements* (New York, 1970), pp. 31-43.
19. See Van Young, "Millennium on the Northern Marches."
20. AGN, Criminal, vol. 204, exp. 10, fols. 191r-205v, 1811.
21. University of Texas at Austin, Benson Latin American Collection, Hernández y Dávalos Collection (hereafter UT-HD), 1.212, 1815.
22. Andrés Lira González, personal communication; and Luis Villoro, *El proceso ideológico de la revolución de Independencia* (Mexico City, 1967), who discusses the same incident, pp. 33-60.
23. In attempting to explain this process, which contrasts with the exaggerated violence frequently directed against European-born Spaniards particularly by village rebels and rioters, I have elsewhere linked it to the psychological mechanism of "splitting" seen in infants, whose dynamics resemble those of scapegoating. For a discussion of "splitting," a concept drawn from the object-relations school of psychoanalytic theory, see Van Young, "Millennium on the Northern Marches" and "Who Was That Masked Man, Anyway?"
24. AGN, Criminal, vol. 226, exp. 5, fols. 267r-361r, 1808; and for another similar incident, see AGN, Operaciones de Guerra, vol. 9, no exp. no., fols. 91r-v, 1817, relating to an occurrence in Tula in 1810.
25. For some instances of this, see AGN, Infidencias, vol. 5, exp. 8, no pagination, Yurirapúndaro, 1810; ibid., exp. 10, no pagination, Huichapan, 1810; AGN, Infidencias, vol. 14, exp. 1, fols. 1r-92v, Sichu, 1811; AGN, Criminal, vol. 241, exp. 4, fols. 106r-115r, Tula, 1811.
26. Jacques Lafaye, *Mesías, cruzadas, utopías: El judeo-cristianismo en las sociedades ibéricas* (Mexico City, 1984), pp. 87-88 and passim; and Lafaye, *Quetzalcóatl and Guadalupe*, p. 28. Lafaye, it seems to me, fails to make a sufficiently sharp distinction between messianic and charismatic leadership, which are not necessarily the same thing. Michael Adas has some perceptive comments to make on this confusion, even in the original formulation of Max Weber; Adas, *Prophets of*

Rebellion: Millenarian Protest Movements against the European Colonial Order (Chapel Hill, 1979), pp. xx-xxi.

27. Allende was supposed to be with King Ferdinand in Querétaro in the spring of 1811; AGN, Criminal, vol. 194, exp. 1, fols. 1r-13r, 1811. For the Cuernavaca incidents, see AGN, Criminal, vol. 47, exp. 15, fols. 443r-574v, 1810.
28. For example, AGN, Criminal, vol. 2, exp. 21, no pagination, 1811.
29. AGN, Operaciones de Guerra, vol. 9, no exp. no., fols. 133r-134r, 1817; AGN, Infidencias, vol. 2, exp. 8, fols. 154r-162v, 1810; AGN, Inquisición, vol. 1416, exp. 11, fols. 173r-178v, 1811; AGN, Operaciones de Guerra, vol. 9, no exp. no., fols. 41r-v, 1817; and AGN, Infidencias, vol. 2, exp. 4, fols. 100r-116v, 1811. Allende's fate (arrest, trial, and death in 1811) was, like that of Hidalgo, the subject of popular speculation, and his return believed imminent; see AGN, Criminal, vol. 262, exp. 19, fols. 235r-256v, 1811.
30. AGN, Criminal, vol. 240, no exp. no., fols. 355r-364r, 1810; ibid., vol. 241, exp. 7, fols. 233r-243v, 1811; ibid., vol. 57, exp. 6, fols. 101r-116r, 1810; ibid., vol. 204, exps. 11-12, fols. 206r-262r, 1810; ibid., vol. 13, exp. 6, no pagination, 1810; ibid., vol. 53, exps. 16-17, fols. 196r-224r, 1810.
31. AGN, Criminal, vol. 163, exp. 18, fols. 307r-320r, 1811.
32. For background on the material antecedents of the rebellion, see Eric Van Young, "Moving toward Revolt: Agrarian Origins of the Hidalgo Revolt in the Guadalajara Region, 1810," in Friedrich Katz, ed., *Riot, Rebellion, and Revolution: Rural Social Conflict in Mexico* (Princeton, in press); Van Young, "The Age of Paradox: Mexican Agriculture at the end of the Colonial Period, 1750-1810," in Nils Jacobsen and Hans-Jürgen Puhle, eds., *The Economies of Mexico and Peru in the Late Colonial Period, 1760-1820* (Berlin, 1986), pp. 64-90; Van Young, "The Rich Get Richer and the Poor Get Skewed: Real Wages and Popular Living Standards in Eighteenth-Century Mexico," All-UC Group in Economic History, Los Angeles, May, 1987; William B. Taylor, "Indian Pueblos of Central Jalisco on the Eve of Independence," in Richard L. Garner and William B. Taylor, eds., *Iberian Colonies, New World Societies: Essays in Memory of Charles Gibson* (n.p., 1986), pp. 161-84; and the recent, excellent studies of Brian R. Hamnett, *Roots of Insurgency: Mexican Regions, 1750-1824* (Cambridge, 1986) and John Tutino, *From Insurrection to Revolution in Mexico: Social Bases of Agrarian Violence, 1750-1940* (Princeton, 1986), which throw much light on questions of long-term structural change in the Mexican countryside.
33. The basic New Testament source on the advent of the Millennium is Revelations 20. Stimulating discussions of millenarian doctrines upon which I have leaned heavily, though not exclusively, in the present treatment, are to be found in Norman Cohn, *The Pursuit of the Millennium: Revolutionary Messianism in Medieval and Reformation Europe and Its Bearing on Modern Totalitarian Movements*, 2nd ed. (New York, 1961), esp. pp. 1-32; Sylvia L. Thrupp, "Introduction," in Thrupp, ed., *Millennial Dreams in Action*, pp. 11-27; Norman Cohn, "Medieval Millenarism," in ibid., pp. 31-43; George Shepperson, "The Comparative Study of Millenarian Movements," in Thrupp, ed., *Millennial Dreams in Action*, pp. 44-52; Janos Bak

and Gerhard Benecke, "Introduction," in Bak and Benecke, eds., *Religion and Rural Revolt* (Manchester, 1984), pp. 2-13 (and the other essays in that volume); J. F. C. Harrison, *The Second Coming: Popular Millenarianism, 1780-1850* (London, 1979), esp. pp. 1-54; Lafaye, *Mesías, cruzadas, utopías*, pp. 7-26 and passim; Adas, *Prophets of Rebellion*; and Eric J. Hobsbawm, *Primitive Rebels: Studies in Archaic Forms of Social Movement in the 19th and 20th Centuries* (New York, 1959).

34. Thrupp, "Introduction," p. 12; and on revitalization movements in general, see the remarks of Adas, *Prophets of Rebellion*, pp. xvii-xxi.

35. See, for example, Miguel León-Portilla, *Aztec Thought and Culture: A Study of the Ancient Nahuatl Mind* (Norman, Okla., 1963); Laurette Sejourné, *Burning Water: Thought and Religion in Ancient Mexico* (London, 1957); Jacques Soustelle, *La Pensée cosmologique des anciens Mexicains* (Paris, 1940); and Burr Cartwright Brundage, *The Fifth Sun: Aztec Gods, Aztec World* (Austin, 1979).

36. The figure of Quetzalcóatl and his association with the Spanish conquest of Mexico has exercised a perennial fascination for scholars of Mexican culture and history. Among modern treatments, all of which deal to some extent with his proto-messianic status and the Aztec prophetic tradition, see Lafaye, *Quetzalcóatl and Guadalupe*, esp. pp. 149-153; Tzvetan Todorov, *The Conquest of America: The Question of the Other* (New York, 1984); R. C. Padden, *The Hummingbird and the Hawk: Conquest and Sovereignty in the Valley of Mexico, 1503-1541* (Columbus, Ohio, 1967); and David Carrasco, *Quetzalcóatl and the Irony of Empire: Myths and Prophecies in the Aztec Tradition* (Chicago, 1982).

37. For the notion of such a cultural substrate among an Indian group both in colonial and modern times, see Victoria Reifler Bricker, *The Indian Christ, the Indian King: The Historical Substrate of Maya Myth and Ritual* (Austin, 1981).

38. Gruzinski suggests that the mythicohistorical lineage of the "hommes-dieux" in fact ended among the Nahuas about 1430 (a century before the Spanish conquest) because of the need for political stabilization in central Mexico, thus divorcing political power and divinity to a certain degree; *Les Hommes-dieux de Mexique*, pp. 18-19.

39. See, for example, the classic investigation of Lesley B. Simpson, *The Ecomienda in New Spain*, rev. ed. (Berkeley, 1966), on the evolution of early Indian labor and tribute policy. There was also present, of course, in Spanish policy a genuine humanitarian, philosophical, and juridical concern with the nature of the Indian and the legitimacy of the conquest, a debate that reached an early crescendo in the sixteenth century. See the classic work of Lewis Hanke, *The Spanish Struggle for Justice in the Conquest of America* (Philadelphia, 1949), and for a more recent view of similar issues, Anthony Pagden, *The Fall of Natural Man: The American Indian and the Origins of Comparative Ethnology* (Cambridge, 1982).

40. On the legal status of Indians, see, among others, Paulino Castañeda Delgado, "La condición miserable del indio y sus privilegios," *Anuario de estudios americanos* 28 (1971), pp. 245-335.

41. For an exhaustive and fascinating treatment of the General Indian Court, an institution unique to New Spain, see Woodrow W. Borah, *Justice by Insurance: The*

General Indian Court of New Spain and the Legal Aides of the Half-Real (Berkeley, 1983).

42. AGN, Tierras, vol. 1494, exp. 4, no pagination, 1783. For a detailed description of such internal socioeconomic differentiation within the Indian pueblos of another region in late colonial Mexico, see Eric Van Young, "Conflict and Solidarity in Indian Village Life: The Guadalajara Region in the Late Colonial Period," *Hispanic American Historical Review* 64 (1984), pp. 55-79; and for a general evaluation of Indian use of legal avenues in land conflicts in the same region, Eric Van Young, *Hacienda and Market in Eighteenth-Century Mexico: The Rural Economy of the Guadalajara Region, 1675-1820* (Berkeley, 1981), esp. pp. 271-342.
43. Indeed, the king occupied an almost suprapolitical position in the Spanish political tradition, and often remained inviolate in the midst of popular rebellion, his authority being split off from the legitimacy of government, as in the traditional cry of rebels and rioters, "Long live the King! Death to bad government!" For a thoughtful treatment of this political habit of mind in the New World, see John L. Phelan, *The People and the King: The Comunero Revolution in Colombia, 1781* (Madison, 1978); and see also MacKay, "Ritual, Violence, and Authority."
44. For example, in analyzing millenarian movements in modern Brazil, René Ribeiro stresses the necessary background conditions of "social isolation...and lack of real religious help" in addition to extreme poverty in making apocalyptic preaching appealing; Ribeiro, "Brazilian Messianic Movements," in Thrupp, ed., *Millennial Dreams in Action*, p. 59. Similarly, Roger Bastide, *Les religions africaines de Brésil* (Paris, 1960), p. 495ff, emphasizes that modern millennial movements have found their origins in "frustration and backwardness through participation in a kind of 'archaic culture' which persists because of geographical and cultural isolation."
45. For more on this point of view, reflecting as it does a subtle mixture of aggression, fear, and racist ideas, see Van Young, "Millennium on the Northern Marches," pp. 400-401.
46. AGN, Historia, vol. 494, exp. 4, fols. 18r-105v, 1774. For a series of interesting reports on the rural Indian schools of several other districts in Mexico, all dating from 1784, see AGN, Historia, vol. 495, exps. 6, 7, 8, 10, 14, 15, and 19; all of these reports discuss similar problems of finance and Indian resistance to the schooling of children, though in some districts the outcome was better.
47. BPE, Civil, caja 49, exp. 4, ser. 637, 1731. It is interesting to note that the pueblo of Mezcala, with other neighboring Indian villages, became a center of prolonged armed rebellion after 1810, and the center of a famous episode of siege by the royalist forces of an insurgent garrison on the island of the same name in Lake Chapala; see Alvaro Ochoa, *Los insurgentes de Mexcala* (Morelia, 1985).
48. Calimaya—AGN, Clero Regular y Secular, vol. 131, exp. 1, fols. 1r-110r, 1792; Apaxtla—ibid., vol. 126, exp. 12, fols. 286r-294r, 1809; Zacualpan—ibid., vol. 5, exp. 8, fols. 418r-453v, 1801; Celaya—AGN, Historia, vol. 500, exp. 3, fols. 168r-187r, 1797.

49. Gruzinski, *Les Hommes-dieux de Mexique*, p. 114ff; AGN, Criminal, vol. 203, exp. 4, fols. 109r-268r, 1778; and see also the interesting remarks on the Indian prophetic tradition by David A. Brading, "Images and Prophets: Indian Religion and the Spanish Conquest," unpublished ms. (1985).
50. AGN, Bienes Nacionales, leg. 663, no exp. no., no pagination, 1817.
51. AGN, Bienes Nacionales, leg. 976, exp. 39, no pagination, 1813.
52. AGN, Bienes Nacionales, leg. 663, no exp. no., no pagination, 1818.
53. David A. Brading, "Tridentine Catholicism and Enlightened Despotism in Bourbon Mexico," *Journal of Latin American Studies* 15 (1983), pp. 1-22; Brading, "Images and Prophets;" Gruzinski, *Les Hommes-dieux de Mexique*, pp. 161-67. See the series of reports and viceregal decrees regarding "abuses" (excess spending by Indians and others, gambling, drinking, commercial activity, etc.) during Holy Week in Mexico City, Pátzcuaro, and Silao in the 1790s, in AGN, Historia, vol. 437, exps. 3, 5-11, 1791-98.
54. See, for example, the case of the riot and murders of several European-born Spaniards by the Indian villagers of Atlacomulco in November, 1810—AGN, Criminal, vol. 229, no exp. no., fols. 263r-413v, 1810, and vol. 231, exp. 1, fols. 1r-59r, 1811; and also the riot during *carnaval*, 1806, by the villagers of Amecameca—AGN, Criminal, vol. 71, exp. 6, fols. 167r-241v, 1806-10.
55. Brading, "Images and Prophets," p. 16, makes much the same point. It should be noted in passing that a possible relationship exists between the occurrence of messianic/millenarian beliefs or movements among Indian populations and earlier missionary activity by the Franciscans, who in the New World retained in their thought and teachings a definite strain of millennial expectation harking back to Joachim of Floris in the twelfth century. Certainly the two Indian pseudo-messiahs of Tepic and Durango originated in regions strongly influenced by Franciscan evangelization. On the other hand, such beliefs among the Indians occurred elsewhere in New Spain as well, in areas missionized by the Dominicans and Augustinians, as Gruzinski demonstrates in *Les Hommes-dieux de Mexique*. Brading suggests that the Franciscan influence may have been important in encouraging millenarian belief among the Yucatec Maya, but leaves the question open for lack of evidence; "Images and Prophets," p. 15. On early evangelization activity in New Spain, see Robert Ricard, *The Spiritual Conquest of Mexico; An Essay on the Apostolate and the Evangelizing Methods of the Mendicant Orders in New Spain: 1523-1572*, trans. Lesley B. Simpson (Berkeley, 1966), especially the map on pp. 62-63. For millenarian thought among the Franciscans, see Lafaye, *Quetzalcoatl and Guadalupe*, pp. 28-34 and passim; and John L. Phelan, *The Millennial Kingdom of the Franciscans in the New World*, 2nd rev. ed. (Berkeley, 1970).

The theme of long-term social and economic causation of popular rebellion in early nineteenth-century Mexico has been passed over in this essay because of space constraints. The interested reader is referred to the following works among the large and growing historiography: Hugh M. Hamill, Jr., *The Hidalgo Revolt: Prelude to Mexican Independence* (Gainesville, 1966); John Tutino, *From Insurrection to Revolution in Mexico: Social Bases of Agrarian Violence, 1750-1940* (Princeton,

1986); and Brian R. Hamnett, *Roots of Insurgency: Mexican Regions, 1750-1824* (Cambridge, 1986), and to the works cited in note 32 above.

56. AGN, Criminal, vol. 157, exp. 3, fols. 93r-155v, 1799.
57. BPE, Civil, caja 143, exp. 5, ser. 1564, 1797.
58. Ibid.
59. See the interesting cases of the kidnapping of wooden religious icons from the village churches of San José de Tateposco and Tucumatlán, both in the Lake Chapala area, in connection with a land conflict and reprisal for rebellious activity, respectively, in BPE, Archivo Judicial de la Audiencia (hereafter AJA), 265:3:3615, 1818, and UT-HD 6-3.316, 1815.
60. The account is the "Relación de lo ocurrido en Guadalajara en 11 de noviembre de 1810," by Prisciliano Sánchez, later an early republican governor of the State of Jalisco; UT-HD, 119-2.27.
61. AGN, Historia, vol. 111, exp. 15, fols. 176r-197v, 1810.
62. In Huichapan, on 14 September 1812, a solemn mass of thanksgiving was sung to celebrate the advent of the insurrection two years previously; Instituto Nacional de Antropología e Historia (Mexico City), Archivo Histórico (hereafter INAH), Colección Antigua, vol. 334, exp. 74, fols. 262r-263v, 1812. The baptism incident is documented in AGN, Operaciones de Guerra, vol. 20, no exp. no., fols. 77r-81v, 1811.
63. INAH, Colección Antigua, vol. 334, no exp. nos., fols. 252r-254r and fols. 154r-v, 1812, respectively.
64. AGN, Inquisición, vol. 1460, no exp. no., fols. 257r-259r, 1816.
65. AGN, Operaciones de Guerra, vol. 4, no exp. no., fols. 163r-167r, 1813, referring to the pueblo of Yautempa, in the Huasteca.
66. For an early reference to the question of regicide, suggested obliquely but unmistakably in connection with King Carlos IV, Ferdinand's father, see the inquiry into the statements of the creole militia officer don Francisco de Solano Gil, in Toluca, in AGN, Criminal, vol. 454, no exp. no., no pagination, 1794; and for the statements of a priest, AGN, Inquisición, vol. 1416, exp. 21, fols. 269r-270v, 1817. For "screwing the King," see AGN, Infidencias, vol. 2, exp. 6, fols. 134r-144r, Oaxaca, 1811 and vol. 2, exp. 2, fols. 40r-57v, also Oaxaca, 1811; and for "shitting on the King," ibid.
67. Ibid. The pun on King Ferdinand's name ("Ferdinand let-me-go" instead of "Ferdinand the Seventh") was a reference to the house arrest imposed by Napoleon at one point on the Spanish royal family.
68. AGN, Infidencias, vol. 6, exp. 8, no pagination, 1809.
69. AGN, Criminal, vol. 251, exp. 10, fols. 309r-319v, 1812.
70. BPE, Civil, caja 140, exp. 5, ser. 1518, 1791. For an interesting recent work on this understudied area, called the region of *los cañones*, see Agueda Jiménez Pelayo, "Historia rural en México colonial: El sur de Zacatecas, 1600-1820," Ph.D. dissertation, University of New Mexico, 1985.
71. See also Van Young, "Who Was That Masked Man, Anyway?" and "Millennium on the Northern Marches."

72. AGN, Criminal, vol. 226, exp. 5, fols. 267r-361r, 1808. Also on the usurpation theme, see AGN, Criminal, vol. 207, exp. 22, fols. 306r-327v, Ocoyoacac (near Toluca), 1810.
73. Gruzinski, *Les Hommes-dieux de Mexique*, pp. 139, 163-67, makes an approach to this question, but from the angle of the widespread popular anticlericalism he sees as a result of the enlightened policies of the Bourbon church, and from the teachings of the Indian messiah Antonio Pérez on the inefficacy of such priestly mediation in the salvation of souls. In passing, it should be mentioned that many more priests in New Spain remained loyal to the Spanish crown than took up arms against it.
74. Gruzinski, *Les Hommes-dieux de Mexique*, p. 18ff. For an equally stimulating but somewhat different point of view, positing a multilevel model of religious understanding of which the Maya Indians lost the uppermost, corresponding to universal religion, see Nancy M. Farriss, *Maya Society under Spanish Colonial Rule: The Collective Enterprise of Survival* (Princeton, 1984), pp. 286-351.
75. See Gruzinski's discussion of Antonio Pérez, for example, in *Les Hommes-dieux de Mexique*. Pérez's uprising seems to have been the last genuinely millenarian episode in the center of the country during the colonial period, leading one to suspect a situation of rapidly changing social conditions and accelerated acculturation there for the next half-century.
76. For the most highly developed discussion to date of the Indian peasant worldview and the relationship of the Indian villages to structures of authority, see William B. Taylor, *Drinking, Homicide, and Rebellion in Colonial Mexican Villages* (Stanford, 1979).

ABOUT THE EDITOR

STEVEN KAPLAN is Associate Professor of African Studies and Comparative Religion at the Hebrew University of Jerusalem. He is currently Chair of the African Studies Department and Director of Graduate Studies at the Rothberg School for Overseas Students. His research interests include the social and religious history of Ethiopia, the history and culture of the Beta Israel (Falasha) and transformations of missionary Christianity. Among his six books and more than three dozen articles are two other books with New York University Press, *The Beta Israel (Falasha) in Ethiopia: From Earliest Times to the Twentieth Century* and *Surviving Salvation: The Ethiopian Jewish Family in Transition*, both published in 1992. The latter was co-authored with Dr. Ruth Westheimer.

ABOUT THE CONTRIBUTORS

DANIEL BAYS is Professor of Modern Chinese History at the University of Kansas, Lawrence, where he has taught since 1971. He is director of an international study program on the history of Christianity in China funded by the Pew Charitable Trusts, 1993-1996. His most recent publication related to this area is "Christian Revival in China, 1900-1937," in *Modern Christian Revivals*, edited by Edith L. Blumhofer and Randall Balmer.

ERIK COHEN is the George S. Wise Professor of Sociology at the Hebrew University of Jerusalem. He has carried out research in Israel, Peru and the Pacific Islands, and, most recently, in Thailand, concentrating on tourism, urban life and social change and folk arts and crafts. He is the author of numerous articles, as well as being co-editor of *Comparative Social Dynamics* and author of *Thai Society in Comparative Perspective.*

JOHN HOWES, after studying Japanese language at the U.S. Navy School of Oriental Languages during World War II, has specialized in teaching, writing and studying about Japan, and in particular its modern intellectual history. He taught Japanese history in the University of British Columbia (Canada) between 1961 and 1990 and since then has taught in Obirin University in Tokyo.

D. DENNIS HUDSON, Professor of World Religions at Smith College, Northampton, Massachusetts, teaches the religious history of South Asia with special attention to Tamil culture. His recent research and writing has been on religious poetry and temples of the eighth century and interactions between Hindus and Christians in the nineteenth century.

JAN SZEMINSKI is Associate Professor in the Department of Spanish and Latin American Studies at the Hebrew University of Jerusalem. His current research interests include the history of central Andean cultures, and oral tradition and Andean languages as a historical source. He is the author of several works in Spanish and in English, including *Manqu Qhapaq Inkap kawsasqankunamanta [De las vidas de Manqu Qhapaq Inka].*

ERIC VAN YOUNG, Professor of History at the University of California, San Diego, is the author of *Hacienda and Market in Eighteenth-Century Mexico: The Rural Economy of the Guadalajara Region, 1675-1810* and editor of *Mexican Regions: Comparative History and Development*. Among his current research projects is a large-scale study of popular participation in the Mexican wars of independence (1810-1821) and the history of psychiatry in Mexico in the last two hundred years.

INDEX